THE GENESIS OF
ISRAEL AND EGYPT

The Genesis of
Israel and Egypt

A Velikovskian View of the Early Civilizations

Vol. 1 in the series "Ages in Alignment"
2nd Edition, Updated and Expanded

Emmet Sweeney

Algora Publishing
New York

Library of Congress Cataloging-in-Publication Data —

Names: Sweeney, Emmet John, author. | Sweeney, Emmet John. Ages in
    alignment ; v. 1.
Title: The genesis of Israel and Egypt : a Velikovskian view of the early
    civilizations / Emmet Sweeney.
Description: 2nd edition, updated and expanded. | New York : Algora
    Publishing, [2023] | Series: Vol. 1 in the series "Ages in alignment" |
    Includes bibliographical references and index. | Summary: "Resolving
    contradictions in accepted history, Velikovsky and Sweeney conclude that
    all the ancient civilizations arose simultaneously around 1100 BC.
    Archaeological evidence of the Flood, the Tower, the rise of the first
    literate cultures, and the great migration westward toward Egypt support
    this view and also reveal Imhotep to be the same person as Joseph, son
    of Jacob"— Provided by publisher.
Identifiers: LCCN 2023012643 (print) | LCCN 2023012644 (ebook) | ISBN
    9781628945065 (trade paperback) | ISBN 9781628945072 (hardcover) | ISBN
    9781628945089 (pdf)
Subjects: LCSH: Jews—History—To 586 B.C.—Chronology. |
    Egypt—History—To 332 B.C.—Chronology. | Palestine—History—To 70
    A.D.—Chronology. | Iraq—History—To 634—Chronology.
Classification: LCC DT83 .S93 2023 (print) | LCC DT83 (ebook) | DDC
    932—dc23/eng/20230322
LC record available at https://lccn.loc.gov/2023012643
LC ebook record available at https://lccn.loc.gov/2023012644

Cover image: Narmer Palette, Egypt's First Dynasty.

Printed in the United States

TABLE OF CONTENTS

List of Illustrations and Tables

The present volume is a revised and expanded edition of the *Genesis of Israel and Egypt*, the first part of a general reworking of ancient history, published originally in 1997. In the years since then it has become apparent to me that the latter volume contained several serious errors. These mainly concerned the identification and date of the first two great natural calamities recalled in biblical and other ancient tradition; the Flood and the event symbolized by the Tower of Babel. In the first edition, I had concurred with Professor Gunnar Heinsohn in identifying the "Great Flood" which Leonard Woolley discovered underneath the city of Ur in Lower Mesopotamia with the Flood of Noah as described in the Bible. Heinsohn placed this event around 1400 or 1300 BC, and equated it with the "Venus Catastrophe" described by Immanuel Velikovsky in *Worlds in Collision* (1950) and elsewhere. In *Worlds in Collision*, Velikovsky had implied that the Venus event coincided with the extinction of the Pleistocene megafauna, whose mangled remains are found in great quantities in northern Eurasia and the Americas. Such a conclusion seemed to be supported by some very detailed geological and paleontological evidence which Velikovsky presented in his 1956 book, *Earth in Upheaval*. Confusingly however, in *Worlds in Collision*, Velikovsky identified the great catastrophe of the mid-second millennium BC with the biblical Exodus, and he appeared to regard the biblical Flood of Noah as an earlier event, to be placed, perhaps, around 3000 BC.

The present writer was similarly confused. However, over the past few years it has become clear that the catastrophic termination of the Pleistocene, which really is to be linked with the biblical Deluge, occurred perhaps around 2300 BC., whereas the "Flood" uncovered by Leonard Woolley in Ur was identical to the disaster known to the Bible as the Destruction of the

Tower of Babel. This latter occurred sometime between 1400 and 1300 BC and directly preceded the rise of literate civilization in Mesopotamia and in Egypt.

It was the cosmic events of 1400–1300 BC that gave birth to the twin concepts of priest-kingship and blood sacrifice, and the construction of large raised altars on which to perform blood sacrifices ultimately stimulated and produced the need for mathematics and record-keeping. But a civilization of some type existed before the Tower episode; the Flood of 2300 BC had made life so precarious for the surviving remnant of humanity that new methods of procuring food and other essentials had to be developed and exploited. The result was a flowering of inventiveness and innovation, giving birth to agriculture and eventually large farming villages and even towns. These were the settlements and cities destroyed by the Tower Catastrophe.

Apart from these changes, there is very little else I have felt the need to alter. In all essentials, therefore, the present edition — from Chapter 3 onwards — is identical to what the reader will find in the first edition.

INTRODUCTION

One of the perennial ambitions of Christian Europeans, throughout the centuries, has been the verification of the Bible. Beginning with Eusebius, in the fourth century, Christian writers sought to enlist the histories of Mesopotamia and Egypt to answer the attacks of those who viewed the Old Testament as fable or, even worse, as propaganda. In this spirit Eusebius, employing the Egyptian history of the Ptolemaic scholar Manetho, constructed a chronology for Egypt based on biblical time scales. Thus for example he followed earlier Jewish commentators in tying the start of Egyptian history with the start of Hebrew history. Such endeavors made Ramses II contemporary with the Exodus, supposedly in the fourteenth or fifteenth century BC (for the simple reason that the Book of Exodus claimed the enslaved Israelites had built a city named Ramses) and identified Menes, the first pharaoh, with Adam (because Menes or Min sounded like "man", a common enough word in ancient languages), thereby making Egyptian civilization commence sometime in the fourth millennium BC, the date of Creation favored by Jewish chroniclers.

Over the centuries, the early Christian and Jewish writers' Egyptian system became the "traditional" chronology for the Kingdom of the Nile, and, incredibly enough — though few contemporary Egyptologists are aware of it — it still forms the basis of our understanding of that history.

With the translation of the hieroglyphs in the years following 1821, it was confidently expected that biblical history was about to receive damatic confirmation. Now that Ramses II for example was more than a name in Manetho's list, it was believed that documents from his time might contain information relating to the Exodus. But such hopes were soon dashed, as it became apparent that the native literature of Egypt was remarkably silent with regard to the Hebrews. Absolutely nothing, it seemed, from the hieroglyphic record, could be recognized as referring to the great events of Hebrew history. As the nineteenth century progressed, such efforts intensified, but always with the same negative result. By 1900 there was a general resignation on the part of orientalists that nothing of the sort would ever be found. Sporadic attempts, it is true, were made over the next half century to locate the missing links. It was found, for example, that a pharaoh named Akhnaton had established a monotheistic cult near the end of the Eighteenth Dynasty and that during his time a semi-nomadic group named "Habiru" had caused much disruption in Palestine. More than one historian and at least one noted psychiatrist (Sigmund Freud) speculated that Moses might have been a contemporary of Akhnaton and derived his own monotheistic ideas from the Egyptian heretic. Yet apart from monotheism, there was nothing to recommend the "fix." Neither Akhnaton nor any of his predecessors, or successors, mentioned the presence in Egypt of Hebrew slaves, and they certainly made no reference to anything remotely resembling the dramatic events described in the Book of Exodus. The consensus to this day, expressed by O. Eissfeldt in 1971 in the pages of *The Cambridge Ancient History*, is that, "There is no evidence outside the Old Testament for the sojourn of Israel in Egypt or for the exodus."

Thus all endeavors to synchronize the two histories came to grief, and eventually the whole idea was abandoned. It now became part of received wisdom that attempts to identify biblical personalities in Egyptian records are futile since the characters mentioned in the Bible — Abraham, Jacob, Joseph, Moses and the rest — were not the great men that the scriptural sources implied. Indeed, if they existed at all, they must have been minor figures whom the Egyptians had not thought worth mentioning. Any attempt now made to find "proof" for the Bible — especially its earlier parts — in archeology is treated with the greatest skepticism, and it is the opinion of almost all orientalists that efforts in this direction be consigned to the realms of the lunatic fringe. Quite simply, such work is not to be taken seriously.

But there have been dissenting voices. An academic storm was raised during the 1950s by the work of Immanuel Velikovsky, who argued that the catastrophic events described so vividly in the earliest parts of the Old Testament (i.e., the Deluge, the Tower of Babel, Sodom and Gomorrah, the Exodus etc.) did actually occur, and occurred very much as they were described in the Scriptures. Velikovsky held that the last of these, the Exodus, which touched directly on Egypt, was in fact a major landmark in Egyptian history. He demonstrated with admirable logic that a series of obscure hieroglyphic documents, collectively known as the "Pessimistic" literature, which spoke of chaos throughout the land and slave rebellion, were Egyptian references to the events described in the Book of Exodus, and argued that modern scholars had missed the identification because they had fundamentally misunderstood what was being spoken of in the Bible. The Ten Plagues and the parting of the Red Sea were not simply "miracles" worked by Yahweh to save the Children of Israel, they were local manifestations of a disturbance in the natural order that had afflicted the entire planet and the "Pessimistic" texts (such as the *Admonitions of Ipuwer*) were the Egyptian recollections of the same event.

Yet allowing Ipuwer and the other "Pessimistic" writers to be contemporaries of the Exodus brought to light an enormous distortion in ancient chronology: For the "Pessimistic" literature was generally believed to have originated six or seven centuries before the Exodus, at the end of Egypt's Old Kingdom — supposedly circa 2200 BC. How then, even if scholars had remarked on the apparent similarities between the two bodies of literature, could they have spoken of the same thing? Yet they did belong together, said Velikovsky, and the chronological error which separated them had effectively made nonsense of both Egyptian and Hebrew history. Realizing that Egyptian chronology was wrong, Velikovsky set about trying to correct it and also to identify the origins of the error. He went part of the way towards a resolution of both questions, yet he never really got to the bottom of either. His "Ages in Chaos" series of books, which were intended to solve the problem, remained incomplete and unfinished when he died. And he failed also to identify the true source of Egypt's faulty time scale.

Velikovsky's most comprehensive discussion of the sources of Egyptian chronology is found in his *Peoples of the Sea* (1977). There he puts the blame squarely on Manetho and on Egyptologists of the nineteenth century, who tried to construct the time scale of pharaonic history around the thirty dynasties mentioned by Manetho. Velikovsky thus assumed that it was Egypt and the Egyptologists who were at fault and that the Bible and biblical chronology was correct. In this however he was very much mistaken.

As it transpired, a comprehensive overview of the sources of ancient Egyptian and Mesopotamian chronology had to await the arrival of Gunnar Heinsohn and his work on the scene in the 1980s. Heinsohn called his readers' attention to an epoch before the advent of scientific archeology, back to the early centuries of the Christian era. It was then, he pointed out, that writers such as Eusebius and Julius Africanus had sought to make the history of Egypt, as it appeared in Manetho, agree with that of the Old Testament. Indeed, Heinsohn noted, the attempt to synchronize the two histories began even before the advent of Christianity, with the Jewish chroniclers of

Ptolemaic Alexandria. In a way, Africanus and Eusebius merely refined and fine-tuned the work these men had done. Thus when European scholars of the nineteenth century founded the science of Egyptology they did not do so in a vacuum. There already existed a "traditional" history of Egypt, one that was taught in universities and which was based firmly upon Old Testament chronology. Illustration of this is seen in the fact that before the Battle of the Pyramids, in 1798, Napoleon pointed to Cheops' famous monument and admonished his men with the words "forty centuries look down on you." He thus placed the Great Pyramid around 2200 BC (very close to the circa 2550 BC in modern textbooks). Yet this was over twenty years before Champollion had read the first line of an Egyptian inscription!

Why then did the historians, in the years after Champollion's break-through, not jettison the Bible-base chronology and start from scratch? The answer is telling: The early archeologists, from Champollion onwards, were almost all devout Christians. The very motivation for the study of Egypt was to prove the Bible correct. One of Champollion's first accomplishments in Egypt was to identify a pharaoh named Sosenk, of the Twenty-Second Dynasty, with the biblical Shishak, who according to the Book of Kings had plundered Solomon's Temple sometime around 920 BC — according to the chronology of the Old Testament.

Champollion and his successors thus did not question the traditional chronology in a radical way; they merely tried to fine-tune it and provide it with some form of scientific justification. This they felt they had found in the so-called Sothic Calendar. I need not go into the details here of the Sothic Calendar and its pseudo-scientific methodology, for it has already been thoroughly debunked — as well as formally repudiated by none other than Wolfgang Helck, the doyen of European Egyptological studies until his death in 1993. Nonetheless, in the nineteenth century it provided the Christian Egyptologists with what they desired. They proceeded, using this, to formulate the definitive Egyptian chronology found to this day in textbooks, a chronology which is essentially the same as that constructed by Eusebius and Africanus all those centuries ago. Thus Menes the first pharaoh was brought down a little from the biblical date of circa 4000 BC to 3300 or 3200 BC, whilst Ramses II was reduced from his biblical date of circa 1400 BC to roughly 1300 BC. Sosenk I, of Manetho's Twenty-Second Dynasty, was kept in precisely the same place, namely around 920 to 900 BC.

These textbook dates are, of course, generally believed by youthful undergraduate students of our time to have nothing to do with the Bible, and to this day (notwithstanding Helck's public statement in the 1980s), they are taught that the chronology they learn from their professors has a scientific basis. Yet in the third edition of *The Cambridge Ancient History*, we find the following comment from a leading scholar concerning the date of the Exodus: "The implication [from the Book of Exodus] that there was some specially energetic activity in building leads to the assumption that the pharaoh who displayed it was Ramesses II (1304–1237 BC), pre-eminent among the rulers of Egypt for his building activity. The mention of the cities Pithom and Ramses [in Exodus] makes the conclusion a practical certainty" (O. Eissfeldt in *The Cambridge Ancient History*, Vol. 2 part 2, pp. 321-2). The writer of these words evidently believed that the date of Ramses II was arrived at independently of the Bible and that this date acted as a check and confirmation of the biblical date. Yet his own statement that the mention of a city called Ramses in Exodus made the connection a "certainty" betrays the true source of his chronology. Thus the date of the Exodus initially provided Ramses II with his place in history, and now Ramses II provides the Exodus with its place, even though the copious records of this pharaoh contain "no evidence" for either the sojourn of the Israelites or the Exodus. The circle of reasoning is complete.

Clearly then, there is strong evidence that Gunnar Heinsohn's ideas, radical though they might be, are correct, and that all of the dates provided for the pharaohs — as well as for the events of the Old Testament — are ficti-tious and need to be discarded.

The present writer, convinced by the arguments of first Velikovsky and then Heinsohn, began work on a general reconstruction of ancient history in the late 1980s. Heeding Heinsohn's call to leave aside all preconceptions, I have attempted to let the archeology, the stratigraphy and the histori-ography, speak for themselves. When that is done, an astonishing picture begins to emerge. Abandoning the biblical idea that high culture arose in the third millennium BC, it soon becomes clear that the ancient civilizations were not nearly as old as is now imagined: And with this realization comes the solution to myriads of anomalies, puzzles and riddles that have perplexed scholars for the past two hundred years. How could the Egyptians of the Early Dynastic and Pyramid Ages for example, cut and carve granite, basalt and the almost diamond-hard diorite using the copper and flint tools of the third millennium BC? And how could those same craftsmen have employed Pythagorean-style geometry in such a remote epoch? These mysteries have led to much wild speculation, but they are resolved instantly when we realize that the pyramids were not constructed in the third millennium, but between the late eleventh and eighth centuries, as shall be demonstrated in the pages to follow. The mysteries and puzzles virtually solve themselves, once the chronology is corrected.

But this is about more than just resolving mysteries. Once the hinges of world history are hung correctly a truly astonishing picture emerges. Great characters and events, long spoken of but previously untraceable in the archeology, now reveal themselves. Catastrophes of nature, clearly and graphically mentioned in all the ancient literatures, including the Bible, are found to show themselves by the signature of devastation and destruction they left in the ground. Most surprisingly of all, however, the histories of Egypt and Israel, which had previously displayed only contradiction and dissonance, now begin to form a single harmonious whole.

The central theme of this work, then, the first volume of my Ages in Alignment series, is the parallel origins of these two neighboring and closely related lands. And we begin, appropriately enough, with an examination of the earliest event recognized by both Egyptians and Hebrews: the Great Deluge. The catastrophe known as the Flood has now, of course, been universally dismissed by establishment academia as a myth, or as an exaggerated account of a local flood or floods. Yet the evidence in the ground, as we shall see, tells a very different tale; here we find abundant proofs that the story told in Genesis and in other parts of the world is not to be so easily dismissed. Indeed, the testimony of geology and paleontology is conclusive in pointing to a world-wide catastrophe at the end of the epoch known as the Pleistocene, the epoch of the mammoth, sabre-toothed tiger and the woolly rhinoceros. Vast numbers of the latter and other species, both extinct and extant, were apparently swept by giant waves into the Polar regions, where their flesh and fur was perfectly preserved by the icy temperatures. The peoples of Egypt and Mesopotamia explicitly dated their origin to the immediate aftermath of this catastrophe; and evidence will be examined to suggest that the disaster did not occur in the remote past, but just before the rise of the first civilizations — in fact, little more than 4,000 years ago! According to the textbooks, of course, 4,000 years ago the civilizations of Mesopotamia and Egypt had already reached an advanced level of development. Indeed, we are told they were at that time over 1,200 years old. But if this is the case, then the scientific evidence for a recent end to the Pleistocene, to be examined the present volume, must be wrong. If however the science is right, then it is the chronologies of Egypt and Mesopotamia that are in error, and 4,000 years ago neither civilization had yet appeared.

The evidence will show that it is the chronologies of Egypt and Mesopotamia that are in error.

After the Flood, the next major event recalled in man's collective memory is the catastrophe of the Tower, known in Genesis as the Tower of Babel and in other traditions as the Battle of the Tower or the War of the Gods and the

Giants, etc. As with the Flood, this was a real event which left a very clear signature in the ground, in the form of burned and devastated settlements throughout the Near East and elsewhere. The Tower event is doubly important in that it represents a chronological marker directly preceding the rise of literate civilization in Mesopotamia, Egypt, India, China, and the Americas, and furthermore signals the moment when the histories of Egypt and the Bible come together. For the characters of Menes/Min, the first pharaoh, and Abraham, the father of the Israelites, are closely bound to the story of the Tower. The latter feature itself was, as we shall see, an apparently electromagnetic phenomenon which manifested itself at the Northern Pole in the direct aftermath of the Great Deluge. Its "destruction" during a subsequent catastrophe was viewed with horror by early man, who reacted to the event by offering propitiary blood sacrifices. These included human sacrifices — performed atop mountains or man-made high places ("altars") — as well as circumcision, the voluntary mutilation of man's own "tower." In Egypt, circumcision was intimately connected with Menes, first pharaoh (himself a euhemerization of the phallic god Min), whilst in Israel the custom was initiated by Abraham.

Thus the epoch of Abraham and the epoch of Menes were one and the same. As well as circumcision, both characters were said to have been the source of many of the arts of high culture, and both of them can be thematically identified with the god Thoth, or Mercury/Hermes, who in ancient tradition was associated with the story of the Tower and the development of literate civilization. The problem here, of course, is that Abraham is conventionally placed around 2100 BC, whereas Menes is dated to 3300 or 3200 BC. How then, could they be contemporary? So, here again we are confronted with the thorny question of chronology. Had the latter not intervened then scholars would long ago have recognized the connection between the two characters and would have begun a correct and properly synchronized reconstruction of the two histories. But this did not happen, with the result being the distorted and utterly confused "history" that we now find in the textbooks. Investigation reveals that the Egyptian founder-hero and his Hebrew counterpart should both have been placed between 1400 and 1300 BC, which means in effect that whilst 1,000 "phantom" years have been added to Hebrew history, over 2,000 years have been added to the Egyptian.

It was just these unnaturally extended chronologies that kept Egyptian and Hebrew histories "out of sync" and contradictory.

Having thus linked the epoch of Abraham with that of Menes, we now find the histories of Israel and Egypt fitting together like matching pieces of a jigsaw. The next "match" comes with Joseph and Imhotep. Egyptian tradition tells us that two centuries or so after Menes there lived a great pharaoh named Djoser ("the Splendid"), whose vizier, Imhotep, was regarded as the greatest of all Egyptian sages. Djoser and Imhotep, the legend says, lived during a famine lasting seven years, and it was a dream of the king's that provided Imhotep with the clue to solving the crisis. Similarly, Hebrew tradition tells us that two centuries or so after Abraham there lived Joseph, the great seer and visionary, who became pharaoh's vizier and helped solve the crisis of a seven-year famine by interpreting the king's dreams.

Historians, of course, have long been aware of the striking resemblances between Imhotep and Joseph, and a great deal has been written on the subject. They would undoubtedly have realized the common identity of the two men a long time ago, but the erroneous chronology, which separated them by over a thousand years, confused the issue.

The next "match" in the two histories comes of course with the Exodus, an event which we find has absolutely nothing to do with either the Eighteenth or Nineteenth Dynasties. Archeology tells us that sometime near the close of the Early Dynastic period, in the Third Dynasty, a great natural catastrophe, whose effects are still plainly visible, struck the entire Near East. This period of darkness, but also of invention and creativity, brought forth the distinctive "Pessimistic" literary *genre* of Egypt. Scribes of the time, most especially Ipuwer and Neferty, described the horrific events which left the country kingless, huge numbers of people dead, cities flattened and the economy destroyed. The parallels between the events described in Exodus and those in the Pessimistic Texts have, of course, been noted by scholars. But once again, the connection was missed because conventional chronology decreed that the Egyptian documents predated the Exodus by many centuries.

In fact, both have been misplaced. The Exodus, as well as the disaster described in the Pessimistic Texts, actually occurred around 1000 BC, some five centuries after the "traditional" date.

In the years following this catastrophe, the Egyptians constructed their greatest monuments — the pyramids. These were erected in honor of the celestial deities whose awesome power had so recently been made manifest. And whilst the Egyptians erected the pyramids, the Hebrews were engaged in the Conquest of Canaan.

Having placed Moses and the Exodus in the early tenth century BC, rather than the remote antiquity of the fifteenth, we might be justified in taking more seriously the biblical claim that there was a man called Moses and that it was he who composed the Torah or Pentateuch, the first five books of the Bible. We end therefore with an examination of the structure of Genesis and the rest of the Torah, one which provides qualified support for such a belief. Here we discover that the books attributed to Moses, as might be expected, are heavily influenced by Egyptian custom, usage, and language. This is in total contrast to the later biblical books, where the Egyptian influence is much diminished. Thus it would appear that a genuine body of tradition, reaching back to the Exodus itself, formed the basis of the Torah. Whether any of this material can be attributed to a man named "Moses" is beside the point: the Egyptian material is genuine.

As might be expected, the sources used in a study such as this are diverse in the extreme. I am particularly indebted to the Trojan work of scholars in many fields over the past century, and I have found publications such as Pritchard's *Ancient Near Eastern Texts* and Breasted's *Ancient Records* absolutely indispensable as sources of documentary material. The meticulous excavating, cataloguing and documenting carried out over the years by great figures such as Maspero, Brugsch, Schaeffer and Breasted has been most helpful, and their scrupulous honesty and attention to detail has provided invaluable assistance in the task of rectifying Egypt's chaotic chronology.

However, as I have already made clear, it is to Immanuel Velikovsky that the present work owes most. Velikovsky's brilliant exposition of the contradictions inherent in ancient chronology is the key that has unlocked the secrets of antiquity. That his Ages in Chaos books failed to deliver a satisfactory reconstruction of history was in no way a major failing of his. He was a pioneer, and the constraints within which he worked made it virtually impossible for him to get everything right. As it was, a great deal of what he said was absolutely right and should have formed the cornerstone of any general reconstruction. Other scholars, failing to profit from Velikovsky's revolutionary insights, threw out all his historical work and constructed revised chronologies of their own, chronologies which repeated all the mistakes made by Velikovsky and added others which had previously not existed. These became yet more impediments to unraveling the truth.

Having said that, I am also indebted to those writers of the Velikovskian school who have carried on the work of reconstruction in a constructive way and have contributed so much to its completion. Above all, Gunnar Heinsohn's insights are of key importance in this regard. His earliest papers, written during the 1980s, focused primarily on the social and economic development of Mesopotamia and provided important pointers to the way forward. In particular, at a time when errors had been identified in Velikovsky's methods and findings, and when many scholars both in America and Britain had begun to jettison the entire corpus of his work, Heinsohn as it were took up the torch of Velikovsky's radicalism and prevented what would perhaps have been the total loss of everything his predecessor had achieved. Heinsohn's first book, *Die Sumerer gab es nicht* (Frankfurt, 1988) demonstrated in a clear and concise way the need for a complete overhaul of our understanding of the Early and Middle Bronze Ages. Here he proved that Mesopotamian history, properly speaking, did not begin until after the middle of the second millennium BC. Utilizing the evidence of stratigraphy, Heinsohn demonstrated that the so-called Sumerians and Akkadians of the third millennium BC were alter-egos of the Chaldeans and Imperial Assyrians of the first millennium BC. This meant a shortening of all ancient Near Eastern history by a full two millennia and called for the reduction of Egyptian history by a commensurate span.

I differ from Heinsohn in a great many details, but to him goes the credit of being the first to identify the true scope of the problem facing ancient historians, as well as pinpointing the source of the fictitious textbook system.

The limitations of a work such as this are obvious. Because of the wide scope of the evidence surveyed, and drawn as it is from many disciplines, only a small portion of what exists has been examined. Some subjects in the book could certainly have been examined in greater detail, though I am aware that this could have obscured the central argument and weakened its general impact. I concede that errors may have crept into the body of the book. In any work, mistakes are inevitable, and this is particularly so in an endeavor such as this. Nonetheless, I hold by the major conclusions reached and am very conscious that I have the full weight of ancient tradition on my side. The conventional history of Egypt is built, ultimately, on a mistaken application of biblical dates to Egyptian; the history that follows is, I contend, how that history would have been written had we not been misled all those centuries ago by the chroniclers of Alexandria and by Eusebius. It is basically a rediscovery of Egypt's history based upon the writings of the Egyptians themselves. The reader may judge for himself which of the two makes most sense.

CHAPTER 1. THE DELUGE AND OTHER CATASTROPHES

A Universal Tradition

Around the globe mankind's most ancient myths and legends speak of an epoch of great natural catastrophes, an epoch inaugurated by a devastating universal Deluge that almost wiped out the human race. This cataclysm was followed by a series of lesser disasters which, though not as severe as the Flood, nonetheless visited great destruction upon the world. Almost everyone is familiar with the biblical version of these events, which, in chronological order, begin with the Flood of Noah, followed by the "fall" or destruction of the Tower of Babel, followed in turn by the destruction of Sodom and Gomorrah (by "fire and brimstone"), followed by the Exodus of the Israelites from Egypt, amidst darkness, devastating plagues, and weird happenings on the Red Sea. Ancient peoples throughout the world, from China to Mexico and back, told similar tales, tales describing an "eruptive age" which saw a succession of mass destructions of humanity by water, fire, hurricane and earthquake. The Greeks told of devastating earthquakes and massive tidal waves which in an earlier age had swept over the land, sometimes almost to the mountaintops. The *Theogony* of Hesiod is a lengthy description of such events, which are presented as the result of titanic battles amongst the gods. As in the Bible and elsewhere, these disasters are initiated with a world-wide Flood.

When such stories began to come to the attention of European scholars, from the sixteenth century onward, they naturally assumed that they referred to the same events as those described in the Bible. This was particularly the case with the various Native American Flood legends which were told to the Spanish Conquistadors and the churchmen who followed them into the New World. Simultaneous European exploration of the Far East, of India and China in particular, revealed analogous traditions in those regions. And ever more material, from virtually every corner of the globe, began to reach the studies of European scholars as the seventeenth and eighteenth centuries progressed. But it was only during the nineteenth century, when Mesopotamia's ancient cuneiform script was finally deciphered, that the biblical tales seemed fully confirmed and verified. Indeed, scholars announced the existence of no less than three separate Mesopotamian Flood legends. The Sumerian version, apparently the oldest, involved a hero named Ziusudra, who occurs as Xisuthros in the account given by Berossus.

1. The "Great Deluge" as imagined by Francis Danby.

Two other versions, the Akkadian and the Old Babylonian, gave the names of the hero who survived the flood as Utnapishtim and Atrahasis. One of these in particular, the Akkadian story of Utnapishtim, displayed striking parallels with that of Noah. Most of the incidents and motifs occurring in the latter also appear in the story of Utnapishtim. Like Noah, Utnapishtim is given a divine warning of the impending cataclysm, and like Noah he constructs a great ship in order to survive it. As with Noah, Utna-pishtim brings various animals into his ark, and he is the sole survivor of all humanity. In one area, however, the two accounts differ. Unlike the biblical, the Mesopotamian flood stories attribute the destruction not to one God, but to various gods and, on occasion, to a dragon-monster named Tiamat.

Such accounts seemed to add weight to the similar stories from virtu-ally every part of the world which learned Europeans had collected in the previous two centuries.

No truly comprehensive cataloging of flood legends has yet been under-taken, though the anthropologist Sir James Frazer lists over two hundred in his encyclopedic *Folklore in the Old Testament*. Here are just a few of the tradi-tions recounted by Frazer, selected from far-reaching and diverse parts of the globe.

From Mexico, one account of the deluge described how a man named Coxcox (or Teocipactli) and a woman called Xochiquetzal saved themselves in a little bark, "having afterwards got to land upon a mountain called by them Colhuaacan, had there a great many children; [and] that these children were all born dumb, until a dove from a lofty tree imparted to them languages, but differing so much that they could not understand one another. The Tlas-calans [by contrast] pretended that the nen who survived the deluge were transformed into apes, but recovered speech and reason by degrees."[1]

Among the myriad stories from the Americas listed by Frazer, one told along the Purus River in South America contains many key elements found around the world. We are told that the Pamarys, Abederys and Kataushys

> relate that at once on a time people heard a rumbling above and below the ground. The sun and moon, also, turned red, blue, and yellow, and the wild beasts mingled fearlessly with men. A month later they heard a roar and saw darkness ascending from the earth to the sky, accom-panied by thunder and heavy rain, which blotted out the day and the earth. Some people lost themselves, some died, without knowing why; for everything was in a dreadful state of confusion. The water rose very high, till the earth was sunk beneath the water and only the branches of the highest trees still stood out above the flood. Thither the people had fled for refuge and there, perched among the boughs, they perished of cold and hunger; for all the time it was dark and the rain fell. Then only Uassu and his wife were saved. When they came down after the flood they could not find a single corpse, no, not so much as a heap of bleached bones. After that they had many children, and they said to one another, 'Go to, let us build our houses on the river, that when the

---

[1] Sir James Frazer, *Folklore in the Old Testament: Abridged version* (London, 1918), p. 107

water comes, we too may rise with it.' But when they saw that the land was dry and solid, they thought no more about it.[2]

The above tradition, which connects the Flood with unusual events in the cosmos, particularly on the sun and the moon, accords very closely with similar accounts in other parts of the world. The darkness, the shaking of the earth, and the terrible cold, are likewise details occurring in other traditions.

Frazer retells flood stories from various parts of Asia, and the ancient lands of India and China supply several of these. Curiously, though, Frazer claims that the Han Chinese (as opposed to ethnic minorities within the country) "did not have a tradition of a universal flood,"[3] a claim which is quite simply untrue. Frazer seems to have been unaware of the legends surrounding the life and times of the Emperor Yahou, a figure whose personality was regarded as "the most auspicious in the Chinese annals,"[4] yet during his reign the country was overwhelmed by an immense catastrophe. "At that time the miracle is said to have happened that the sun during a span of ten days did not set, the forests were ignited, and a multitude of abominable vermin were brought forth."[5] Elsewhere we read that, "In the lifetime of Yao [Yahou] the sun did not set for ten full days and the entire land was flooded."[6]

This phenomenon of a brilliant light that lasted many days just prior to the onset of the Deluge is encountered in traditions throughout the globe. We are told that an immense wave that "reached the sky" fell down on China. "The water was well up on the high mountains, and the foothills could not be seen at all."[7] It was said that the cataclysm which struck China in Yahou's time took many years from which to recover. "Destructive in their overflow are the waters of the inundation," said the emperor. "In their vast extent they embrace the hills and overtop the great heights, threatening the heavens with their floods."

Although Frazer seems to have discounted the legend of Yahou as referring to a universal Flood, he freely admits to and lists a multitude of Deluge legends indubitably referring to a worldwide calamity amongst the various minority nations of China, as well as among the other peoples of East Asia. One of these is that of the Lolos, an aboriginal race from Yunnan in south-

---

[2] Ibid., p. 100
[3] Ibid., p. 131
[4] H. Murray, J. Crawfurd, and others, *An Historical and descriptive Account of China* (London, 1836)
[5] "Yao," *Universal Lexicon*, Vol. XL (1749).
[6] J. Hubner, *Kurze Fragen aus der politischen Historie* (Leipzig, 1729)
[7] *The Shu King, the Canon of Yao* (trans. Legge, 1879)

western China. According to the Lolos, the catastrophe was unleashed by Tse-gu-dzih, one of the early and long-lived patriarchs. We hear that,

> Men were wicked, and Tse-gu-dzih sent down a messenger to them on earth, asking for some flesh and blood from a mortal. No one would give them except only one man, Du-mu by name. So Tse-gu-dzih in wrath locked the rain-gates, and the water mounted to the sky. But Du-mu, who complied with the divine injunction, was saved, together with his four sons, in a log hollowed out of a *Pieris* tree; and with them in the log were likewise saved otters, wild ducks, and lampreys. From his four sons are descended the civilized peoples who can write, such as the Chinese and the Lolos. But the ignorant races of the world are descendants of the wooden figures whom Du-mu constructed after the deluge in order to people the drowned earth.[8]

India of course supplied a substantial number of Flood stories, the most famous of which concerned Manu, the progenitor of the human race. The legend, as related in the Sanskrit *Satapatha Brahmana*, goes thus:

> In the morning they brought to Manu water for washing, just as now they are wont to bring water for washing the hands. When he was washing himself, a fish came into his hands. It spake to him the word, 'Rear me, I will save thee!' 'Wherefrom wilt thou save me?' 'A flood will carry away all these creatures: from that I will save thee!' 'How am I to rear thee?' It said, 'As long as we are small, there is great destruction for us: fish devours fish. Thou wilt first keep me in a jar. When I outgrow that, thou wilt dig a pit and keep me in it. When I outgrow that, thou wilt take me down to the sea, for then I shall be beyond destruction.' It soon became a ghasha (a large fish); for that grows largest of all fish. Thereupon it said, 'In such and such a year the flood will come. Thou shalt then attend to me by preparing a ship; and when the flood has risen thou shalt enter into the ship, and I will save thee from it.' After he had reared it in this way, he took it down to the sea. And in the same year which the fish had indicated to him, he attended to the advice of the fish by preparing a ship; and when the flood had risen, he entered into the ship. The fish then swam up to him, and to its horn he tied the rope of the ship, and by that means he passed swiftly up to yonder northern mountain. It then said, 'I have saved thee. Fasten the ship to a tree; but let not the water cut thee off, whilst thou art on the mountain. As the water subsides, thou mayest gradually descend!' Accordingly he gradually descended, and hence that slope of the northern mountains is called 'Manu's descent.' The flood then swept away all those creatures, and Manu alone remained here.[9]

---

[8] Frazer, op cit., p. 83
[9] Frazer, op cit., pp. 78-9

The tale goes on to describe how Manu produced a woman by offering a sacrifice to the waters of clarified butter, sour milk, whey and curds. With this woman, he re-peopled the earth.

Frazer listed a veritable plethora of Flood legends from Australia and the Pacific islands, as well as from virtually every region of the world, though he regarded those from Africa as being perhaps influenced by biblical ideas and so generally discounted them. Those from Europe he treated in the same way — though with no good reason. How could an Irish tradition, for example, which spoke of a vast wave overwhelming the entire island of Ireland have been in any way inspired by the Bible? Genesis makes no mention of tidal waves, only rain and water from the "fountains of the deep." A similar tradition among the Sami people (Lapps) told how the creator god Jubmel unleashed devastation upon the world to punish the misdeeds of men.[10] We are told that "when the wickedness increased among the human beings," the center of the earth "trembled with terror so that the upper layers of the earth fell away and many of the people were hurled down into those caved-in places to perish." "And Jubmel, the heaven-lord himself, came down.... His terrible anger flashed like red, blue, and green fire-serpents, and the people hid their faces, and the children screamed with fear.... The angry god spoke: 'I shall reverse the world. I shall bid the rivers flow upward; I shall cause the sea to gather itself up into a huge towering wall which I shall hurl upon your wicked earth-children, and thus destroy them and all life.'" At this point,

> Jubmel set a storm-wind blowing,
> and the wild air-spirits raging....
> Foaming, dashing, rising sky-high
> came the sea-wall, crushing all things.
> Jubmel, with one strong upheaval,
> made the earth-lands all turn over;
> then, the world again he righted.
> Now the mountains and the highlands
> could no more be seen by Beijke [the sun].
> Filled with groans of dying people,
> was the fair earth, home of mankind.
> No more Beijke shone in heaven.

The mention here of vast earthquakes and chasms that opened in the ground, of the appearance of a celestial body with serpent-like features, a sea-wall that crushed all in its path, mountains levelled or covered in water, the world turned over and then righted, and the disappearance of the sun —

---

[10]Leonne de Cambrey, *Lapland Legends* (Yale, 1926)

all of these ideas occur in Flood legends throughout the world, though most do not appear in the biblical account.

The Deluge in Mesopotamian and Egyptian Tradition

As the present work is aimed at recovering the histories of the civilizations of the Near East, it behooves us to take a closer look at the Flood legends current among the ancient Mesopotamians and Egyptians.

The scholars who deciphered Mesopotamia's cuneiform script in the mid-nineteenth century were somewhat surprised at the centrality of the Flood to the culture and religion of the region. There were many parallels, of course, with the biblical account, yet there were also many differences. Whereas the story found in Genesis is rather matter of fact and even pedestrian, the Mesopotamian version is replete with the most colorful imagery and high drama. Consider for example Utnapishtim's description of the event to the hero Gilgamesh, where he tells how Ishtar or Inanna — the goddess Venus — orders the general destruction of mankind:

> The Annunaki lifted up their torches;
> setting the land ablaze with their flare;
> Stunned shock over Adad's deeds overtook the heavens
> And turned to blackness all that had been light.
> The [...] land shattered like a [...] pot.
> All day long the South Wind blew [...],
> blowing fast, submerging the mountain in water,
> overwhelming the people like an attack.
> No one could see his fellow,
> they could not recognize each other in the torrent.
> The gods were frightened by the Flood,
> Retreated, ascending to the heaven of Anu.
> The gods were cowering like dogs, crouching by the outer wall.
> Ishtar shrieked like a woman in childbirth,
> The sweet-voiced Mistress of the Gods wailed:
> 'The olden days have alas turned to clay,
> because I said evil things in the Assembly of the Gods!
> How could I say evil things in the Assembly of the Gods,
> Ordering a catastrophe to destroy my people?!
> No sooner have I given birth to my dear people
> Than they fill the sea like so many fish!'
> The gods — those of the Annunaki — were weeping with her,
> The gods humbly sat weeping, sobbing with grief(?),
> Their lips burning, parched with thirst.

Six days and seven nights
Came the wind and flood, the storm flattening the land.
When the seventh day arrived, the storm was pounding,
The flood was a war — struggling with itself like a woman writhing (in labor).[11]

Leaving aside such differences between the Mesopotamian story and the biblical, scholars were nonetheless surprised by many striking parallels in the two accounts. Just as Noah is warned by God of the impending cataclysm, so too Utnapishtim is forewarned in a dream, and he, like Noah, is ordered to build a boat/ark with which to save himself, his family, some friends, and two of every species of animal. As in the Genesis account, the outside of the ark is covered in pitch, and has only one door. When the rain comes, it lasts six days, in contrast to the biblical forty, yet the endings are remarkably alike. Utnapishtim, like Noah, releases a series of birds to test whether dry ground exists. These are a dove, a raven and a swallow, in contrast to the raven and three doves released by Noah. And both arks find land on a mountaintop: Ararat in the Bible and Mt. Nisir in the Babylonian story. Finally, just as Noah offers a sacrifice to God upon reaching dry land, so too does Utnapishtim. Finally, like Noah, Utnapishtim offers a blood sacrifice upon disembarking from the Ark.

2. Image from Mesopotamia, thought to represent Utnapishtim and his Ark.

The significance of blood sacrifice in relation to past cataclysms will be examined more fully at a later stage.

Some versions of the Mesopotamian myth linked it to a conflict amongst the gods, with Marduk defending heaven from an assault by the dragon-monster Tiamat. This creature he gutted and dismembered, using its parts to

---

[11] M. G. Kovacs, *The Epic of Gilgamesh* (Stanford, 1989), pp. 100f.

create as it were a new heaven and a new earth. And it was immediately after the Flood that, as the cuneiform records state, "Kingship descended from Heaven." In short, civil societies governed by priest-kings were established. The Babylonian Creation Epic tells us how immediately after destroying Tiamat, Marduk orders the building of the first temple:

> I shall make a house to be a luxurious dwelling for myself
> And shall found his [Marduk's] cult center within it ...

In gratitude for saving the universe from Tiamat, the other gods offer to build Marduk's home for him, at which point,

> His face lit up greatly, like daylight.
> 'Create Babylon, whose construction you requested!
> Let its mud bricks be molded, and build high the shrine.'

During the space of an entire year the gods manufacture bricks, and by the end of the second year they have built the great shrine and ziggurat of Esagila, Another well-known Mesopotamian text has the work of rebuilding guided by the goddess Ishtar, who is herself the bringer of destruction:

> My mankind, in its destruction I will ...
> I will return the people to their settlements
> After the ... of kingship had been lowered from heaven,
> After the exalted tiara and the throne of kingship had been lowered from heaven,
> He perfected the rites and the exalted divine laws ...,
> Founded the five cities in ... pure places,
> Called their names, apportioned them as cult centers.[12]

The Mesopotamian sources therefore connect not only the establishment of religious customs, but the very idea of priest-kingship, to the aftermath of the cataclysm. The whole concept of kingship was everywhere initially inseparable from priesthood, and all the early kings were at the same time High Priests, one of whose major functions was the offering of blood sacrifices on high altars. This is further emphasized in another Mesopotamian text, The Epic of Etana, which states that immediately after the Flood:

> The great Annunaki, who decree the fate,
> Sat down, taking counsel about the land.
> They who created the regions, who set up the establishment,

---

[12] S. N. Kramer, *History Begins at Sumer: Thirty-Nine Firsts in Man's Recorded History* (Pennsylvania, 1981), p. 149.

> The Igigi were too lofty for mankind,
> A stated time for mankind they decreed.
> The beclouded people, in all, had not set up a king.
> At that time, no tiara had been tied on, nor crown,
> And no scepter had been inlaid with lapis;
> The shrines had not been built altogether.
> The seven [Igigi] had barred the gates against the settlers [settlements].
> Scepter, crown tiara, and [shepherd's] crook
> Lay deposited before Anu in heaven,
> There being no counseling for its people.
> [Then] kingship descended from heaven.[13]

Ideas of exactly the same kind are encountered in Egypt.

It is often stated that the Egyptians did not have a Flood story, and yet, in the words of Professor William Mullen of Bard College, New York, "the phrase 'great flood' appears several times in the Pyramid Texts and it is quite distinct from the standard phrase for the annual inundation; usually it forms part of the longer phrase 'the great flood which came forth from the great lady, Heaven.'"[14] As a matter of fact, the "Great Flood" — *Mehet Weret*, occupied a central position in Egyptian cosmology. Mehet Weret was portrayed as a goddess, one who bore a close relationship to Hathor. The latter, like Mehet Weret, was known as the "Eye of Ra" and wore a horned solar disc. She was, furthermore, responsible for a catastrophe which destroyed much of humanity, as we shall see. Manetho, although writing in Greek, was an Egyptian, and he refers to the first three dynasties of pharaohs as "kings who reigned after the Flood." Again, Egyptian cosmology had much to say of a "watery abyss" which existed before the act of creation and before the emergence of the first land. This they named the Nun, or Nu, an idea suggestive, as it also is in Genesis, of an ancestral memory of a world-engulfing inundation. Furthermore, the term Nu is more than a little reminiscent of Noah, a name which has an uncertain etymology and may not even be Hebrew.[15] In addition to all this, we need to remember that the Egyptians had a legend of World Destruction (in the so-called "Book of the Heavenly Cow") which, though not specifically speaking of a flooded world, strongly hints at it. Here

---

[13] J. Pritchard (ed.), *Ancient Near Eastern Texts* (Princeton, 1949), p. 114
[14] William Mullen, "Myth and the Science of Catastrophism: A Reading of the Pyramid Texts," *Pensée*, Vol. 3, No. 1 (1973).
[15] The name Noah is generally believed to derive from the Hebrew *noach*, meaning "rest," but this is by no means certain. As we shall see later, the Book of Genesis is replete with Egyptian cultural influence, so the possibility of it being derived from the Egyptian watery abyss, the Nu, cannot be easily dismissed.

the great destroyer is Hathor, the "Eye of Ra," a goddess closely identified with Mehet Weret, the Great Flood.

The story, told in several surviving papyri, recounted how Ra, tiring of the wickedness of mankind, sent out his eye, in the form of the goddess Hathor, to punish the human race mercilessly. Before she could complete the job however Ra repented of his actions, and, in order to save a remnant of humanity, made Hathor drunk with vast quantities of beer, which he dyed red to resemble the blood of millions of people. The ruse worked, and Hathor desisted from her work of destruction. An excerpt from the story, translated by Erik Hornung, reads thus (and note the prominent position in the story occupied by Nun, the watery abyss):[16]

> Then said Ra to Nun, "O eldest god in whom I originated and you ancestral gods, see, mankind, who originated from my Eye, has contrived a plot against me. Tell me what you would do about this, since I am seeking a solution. I cannot slay them until I have heard what you might have to say about this."

> The Majesty of Nun replied, "O my son Ra, the god mightier than the one who produced you and greater than those who created you, stay put on your throne! The fear of you is great; your Eye shall proceed against those who conspire against you." The Majesty of Ra said, "See, they have fled into the desert [the lands of chaos without order], their hearts fearful over what I might say to them." Then they said unto His Majesty, "Send out your Eye that it may smite them for you, those who have conspired so wickedly. No Eye is as capable as it to smite them for you. May it descend it the form of Hathor."

> Then this goddess returned after she had slain mankind in the desert. The Majesty of this god said, "Welcome, Hathor! Have you accomplished that for which you set out?" This goddess replied, "As you live for me, I have overpowered mankind and it was agreeable to my heart." The Majesty of Ra said, "I shall gain power over them as king. Hold off decimating them!" [at this point Sekhmet came into being whose bloodlust was unquenchable and so Ra must devise a plan to stop her].

This Egyptian tale of World Destruction is thus strongly reminiscent of the Mesopotamian one, quoted above, which clearly identifies the goddess Ishtar/Inanna as the agent of divine wrath. Hathor was without question identifiable with the latter goddess, and both represent the goddess and planet Venus. We therefore have very strong grounds for supposing the

---

[16]E. Hornung in (ed. William Kelly Simpson) *The Literature of Ancient Egypt* (Yale, 2003)

World Destruction inflicted by Hathor is identifiable with the Great Flood inflicted by Ishtar.[17]

As in the Land of the Two Rivers, the founding of cities and the establishment of kingship were believed by the Egyptians to have occurred in the aftermath of a great catastrophe, though, as we shall see, a second cosmic upheaval struck the earth before the emergence of literate civilization.

The Evidence of Geology and Paleontology

Whilst anthropologists, linguists and historians were collecting Flood stories from throughout the world, scientists were finding manifold proofs of cataclysmic events on the earth at various epochs in the past. Early geologists noted that large parts of our planet's surface were covered with what is called "the drift." This comprises entire geological strata of material such as gravel, sand, or clay, which had "drifted" from some other destination and shaped itself into rolling hillocks, mounds, and "drumlins." These features looked to early geologists as if they had been shaped by the action of onrushing and retreating water; and that impression was strengthened by the presence of rounded pebbles, rocks and boulders in the drift material. Such shaping can only be accomplished by the action of water. Also noted over large parts of the earth were huge numbers of "erratics," rocks — sometimes of great size — which do not belong to the geological strata of the region in which they are found and which evidently had been deposited there by some external force.

In order to account for these features, researchers of the eighteenth and early nineteenth centuries invoked vast tidal waves, which, it was assumed, had swept over the surface of the earth, and which were named "waves of translation."[18]

Even as geologists sought to make sense of the earth's history through the study of its rocks and clays, zoologists were in the process of forming a new science; that of paleontology: the study of the history of life. From the time of Georges Cuvier, the French founder of paleontology, it became clear that the earth had once harbored myriads of creatures no longer in existence. Some of these, such as the mammoth and the woolly rhinoceros, were closely related to modern species, and there seemed little doubt that the extinct animals had died in some great catastrophe. That at least was the opinion of Cuvier and

---

[17]"The work [Book of the Heavenly Cow] has been compared with the Mesopotamian Atrahasis and the biblical tale of Noah's Ark and the Great Flood ..." Joshua J. Mark, "The Book of the Heavenly Cow," 22 August, 2019 www.worldhistory.org

[18]All of these features are now – without any compelling reason in most cases – attributed to the action of ice during what are now termed the "Glacial Periods."

most other natural historians of his epoch — the early and mid-nineteenth century. From the frozen wastelands of the north, from Siberia and Alaska, came reports of the remains of vast numbers of creatures, their flesh perfectly preserved by the intense cold, but their bones smashed and limbs torn off. Often these beasts were found heaped on top of each other, in immense deposits, and their bodies intermingled with uprooted trees, boulders and gravel. From less remote lands too, such as Great Britain, came reports of sensational discoveries, of mountain caves filled with the shattered bones of bison, rhinoceros, elephant and hippopotamus. Only a great and terrible flood, it was surmised, could have lifted herds of such animals, from such varied and remote environments, and thrown them into the deepest and most inaccessible reaches of Britain's cave systems.[19]

Cuvier himself, the chief proponent of the flood theory, was by no means a biblical scholar or in any way influenced by the Bible. Indeed, as a child of the Enlightenment he was, if anything, quite hostile to the Scriptures. Nevertheless, some other "catastrophists" of the time were far more favorably disposed towards the sacred writings and they attempted to link the geological evidence with the biblical account. Such men identified the last great extinction, which occurred at the end of the Pleistocene (the age of the mammoth, woolly rhinoceros, sabre-toothed tiger, etc.), with the Flood of the Bible, and accordingly dated it to around 3000 BC. In time, "Catastrophism" or the belief that great cataclysms of nature had fundamentally affected the course of earth's history, came to be linked, in part at least, with a biblical view of the past.

By the 1850s, however, a revolution in scientific thinking was underway. After the acceptance of Darwin's theory of evolution through natural selection, scientists distanced themselves from a biblical world-view, or indeed a world-view that could be construed as in any way favorable to the Bible. Quite simply, the evolution controversy seemed to have thoroughly discredited the first part of the Bible in scholarly eyes. In addition, a group of scholars in Germany, most especially Karl Heinrich Graf, Albrecht Alt, Martin Noth and above all Julius Wellhausen (the so-called "Berlin School"), began to subject the Bible to critical examination and to interpret the Book of Genesis in a way that had never been done before; as a work of literature rather than Revealed Truth. The early patriarchs, it soon became clear, were most probably not real people but humanized gods, whilst large parts of Genesis could only have been written in the seventh or sixth centuries BC — or even later

---

[19]See e.g., J. McEnery, Cavern Researches, or discoveries of Organic remains and of British and Roman Relics, in the caves of *Kent's Hole, Anstis Cove, Chudleigh and Barry Head* (London, 1859).

— as they contained ideas, symbols and technologies that were unknown before that time.[20] Thus it was that the German critics, together with the Darwinian natural historians, put paid by the end of the nineteenth century to the idea of a world-wide Flood.

But if no such event occurred, this raised the problem of explaining the legend and, even more worryingly, explaining the similar traditions found throughout the world. This was by no means an easy task, because it meant too the reinterpretation of the geological and paleontological evidence which Cuvier and his associates had identified. The literary material was eventually "explained away" as exaggerated memories of local events which early man, in his ignorance, had imagined had engulfed the entire earth.[21] The paleontological and geological evidence was not so easy to deal with, though in time a novel expedient was employed: it was decided that mass extinctions, for example, were a "mystery" which future research would undoubtedly solve.[22]

This has been the scholarly consensus since the late nineteenth century, yet it is a consensus never shared by the "man in the street" and it is one which continually has had to explain disturbing evidence which repeatedly brought the Flood story back to the public eye. The most striking, and perhaps most talked about of this evidence, comes from the Arctic; more specifically from the permafrost regions of Siberia and Alaska. Findings from these areas have been repeatedly cited by alternative thinkers over the past century-and-a-half — though these same findings are invariably and even studiously ignored in modern textbooks. Yet this is evidence of such importance that it demands the attention of anyone honestly seeking the truth; and as such I wish to present a small sample here.

In the Fairbanks district of Alaska, for example, where the Tanana River joins the Yukon, gold is mined out of gravel and "muck". This muck is a frozen mass of animals and trees. Froelich Rainey, of the University of Alaska, describes the scene:

> Wide cuts, often several miles in length and sometimes as much as 140 feet in depth, are now being sluiced out along stream valleys tributary to the Tanana in the Fairbanks District. In order to reach the gold-bearing gravel-beds an over-burden of frozen silt or "muck" is removed with hydraulic giants. This "muck" contains enormous numbers of

---

[20]See e.g., Julius Wellhausen, *Prolegomena zur Geschichte Israels* (Berlin, 1883).
[21]This was the explanation favored by James Frazer, who also claimed that Flood stories represented a rationalization of such mysterious phenomena as sea-shells occurring on mountains-tops, etc. See e.g., *Folklore in the Old Testament*, pp. 135-143
[22]There are several "possibilities" now in vogue, the most frequently-cited of which tend to be "climate-change" or, even more outlandishly, "over-hunting" by early humans.

frozen bones of extinct animals such as mammoth, mastodon, super-bison and horse."[23]

Professor Rainey was in no doubt that these animals perished in comparatively recent times. Along with extinct species were found enormous quantities of animals of species still surviving. Mixed with the bodies of the animals, most of whom were dismembered and whose bones were smashed — although their flesh and skin are often well preserved — were found millions upon millions of uprooted and smashed trees, along with other types of debris, such as sand and gravel. The whole mass of animals, trees and gravel was found thoroughly mixed in a promiscuous mass, as though thrown together by some immense and virtually random force.

3. Geologist Otto Geist surveys "Muck" deposits in Alaska, 1941. The uprooted and mangled trees are intermingled with the bodies of billions of Pleistocene creatures, some with flesh and fur intact, though bones are smashed and bodies often dismembered.

---

[23] F. Rainey, "Archeological Investigation in Central Alaska," *American Antiquity*, V (1940), p. 305

According to Frank C. Hibben of the University of New Mexico:

> Although the formation of the deposits of muck is not clear, there is ample evidence that at least parts of this material were deposited under catastrophic conditions. Mammal remains are for the most part dismembered and disarticulated, even though some fragments yet retain, in their frozen state, portions of ligaments, skin, hair, and flesh. Twisted and torn trees are piled in splintered masses.... At least four considerable layers of volcanic ash may be traced in these deposits, although they are extremely warped and distorted....[24]

It was apparent to geologists that when these deposits were laid down, the area was subjected to repeated and violent volcanic activity; yet the scale and nature of the devastation goes well beyond anything attributable to volcanoes alone. Evidently great waves from the ocean had uprooted entire forests and lifted herds of animals, of every kind and variety, and thrown them together, twisted, smashed and dismembered, along with billions of tons of sand and gravel, into the polar regions.

The permafrost regions of the Russian north revealed a situation precisely paralleling that in Alaska. From the sixteenth and seventeenth centuries, when Russian explorers and trappers began to penetrate the frozen wastelands of Siberia, there came reports of elephants, of a type no longer in existence, found in great quantities in the icy ground. A lucrative trade in mammoth ivory quickly developed. By the middle of the nineteenth century so much of this material was reaching Europe that people began to talk about the "ivory mines" of the region, and soon Northern Siberia was to provide more than half the world's supply of the material.

One remarkable feature of these creatures was the state of preservation of the soft tissue. Flesh, skin and hair are often seen, and the flesh so well preserved by the cold that it can, on occasion, be safely eaten.

It soon became clear that many areas of the Russian east, but most especially north-eastern Siberia, held vast quantities of these creatures just beneath the surface. They are found, as a rule, in conditions very similar to those of the "muck" deposits in Alaska, where, as we saw, the bodies of mammoths are found intermingled with those of other species, both extinct and extant, mixed along with other kinds of debris, but most especially sand and gravel, as well as smashed and uprooted trees.

In the Arctic Ocean, just to the north of Siberia, lie various groups of islands. The earliest of these to be explored, the Liakhov Islands, were found to be absolutely packed with the bones of mammoths and other creatures. "Such was the enormous quantity of mammoths' remains that it seemed ...

---

[24] F. C. Hibben, "Evidence of Early Man in Alaska," *American Antiquity*, VIII (1943), p. 256

that the island was actually composed of the bones and tusks of elephants, cemented together by icy sand."[25] The New Siberian Islands, discovered in 1806 and 1806, present the same picture. "The soil of these desolate islands is absolutely packed full of the bones of elephants and rhinoceroses in astonishing numbers."[26] Again, "These islands were full of mammoth bones, and the quantity of tusks and teeth of elephants and rhinoceroses, found in the nearby island of New Siberia, was perfectly amazing, and surpassed anything which had as yet been discovered."[27]

It would appear that these islands were formed, at least in part, by billions of tons of animal and vegetable matter, as well as sand and gravel, which was swept into the polar regions by enormous waves, waves which were, by the nineteenth century, termed "waves of translation." These waves, it appears, were accompanied by a sudden and dramatic climate change. Temperatures dropped catastrophically. James D. Dana, the leading American geologist of the second half of the nineteenth century, wrote: "The encasing in ice of huge elephants, and the perfect preservation of the flesh, shows that the cold finally became *suddenly* extreme, as of a single winter's night, and knew no relenting afterward."[28]

It has often been emphasized, rightly, that the mammoth, as well as the woolly rhinoceros, so many of whose bodies are found in Siberia, are *not*, in spite of their hairy coats, creatures of the Arctic. Elephants in particular, whose daily calorie intake is enormous, could never survive on the sparse mosses and lichens which now cover the barren wastelands of northern Siberia. These were animals of the temperate zones, a fact confirmed by the contents of their mouths and stomachs. Here were found plants and grasses that do not now grow in northern Siberia. "The contents of the stomachs have been carefully examined; they showed the undigested food, leaves of trees now found in Southern Siberia, but a long way from the existing deposits of ivory. Microscopic examination of the skin showed red blood corpuscles, which was proof not only of a sudden death, but that the death was due to suffocation either by gases or water, evidently the latter in this case. But the puzzle remained to account for the sudden freezing up of this large mass of flesh so as to preserve it for future ages."[29]

On the islands of the Arctic Ocean, "neither trees, nor shrubs, no bushes, exist ... and yet the bones of elephants, rhinoceroses, buffaloes, and horses

---

[25] D. Garth Whitley, "The Ivory Islands of the Arctic Ocean," *Journal of the Philosophical Society of Great Britain*, XII (1910), p. 35

[26] Ibid., p. 36

[27] Ibid., p. 42

[28] J. D. Dana, *Manual of Geology* (4th ed., New York, 1894), p. 1007

[29] D. Garth Whitley, loc. cit., p. 56

are found in this icy wilderness in numbers which defy all calculation."[30] Clearly, either the climate of the region was much warmer when the above creatures lived or they were swept into these latitudes by some titanic force, almost certainly tidal waves. Or, alternatively, both these options might be correct. The cataclysm which threw together the animals and extinguished their lives also changed the climate suddenly and dramatically — a freezing so rapid that flesh and hair was preserved intact.

Notwithstanding its suppression in the halls of academic respectability, evidence of this sort emerged in a never-ending stream throughout the entire nineteenth and twentieth centuries. Much of the material was so startling that it even caught the attention of mainstream publications. Such was the case, for example, with the Berezovka mammoth, unearthed in eastern Siberia in 1901, with its flesh remarkably-well preserved by the cold. But it was the contents of the creature's stomach that really caught the public's attention. Remains of the animal's last meal, not fully digested, were detected; and this meal included flowering plants, such as buttercups, *in full bloom.* Evidently the beast had been grazing, on a summer's day, and had then been killed and frozen so quickly that thousands of years later its flesh was so well-preserved that it could be, as it was, partly eaten by wolves. It is absolutely impossible to explain this without recourse to some cataclysmic event. The words of American zoologist Ivan T. Sanderson say it all:

> [N]ot one trace of pine needles or of the leaves of any other trees were in the stomach of the Berezovka mammoth; little flowering butter-cups, tender sedges and grasses were found exclusively. Buttercups will not even grow at forty degrees (4.4°C), and they cannot flower in the absence of sunlight. A detailed analysis of the contents of the Berezovka mammoth's stomach brought to light a long list of plants, some of which still grow in the arctic, but are actually much more typical of Southern Siberia today. Therefore, the mammoths either made annual migrations north for the short summer, or the part of the earth where their corpses are found today was somewhere else in warmer latitudes at the time of their death, or both.[31]

The circumstances surrounding the deaths of these creatures constitute, in Sanderson's admission, a profound mystery:

> Here is a really shocking — to our previous way of thinking — picture. Vast herds of enormous, well-fed beasts not especially designed for extreme cold, placidly feeding in sunny pastures, delicately plucking flowering buttercups at a temperature in which we would probably

---

[30] Ibid., p. 50

[31] Ivan T. Sanderson, "Riddle of the Frozen Giants," Saturday *Evening Post*, No. 39 (January, 1960)

not even have needed a coat. Suddenly they were all killed without any visible sign of violence and before they could so much as swallow a last mouthful of food, and then were quick-frozen so rapidly that every cell of their bodies is perfectly preserved, despite their great bulk and their high temperature. What, we may well ask, could possibly do this?

What, indeed?

This was a mystery pondered over a hundred years earlier, in 1834, by no less a person than Charles Darwin who, upon contemplating the extermination of life, both large and small, on every continent, asked this very question:

> The greater number, if not all, of these extinct quadrupeds lived at a late period, and were the contemporaries of most of the existing seashells. Since they lived, no very great change in the form of the land can have taken place. What, then, has exterminated so many species and whole genera?

> The mind at first is irresistibly hurried into the belief of some great catastrophe; but thus to destroy animals, both large and small, in Southern Patagonia, in Brazil, on the Cordillera of Peru, in North America up to Behring's Straits, we must shake the entire framework of the globe.[32]

As Darwin said, that indeed is the conclusion to which the evidence inexorably draws us, yet, almost in the same breath, in the very next sentence, the great scientist goes on to deny even the possibility of such an event. What could have caused him — and thousands like him since — to deny the evidence of his own eyes and postulate the most improbable and evidence-free alternatives? That, unfortunately, is a question for psychology and not for either history or natural history. And irrespective of what Darwin claimed, proofs that the entire framework of the globe was indeed shaken at the end of the Pleistocene has accumulated further in ever-increasing quantities over the past century and a half.

Seismic Upheaval and Sea-Level Change

The extinction of the Pleistocene megafauna was accompanied by a massive outburst in seismic activity which simultaneously raised mountain ranges thousands of feet and consigned other regions to the depths of the sea. This violent volcanic activity coincided with a significant increase in ocean-levels across the globe.

The modern student of geology is assured by his professors that mountain ranges took millions of years to raise, with slow and steady tectonic

---

[32]Darwin, "Voyage of the Beagle," January, 1834.

forces adding centimeters or even millimeters every year. Yet if this were the case, erosion would have reduced those same ranges to ground level before they could reach the status of mountains.

During his famous voyage, Darwin noted the existence of a raised beach, about 3,000 feet up in the Andes, complete with sand, rounded pebbles and sea shells belonging to shellfish of modern species, which ran down the Pacific coast of the South American continent. Commenting upon this feature, Darwin noted that the Cordillera looked as if it had been raised with immense speed, owing to the absence of intermediate beaches.[33] All of which was of course perfectly correct. Had the Andes risen over millions of years, as the textbooks now of tell us, there would be many beaches between the present sea level and the one at 3,000 feet elevation. Beaches form very quickly, with shore-dwelling molluscs quickly colonizing new shorelines. The fact that they do not appear between the two means that they did not have time to do so.

The existence of the raised Andean beach, and similar features in many other parts of the world, suggests that, in the relatively recent past, titanic forces moved the earth's tectonic plates against each other. The South American plate must have crashed with great force against the Pacific plate, with the entire continent moving in a western trajectory. This means that the topography of the Atlantic Ocean too must have changed dramatically, and has a direct bearing on the age of that vast body of water.

But the sheer speed of mountain-building, which Darwin remarked upon, almost certainly cannot be explained by a cataclysm of the type now generally admitted by mainstream scholarship — i.e., by an asteroid impact of some sort. Since the work of Luis Alvarez and his son Walter in the early 1980s it has become part of received wisdom that some kind of asteroid impact annihilated the dinosaurs — supposedly 65 million years ago — and that other cataclysms of similar type may have terminated geological epochs at other times. It is now even mooted in mainstream publications that the Pleistocene may have been terminated in the same way — around 12,000 years ago. Whilst it is gratifying to again see some form of catastrophism gaining traction in mainstream academia, it has to be pointed out that asteroid impacts or such like would probably be incapable of producing the massive tectonic disruption observed by geologists. As Darwin said, we need to shake the entire framework of the globe to explain what exists.

The tectonic upheavals of the Pleistocene signaled an immense outbreak of volcanic activity, of a scale and intensity which dwarfs anything in the experience of modern man.

---

[33]Ibid.

Perhaps the best-known example of Pleistocene super-vulcanism is the gigantic caldera (volcanic crater) on the Aegean island of Santorini. The Santorini crater, which reaches to a depths of over 900 meters below sea level, is often popularly believed to have been the result of the volcanic eruption which buried the Minoan city at Akrotiri. But this is not the case. The eruption which buried Akrotiri under 15 meters of ash occurred during the Bronze Age and was a much smaller event (though still enormous by modern standards) than the eruption or eruptions which created the gigantic caldera. The latter feature is in fact said to have formed in three eruptions during the Pleistocene, the last of which occurred at the end of the epoch — supposedly 10,000 years ago.[34] The latter event was of an intensity quite unlike anything in modern experience. We are talking about an explosion many times more powerful than the eruption of Krakatoa in 1883. Now, if the Santorini event had been an isolated one, it would still pose a major problem; however, evidence from all over the planet shows a mass outbreak of super-vulcanism at the time, an outbreak which is quite simply inexplicable in terms of conventional geological theory.[35]

In recent years, for example, it has become clear that the whole of the Yellowstone National Park is the result of a series of immense 'super volcano' eruptions during the Pleistocene,[36] massive events which shook the whole of the North American continent. A similar picture emerges on the other side of the planet. Thus in 1968 it was reported that proof of large scale volcanic eruptions in New Zealand in the Pleistocene had been detected in deep-sea cores taken within around 1,000 kilometers east of the country.[37] In 1982 it was reported that there had been a "large magnitude" volcanic eruption in Alaska near the end of the Pleistocene.[38] No part of the world escaped these upheavals. Professor Maurice Ewing, who led an oceanographic expedition to the Atlantic in 1948, spoke of titanic eruptions in the Mid-Atlantic Ridge near the end of the Pleistocene. In the area of the Azores his expedition found an uncharted submarine mountain, 8,000 feet high, with "many layers of volcanic ash," and farther on, a great chasm dropping down 1,809 fathoms (10,854 feet), "as if a volcano had caved in there at some time in the

---

[34]See e.g., Chris Satow et al. "Eruptive activity of the Santorini Volcano controlled by sea-level rise and fall," *Nature Geoscience* 14 (2021), 586-592

[35] E. Venzke, (ed.) Global Volcanism Program, 2013. *Volcanoes of the World*, v. 4.4 10. 4. Smithsonian Institution. Downloaded 16 Dec. 2021. https://doi.org/10.5479/si.GVP. VOTW4-2013

[36]There exists a large literature on this topic. See, e.g.,, Victoria Jaggard, "Yellowstone Supervolcano may rumble to life sooner than thought," *National Geographic*, October, 2017.

[37]Dragoslav Ninkovich, *Earth and Planetary Science Letters*, Vol. 4, No. 2 (1968).

[38]John A. Westgate, *Science* November (1982)

past."[39] All of this accords with the findings of Russian and Scandinavian geologists and oceanographers, who state that the entire Mid-Atlantic Ridge sank beneath the waves in one cataclysmic paroxysm at the termination of the Pleistocene.[40]

Now, the earth was already a very old planet by the beginning of Pleistocene epoch, so the volcanic activity of the time cannot have been the consequence of a young planet still settling down, as it were. Something must have triggered a renewed and spectacular outburst of seismic activity. In 1925 the great English explorer Colonel Percy Fawcett noted that in South America, "Devastating earthquakes seem to take place ... once or twice in a century. ... The whole of South America trembles periodically in the recurrent but diminishing waves of a vast eruptive age, the history of which can only be found in Indian legend."[41] Evidently Fawcett did not believe this "eruptive age" to lie in the distant past.

Immanuel Velikovsky, whose ideas will be examined presently, held that the seismic eruptions of the Pleistocene were the direct the result of major upheavals within the solar system: A simple asteroid or small comet impact is insufficient to account for what we see. In Velikovsky's scheme, the Pleistocene disturbances would have been the result of a close encounter between the earth and a very large body; the resulting gravitational stresses producing major convulsions of the earth's tectonic plates — convulsions that would have continued for centuries, though diminishing in strength with the passing of time — much as Fawcett claimed. As such, Velikovsky pointed to the strength and frequency of seismic activity in ancient times, evidence for which is found both in literature and in archaeological excavation. The great eruption of Vesuvius, which buried Pompeii in AD 79, was far from being unique or even unusual in the ancient world. In the words of Velikovsky, "earthquakes result from torsion of the crust following a change in the position of the equator and the displacement of matter inside the globe caused by the direct attraction of a cosmic body when in close contact. Pull, torsion, and displacement were responsible for mountain-building too." He continues, "If this conception of the causes of earthquakes is correct, then there must have been fewer and fewer earthquakes during the course of time since the last cosmic earthquake. The regions of the Apennine Peninsula [Italy], the eastern Mediterranean, and Mesopotamia, for which we have reliable records, can be compared in this respect to the same regions today. Earthquakes in Asia Minor, Greece, and Rome described or mentioned by

[39]Maurice Ewing, "New Discoveries on the Mid-Atlantic Ridge," *National Geographic* Vol. XCVI, No. 5 (November, 1949)

[40] N. Zhirov, *Atlantis: Atlantology, Basic Problems* (English ed., London, 1970).

[41]Percy Fawcett, *Exploration Fawcett* (London, 1953), p. 174

many classic authors. For the purpose of comparison with earth-tremor activity of the present day, it is enough to point to fifty-seven earthquakes reported in Rome in a single year during the Punic wars (-217)."[42]

The cataclysmic volcanic activity of the Pleistocene epoch did not occur in the distant past; it occurred when men had already reached a high level of culture. As we shall see, the cosmic body which brought these events, apparently a gigantic comet, came to be worshipped by humanity and sacrifices offered it. With its long 'tail' of debris stretching across the sky, the comet appeared to an awe-struck humanity as a gigantic serpent, and was honored — under the name of the Cosmic Serpent, or Dragon — in every corner of the globe. The dragon, all men insisted, brought with it the Flood, and the creature, in all its guises, was always associated with water (e.g. the Hydra). And it was in response to these events that mankind first built temples and established priesthoods — events which occurred in the centuries after 2000 B.C.

According to geologists and oceanographers, the oceans rose by something between 100 and 130 meters at the end of the Pleistocene epoch.[43] That this rise actually occurred is beyond question and demonstrated in a multitude of ways. During the Pleistocene, Britain and Ireland were not islands, but were joined to the European continent. The water separating Britain from Denmark and northern Germany, now called the North Sea, was then a large and fertile plain, named Doggerland by geologists. Remains of Paleolithic man, as well as extinct creatures such as mammoths, are regularly dredged from the sea floor in the region.[44] At this time, the continental shelf, which extends far into the Atlantic to the west of Ireland, formed Eurasia's shoreline. And a similar picture emerges from North America. Newfoundland was then connected to the mainland of Canada, and the Grand Banks, which form the easternmost part of North America's continental shelf, were dry land and part of the continent.[45] Indeed, North America's landmass extended hundreds of miles eastward all the way down to Florida, and the Hudson River emptied itself into a much smaller and shallower Atlantic a long distance to the south and east of New York City.[46]

[42]Immanuel Velikovsky, *Worlds in Collision*, New York, 1950), p. 267

[43]See e.g., Kurt Lambeck, "Late Pleistocene, Holocene and present sea-levels: constraints on future change," *Palaeogeography, Palaeoclimatology, Palaeoecology*, Vol. 89, Issue 3 (December, 1990)

[44]Mark J. White, "Things to do in Doggerland when you're dead: Surviving OIS3 at the northwesternmost fringe of Middle Palaeolithic Europe," *World Archaeology*. 38, 4. (2006), pp. 547–575

[45]John Shaw, "Palaeogeography of Atlantic Canadian Continental Shelves from the Last Glacial Maximum to the Present, with an Emphasis on Flemish Cap," *Journal of Northwest Atlantic Fishery Science*. 37: (2006), pp. 119–126.

[46]See Harley J. Knebel et al., "Hudson River: Evidence for extensive migration on the exposed continental shelf during Pleistocene time," *Geology*, Vol. 7, No. 5 (May, 1979).

From the opposite side of the world a similar picture emerges: Here we find that during the Pleistocene, Australia was joined to New Guinea in the north and Tasmania in the south, forming a continent much larger than that of the present day. Huge marsupials, birds and reptiles, now extinct, roamed the length and breadth of this landmass.[47]

Establishment academics now see the post-Pleistocene sea-rise as the result of the melting of great ice sheets which supposedly covered large parts of Eurasia and North America during an "Ice Age" which is said to have occupied the last few thousand years of the Pleistocene.[48] Yet human tradition, as we have seen, knew about rising ocean levels long before science confirmed it. Why then is this tradition derided and ignored? And whence comes the notion of an Ice Age, a concept which "explains" not only altered sea-levels, but also all the other evidence — such as mass extinctions, erratics, boulder-clay and drift, etc., which was formerly believed to confirm the reality of the Great Deluge?

I do not intend to go into the question of the Ice Age in any detail, since it represents a diversion away from the central goal of the present work, which is to recover and elucidate the histories of the ancient peoples of the Near East. Suffice to note here that early geologists found very real evidence that at some period or periods in the past earth's overall temperature was substantially cooler than now, and that great ice sheets once covered regions which currently have temperate climates. This was noted by many natural historians in the early nineteenth century and culminated in 1837 in Karl Schimper's concept of an "Ice Age" — a concept then further developed by his friend and colleague Louis Agassiz. That certain regions of Europe, such as the Highlands of Scotland, once had glaciers, is correct and easily demonstrated. Accumulations of gravel and other debris, named "moraines," which are typical of the detritus left behind by retreating glaciers, can be viewed in certain locations in the north of Scotland. As the nineteenth century progressed, and the spirit of the age, which was one that lauded human progress, sought to divest itself of the constraints of religion, the idea of an Ice Age came more and more into the fore as a means of explaining away the evidence which had hitherto pointed so overwhelmingly to a catastrophist view of the past. And so the idea of expanded glaciers, earlier confined to

---

[47]See e.g., Chris Ballard, "Stimulating minds to fantasy? A critical etymology for Sahul," *Sahul in review: pleistocene archaeology in Australia, New Guinea and island Melanesia.* (Canberra, 1993), p. 17. See also, George W. Earl, "On the physical structure and arrangement of the islands of the Indian Archipelago," *Journal of the Royal Geographical Society* Vol. 15. (1845), pp. 358–365.

[48]Ibid. The last Ice Age is now termed the Younger Dryas and placed between the end of the Pleistocene and the start of the Holocene – the most recent of Earth's geological epochs.

specific regions such as Highland Scotland and other cooler parts of Europe, was now extended to include most of Europe, where erratic boulders, as well as the drift, with its gravel, boulder-clay and sand, had previously been regarded as proof of a great Flood. These were now viewed, on the contrary, as evidence of a universal glaciation.

Yet a gradual cooling of the climate could in no way explain most of the geological and paleontological evidence, such as the mass extinctions at the end of the Pleistocene. Nor, in reality, could it even properly explain the existence of erratics or the drift and its associated features. No matter, it served its purpose in giving an apparent explanation to some of the most glaringly catastrophist features of the earth's topography.

From the point of view of the reconstruction proposed here, it will be apparent, as we proceed, that the entire notion of an Ice Age or Ice Ages is unnecessary, and that any cooling of the earth which occurred in the past was short-lived and actually the result of cataclysmic upheavals of the planet's surface which were themselves the result of earth's encounters with extra-terrestrial bodies. Descriptions of the Flood from throughout the world speak of vast seismic upheavals which unleashed clouds of volcanic dust into the atmosphere, simultaneously causing a profound darkness and plunging temperatures. But the selfsame volcanic activity, whilst darkening and cooling the landmasses, also temporarily heated the seas, which then gave forth immense quantities of water-vapor. This condensed over the colder continents as snow. Many descriptions of the Deluge speak of a terrible cold enveloping the world. The rapid build-up of snow, of course, caused — in some regions of the earth at least — the formation of ice-caps and glaciers.

This then was an Ice Age of sorts, but it was short-lived and caused none, or very few, of the major geological features now attributed to it. As soon as the earth's tectonic plates stabilized and the volcanoes ceased pouring forth masses of dust, the darkness dissipated and temperatures rose; a process which probably took little more than a century.

But if the rising oceans at the end of the Pleistocene were not the result of melting ice-caps, whence came the extra water that deluged the planet? Ancient peoples, we have seen, held that it came out of the sky, in the form of torrential rain; yet normal rain itself comes from the oceans and does not deepen the seas or add to the earth's overall supply of water. Clearly the surplus water must have had an extra-terrestrial origin, a source elsewhere in the Solar System. It is to that question that we now turn.

A Catastrophist Perspective

As noted earlier, not everyone has been willing to "toe the academic line" in dismissing the evidence for past catastrophes. No sooner had the gradualist or "uniformitarian" view of the past, with its Natural Selection and Ice Ages, gained the upper hand in the 1870s than a host of "alternative" historians brought the evidence for catastrophes, both textual and geological, to the public's attention in a most forceful way. The first and perhaps most famous of these was maverick writer and politician Ignatius Donnelly, whose best-selling books *Atlantis: the Antediluvian World* (1882) and *Ragnarok: the Age of Fire and Gravel* (1883) caused a sensation at the time. Donnelly was at pains, particularly in *Ragnarok*, to cite the geological and paleontological evidence, and there is no question that he presented a major challenge to the then-consolidating anti-catastrophist consensus. In *Ragnarok*, he claimed that the biblical Flood, as well as the destruction of Atlantis and the various other "floods" mentioned in ancient tradition, had been caused by the close passage near the earth of a gigantic comet, which had quite literally shaken our planet off its axis, as well as deposited hundreds of billions tons of debris on the terrestrial sphere — debris now known to geologists as the drift. The evidence presented in *Ragnarok* was first-class, and is replete with quotes from professional geologists; quotes affirming a clearly catastrophist interpretation for what they were describing. Nonetheless, Donnelly's thesis went very much against the scholarly *esprit du temps*, and reasons were sought — and of course found — to dismiss his work *in toto*. These reasons came mainly from his *Atlantis* book, but no matter; they served their purpose in enabling establishment academics to dismiss him as a pseudoscientist — a judgement encountered now in Donnelly's Wikipedia page.

In *Ragnarok*, Donnelly had followed earlier catastrophists in placing the Flood at the end of the Pleistocene. However, in keeping with the greatly-lengthened chronology of prehistory then in vogue, he placed this event around 10000 BC — as opposed to the circa 3000 BC favored by Cuvier and earlier catastrophists.

Since Donnelly's time many "alternative" historians — men such as Comyns Beaumont and Lewis Spence, and more recently Charles Hapgood (*Earth's Shifting Crust* (1958) and *Path to the Pole*, 1970), Hugh Auchincloss Brown (*Cataclysms of the Earth*, 1967) and a host of others — have agreed that it was the Flood, or a flood-cataclysm of some sort, which ended the Pleistocene, and they have tended to follow Donnelly's date of *circa* 10000 BC for it.[49] There was one notable exception; Immanuel Velikovsky. He agreed that

---

[49]Some of the more recent examples of the genre include: D. S. Allan and J. B. Delair, *When the Earth Nearly Died* (London, 1994); R. Firestone, A. West and S. Warwick-Smith, *The*

the Pleistocene was ended by the Flood, but dated it far closer to the biblical date: 3000 BC.

When Velikovsky published his first book, *Worlds in Collision* in 1950, it precipitated a scholarly controversy unheard of since the battle over Darwin's ideas a hundred years earlier. As the title of the book suggested, Velikovsky held that at various periods in the geologically recent past, large cosmic bodies had come near to colliding with our own planet, with devastating results on earth. *Worlds in Collision* dealt chiefly with the final two series of these disasters, which Velikovsky synchronized with the Exodus from Egypt and with the destruction of Sennacherib's army outside Jerusalem some 750 years later. Each close encounter between the earth and the other cosmic body, he claimed, caused our planet to be shaken from its very axis. The earth's solar orbit, as well as the length of the year, was altered, whilst tremendous seismic disturbances seized the globe. Thousands of volcanoes burst into activity, and the skies were darkened. Tremendous tidal waves swept the continents, wiping out whole species and civilizations. Showers of meteorites and electrical discharges bombarded the earth.

Worlds in Collision represented an encyclopedic collection of catastrophe legends from throughout the earth, and Velikovsky was able to demonstrate that these agreed very precisely with what physicists tell us would happen to our planet should a large cosmic body come near to us. Albert Einstein, with whom Velikovsky was in continuous contact during the months and years following appearance of the book, was in total agreement. He accepted that Velikovsky had proved "without question" that ancient man was witness to cataclysmic events outside the experience of modern man, though he held that Velikovsky was in error in concluding that the cosmic body or bodies responsible was of planetary dimensions. He concurred with prevailing astrophysical theory in insisting that it can only have been an asteroid or comet of normal side which caused the damage.

In 1956 Velikovsky published a follow-up volume named *Earth in Upheaval* in which he turned his attention to the geological and paleontological evidence. In some ways, *Earth in Upheaval* was an even more important work than *Worlds in Collision*, and that was certainly the opinion of Einstein, who read it in manuscript form before its publication. Velikovsky went over the ground covered by earlier catastrophists, though he did so in more detail, and furthermore emphasized the point — generally ignored by more recent catastrophists — that the destruction of the Pleistocene megafauna must

---

Cycle of Cosmic Catastrophes: How a Stone-Age Comet changed the Course of World Culture (Bear and Company, 2006); and J. L. Powell, *Deadly Voyager: The Ancient Comet Strike that changed Earth and Human History* (Bowker, 2020).

have been an event of recent history. Again and again he showed, quoting the geologists and paleontologists themselves, that the major topographic changes which marked the transformation from the Pleistocene to the Holocene (recent age) could not have occurred more than 4,000 years ago, give or take a couple of centuries.

As noted above, *Worlds in Collision* argued that our planet had been struck by not one but a series of cosmic catastrophes which began with the biblical Deluge, around 3000 BC, and ended with certain calamitous events described in the Bible and there dated to the seventh century BC. He held, for example, that the Exodus of the Israelites from Egypt was accompanied by a natural catastrophe associated in the minds of the ancients with a great comet, known by various names in various lands, but especially linked to the cosmic serpent or dragon monster. Velikovsky was able to show that in traditions from throughout the world the dragon, or cosmic serpent, is invariably associated with a myth of World Destruction, and almost as frequently associated with water (e.g. the Greek "Hydra"). What was outrageous, from the point of view of establishment academia, was that he held that this comet was planet-sized and that it had erupted in a tremendous explosion from the planet Jupiter. As proof of this he cited evidence of various kinds, both from the natural and human sciences. All ancient peoples, he said, seemed to have regarded the planet Jupiter as the father of the gods. We now know that Jupiter is the largest planet in the Solar System. But how could the ancient astronomers have known this — or how could they have given primacy in the planetary system to Jupiter? Even if they (as now seems to be the case) possessed some form of magnifying lenses — fashioned either from glass or rock crystal — they would still have had no inkling of Jupiter's true size, for through a telescope the planet looks no bigger than Mars. When Velikovsky presented this problem to Einstein, who had hitherto been extremely skeptical of Velikovsky's claims, the great physicist began to look seriously at the whole scenario.[50]

According to early legends, the "sky father" Jupiter had decided to chastise the human race for its incorrigible wickedness. In some accounts, the great god/planet then gave birth to a new god, or new star, who was to carry out the punishment. In Greek mythology the task was assigned to Athena, who sprang fully armed from the head of Zeus (Jupiter) with a mighty roar. In Egyptian mythology the goddess assigned to the task was named Hathor (also Isis or Neith), whose slaughter of humanity we have already mentioned.

---

[50]The story of Velikovsky's debates with Einstein are told in his as yet unpublished *Before the Day Breaks*. Velikovsky however relates his discussion on the nature of Jupiter in his 1983 book, *Stargazers and Gravediggers*.

According to Velikovsky, another name for the avenging deity was Typhon, and the Roman writer Pliny, who had access to volumes of Greek, Egyptian and Babylonian literature that are now lost, describes Typhon as an enormous blood-red comet that had brought the earth to the brink of destruction.[51] Velikovsky demonstrated in great detail the link between Typhon and the goddess known as Venus/Ishtar/Isis/Athena/Hathor, all of whom were linked either to a World Destruction or to the great Deluge itself.

Velikovsky worked for many years on a book dealing specifically with the Flood, though he died before it could be published. The manuscript however, *In the Beginning*, was finally published in 2021, and in it he links the Deluge to the planet Saturn, rather than the Hathor/Ishtar comet. Why he did so is complex, though it must be borne in mind that he was constrained by the chronology and history outlined in the Old Testament, particularly the Book of Genesis. Yet even a cursory viewing of the material presented in *Worlds in Collision* and *Earth in Upheaval* shows that the catastrophic destructions described therein can only have referred to the Great Deluge and that furthermore these must have been the consequences of earth's close encounter with a large cosmic body — the Typhon comet, in short. And that is precisely the conclusion reached by the present author. As such, it will be apparent that the extra water which poured onto the earth during the Deluge must have come from a comet's tail. Had the latter originated in one of the gas giants, Jupiter or Saturn, then that tail would likely have included huge amounts of hydrogen gas — one of the components of water. Oxygen in the earth's atmosphere could then have combined with hydrogen from the tail of the comet due to electromagnetic activity in the upper atmosphere, and fallen as water over our planet.

Seismic activity, also a feature of the Deluge, would have resulted from the head of the comet, which was enormous, exerting tremendous gravitational stresses upon the terrestrial sphere. These would have resulted in volcanic and seismic disturbances and massive alterations of the earth's topography — all of which are reported in many of the Deluge traditions.

When did the Pleistocene end?

It is still routinely stated in textbooks, journals and other academic media that the Pleistocene ended between 11,000 and 12,000 years ago. Yet evidence collected over the past two centuries, much of it cited in Velikovsky's *Earth in Upheaval*, categorically refutes that assertion. On the contrary, the data, of an overwhelming quantity and variety, tell us that the end of the Pleis-

---

[51]Pliny, *Natural History*, ii, 23.

tocene, and the catastrophe which marked its end, cannot have occurred much before 2200 or 2300 BC. Relics of early man, often at a surprisingly advanced cultural level, were regularly found alongside the bones of extinct creatures. Such was the case, for example, on the Atlantic coast of Florida, at Vero Beach in the Indian River region, where in 1915 and 1916 human remains were found in association with the remains of Pleistocene animals, some of which, like the saber-toothed tiger, became extinct, and others of which, like the camel, have disappeared from America.

The find, according to Velikovsky, "caused immediate excitement among geologists and anthropologists."[52] This was due to the fact that along with the human bones "pottery was found, as well as bone implements and worked stone."[53] According to Aleš Hrdlika, of the Smithsonian Institute, the "advanced state of culture, such as that shown by the pottery, bone implements, and worked stone brought from considerable distance, implies a numerous population spread over large areas, acquainted thoroughly with fire, with cooked food, and with all the usual primitive arts." Hrdlička however held that the human remains could not be of an antiquity "comparable with that of fossil remains with which they are associated."[54] But the bones and artifacts were found among the extinct animals. E. H. Sellards, the discoverer of the deposits and a very capable anthropologist, wrote that "the human bones and fossils normal to this stratum and contemporaneous with the associated vertebrates is determined by their place in the formation, their manner of occurrence, their intimate relation to the bones of other animals, and the degree of mineralization of the bones." In his view the evidence "affords proof that man reached America at an early date and was present on the continent in association with a Pleistocene fauna."[55]

Yet the human artifacts at Vero were of a relatively advanced cultural stage. The art of the potter was practiced, and the work produced did not differ in any significant way from that of the mound-building cultures of Florida of the first millennium B.C.[56]

During the 1920s another such association of human remains and extinct animals was found. The discovery, at Melbourne, just to the north of Vero and still in the state of Florida, was of "a remarkably rich assemblage of animal bones, many of which represent species which became extinct at or

[52]Velikovsky, *Earth in Upheaval* (London, 1955), p. 146
[53]Ibid.
[54]Aleš Hrdlička, "Preliminary Report on Finds of Supposedly Ancient Human Remains at Vero, Florida," *Journal of Geology*, XXV (1917).
[55] E. H. Sellards, "On the Association of Human Remains and Extinct Vertebrates at Vero, Florida," *Journal of Geology*, XXV (1917).
[56]*Earth in Upheaval*, p. 146

after the close of the Pleistocene epoch."[57] In the words of Velikovsky, the discovery "established unequivocally that in Melbourne — and in Vero — the human bones were of the same stratum and in the same state of fossilization as the bones of the extinct animals."[58] According to Velikovsky, "It follows that the extinct animals belonged to the recent past. It follows also that some paroxysm of nature heaped together these assemblages; the same paroxysm of nature may have destroyed numerous species so that they became extinct."[59]

To these discoveries in Florida we must add, from several parts of the North American continent, artistic portrayals of Pleistocene creatures, in particular elephants of the mammoth and mastodon species. These representations have been found associated with remains that invariably look remarkably modern, and, although such artifacts continue to come to light, doubt has been cast on their authenticity or their interpretation. As recently as September 2007, Mark Holley, an underwater archeologist with the Grand Traverse Bay Underwater Preserve Council, announced the discovery of a remarkably well-preserved carving of a mammoth in the waters of Lake Michigan. Holley, who teaches at Northwestern Michigan College in Traverse City, Michigan, describes the artifact as a granite boulder 3.5 to 4 feet high by 5 feet long, inscribed with markings that resemble a mastodon with a spear in its side. Confirmation that the markings are an ancient petroglyph will require more evidence. Nevertheless, the find seems likely to be genuine.[60]

Evidence from the Arctic, both in America and Asia, tells a similar tale. In various levels of the icy muck near Fairbanks, Alaska, stone implements were found "frozen *in situ* at great depths and in apparent association" with the Ice Age fauna, implying that "men were contemporary with extinct animals in Alaska."[61] In Velikovsky's words, "Worked flints, characteristically shaped, called Yuma points, were repeatedly found in the Alaskan muck, one hundred and more feet [about thirty meters] below the surface. One spear point was found there between a lion's jaw and a mammoth's tusk."[62] Yet similar weapons were used only a few generations ago by the Athapascan Indians, who camped in the Upper Tanana Valley.[63] According to Hibben, "It

---

[57] J. W. Gidly, "Ancient Man in Florida," *Bulletin of the Geological Society of America*, Vol. XL, (1929)

[58] *Earth in Upheaval*, p. 147

[59] Ibid., p. 148

[60] John Flesher, "Possible mastodon carving found on rock," Associated Press, 2007-09-04. Retrieved on 2007-09-05

[61] Rainey, loc. cit., p. 307

[62] Earth in Upheaval, p. 5. Cf. Hibben, *American Antiquity*, VIII, 257

[63] Ibid. Cf. Rainey, loc. cit., p. 301

has been suggested that even modern Eskimo points are remarkably Yuma-like," all of which, as Velikovsky noted, "indicates that the multitudes of torn animals and splintered forests date from a time not many thousand years ago."

Such discoveries recall the opinion of a number of American geologists in the latter part of the nineteenth and the first part of the twentieth centuries, among them George Frederick Wright (1838–1921), Newton Horace Winchell (1839–1914), and Warren Upham (1850–1934). Wright came to the conclusion that the Ice Age "did not close until about the time that the civilization of Egypt, Babylonia and Western Turkestan had attained a high degree of development," a view opposed to the "greatly exaggerated ideas of the antiquity of the glacial epoch."[64]

The evidence from geology supports that of the archaeologists.

Velikovsky stressed that in many localities, geologists found to their astonishment that lakes, river-valleys, deltas and cataracts were often no more than three to four thousand years old. Often it was possible to be much more precise, and it was discovered that a great many of these features were between 3,500 and 4,000 years old.

Such was the case, for example, with a number of inland lakes with no outward flow, whose salt and chlorine content could be compared with the salt and chlorine of the feeder rivers. Two of these, Abert and Summer lakes in southern Oregon, are regarded as remnants of a once large glacial lake, Chewaucan. W. Van Winkle of the United States Geological Survey examined the saline content of these two lakes and wrote: "A conservative estimate of the age of Summer and Abert Lakes, based on their concentration and area, the composition of the influent waters, and the rate of evaporation, is 4,000 years."[65] Velikovsky comments that van Winkle, "startled by his own result ... conjectured that salt deposits of the early Chewaucan Lake may be hidden beneath the bottom sediments of the present Abert and Summer lakes."[66]

Yet the same astonishingly recent result was obtained for lake after lake. Thus for example Owens Lake in California, which lies to the east of Sequoia National Park, was examined by H. S. Gale with the object of determining its content of chlorine and sodium. These were compared to the chlorine and sodium of the feeder river, and the conclusion reached was that the river required 4,200 years to supply the chlorine and 3,500 to supply the sodium.[67]

---

[64]   G. F. Wright, *The Ice Age in North America*, (1891), p. 683

[65] Walton van Winkle, "Quality of the Surface Waters of Oregon," US Geological Survey, Water Supply Paper 363 (Washington, 1914). Quoted from *Earth in Upheaval*, p. 148

[66] Ibid.

[67] Ibid., pp. 148-9

A prehistoric basin in Nevada, named Lake Lahontan, which previously covered an area of 8,500 square miles, was also investigated. As its water level fell, the ancient lake split up into a number of lakes divided by a desert terrain. In the 1880s Lake Lahontan and its basin was examined by I. Russell of the United States Geological Survey, and it was established that the lake never completely dried out and the present-day Pyramid and Winnemucca lakes north of Reno and the Walker Lake south-west of it are the remnants of the older and larger lake. Russell concluded that Lake Lahontan existed during the Ice Age and was contemporaneous with the different stages of glaciation of the epoch. He also discovered the bones of various Pleistocene animals in the deposits of the ancient lake. In more recent times, Lake Lahontan was explored anew by J. Claude Jones, and the results of this investigation were published as "Geological History of Lake Lahontan" by the Carnegie Institution in Washington. Jones investigated the saline content of Pyramid and Winnemucca lakes and of the Truckee River that feed them. He discovered that the river could have supplied the entire content of chlorine of these two lakes in 3,881 years. "A similar calculation," he wrote, "using sodium instead of chlorine, gave 2,447 years necessary." Jones' work led him to agree with Russell that Lake Lahontan never fully dried up and that the existing Pyramid and Winnemucca lakes are its residuals.

Yet, as Velikovsky commented, "these conclusions require that the age of the mammals of the Ice Age, found in the deposits of Lake Lahontan, be not greater than that of the lake. This means that the Ice Age ended only twenty-five to thirty-nine centuries ago."[68]

The formation of these lakes was associated with the event which brought to an end the Pleistocene, for many of the creatures of that epoch were found in the Lahontan sediments. These included bones of horses, elephants and camels. There was also a spear point of human manufacture.[69] Velikovsky notes that when a branch of the Southern Pacific Railroad was laid through Astor Pass, a large gravel pit of Lahontan age was opened. J. C. Merriam of the University of California identified there the bones of many species of extinct animals, among them the skeletal remains of *Felix atrox*, a species of lion found also in the asphalt pit of Rancho la Brea, as well as a species of horse and a camel, also found at la Brea. In Jones's words: "All of these forms are now extinct and neither camels nor lions are found on this continent as a part of the native fauna." According to Velikovsky, "the similarity of the fauna of the asphalt pits of La Brea and the deposits of Lake

---

[68] Ibid., p. 149
[69]   I. Russell, "Geologic History of Lake Lahontan," U.S. Geological Survey, Monograph 11, p. 143

Lahontan led Merriam to decide that they were contemporaneous," and, "On the basis of his analysis Jones came to the conclusion that the extinct animals lived in North America into historical times." This, of course, was an unusual and controversial statement, and it was opposed at first on the ground that his interpretation of his observations was "obviously erroneous, since [it] led him to the conclusion that the mastodon and the camel lived in North America into historical times." Yet, as Velikovsky points out, this was "an argument of a preconceived nature, not based on the findings of field geology."

River-systems, as well as lakes, leave their own signatures on the landscape. As with lakes, earthquake and other seismic activity has a great impact upon rivers. Old water-courses are dammed and form lakes, others are diverted into new channels. Sometimes these channels take the river far from its prior course. If what Velikovsky claimed is true, if mountain-ranges were raised hundreds and even thousands of meters only three thousand years ago, then we must expect that many river-systems are entirely new. Or rather that they are but three millennia old. And this is exactly what we do find.

As Velikovsky noted in *Earth in Upheaval*, when Charles Lyell visited the United States, he was told by a resident of the Niagara Falls region that the cataract retreats about three feet per year. Taking the rather superior attitude that the natives of a country are likely to exaggerate, Lyell announced that one foot per annum would be a more likely estimate. From this he concluded that the St. Lawrence River would have needed over thirty-five thousand years, from the time the land was freed from the ice cover and the water started its work of erosion, to cut the gorge from Queenston to the place it occupied in the year of Lyell's visit. Since then this span has often been mentioned in textbooks as the length of time from the end of the glacial period.

Yet subsequent research proved that the local interviewed by Lyell had not exaggerated, but under-estimated the rate of erosion. Records were to show that since 1764 the falls had retreated from Lake Ontario towards Lake Erie at the rate of five feet per year. If the process of wearing down the rock had gone on at this rate from the time of the disappearance of the ice cover, seven thousand years would have been sufficient to do the work. However, if in the beginning, when the ice first melted, the river system was swollen with extra water and detritus, the erosion rate must have been much more rapid, and the age of the gorge must therefore be reduced further. According to G. F. Wright, author of *The Ice Age in North America*, five thousand years may be regarded as adequate.

But even this figure, it seems, needs to come down, for it was subsequently discovered that a large part of the falls predated the Ice Age. In the 1920s borings made for a railway bridge showed that the middle part of Whirlpool Rapids Gorge contained a thick deposit of glacial boulder clay, indicating that it had been excavated once, had been filled with drift and then partly re-excavated in post-glacial times. According to R. F. Flint of Yale, Upper Great Gorge, the uppermost segment of the whole gorge, appears to be the only part that is genuinely post-glacial. Yet this poses a great problem. Here, the present rate of recession is 3.8 feet per year, and "Hence the age of the Upper Great Gorge is calculated as somewhat more than four thousand years — and to obtain even this [high] figure we have to assume that the rate of recession has been constant, although we know that discharge has in fact varied greatly during post-glacial times." Velikovsky comments, "If due allowance is made for this last factor, the age of the Upper Great Gorge of Niagara Falls would be somewhere between 2,500 and 3,500 years. It follows that the ice retreated in historical times, somewhere between the years 1,500 and 500 before the present era."

Geological investigation of the Mississippi River produced a similar result. In 1860 A. A. Humphreys and H. L. Abbot, of the U. S. Army Corps of Topographical Engineers, extensively studied the river and its delta. They determined the latter's age by dividing its average annual growth into the distance from the continental shoreline. They concluded: "Adopting this rate of progress (262 feet per annum), four thousand four hundred years have elapsed since the river began to advance into the gulf."[70]

Numerous river-systems throughout the world are likewise shown to have begun flowing in their present courses only three to three and half thousand years ago.

A point stressed by Velikovsky was that what we now call the Ice Age was a much shorter period of time (or rather periods of time) than is now believed and that the episodic lowering of the earth's temperature was the direct result of the cosmic upheavals described in ancient literature. Essentially, as the earth found itself in close contact with extra-terrestrial bodies, the tectonic plates went into upheaval and volcanoes everywhere erupted, unleashing huge amounts of dust and ash into the atmosphere. With the sun effectively blotted out, a dramatic lowering of the planet's temperature followed. Glaciers expanded and ice sheets moved south. Yet within a few years, less perhaps than a single decade, most of the volcanic dust had settled and the environment began to warm, to emerge from the Ice Age. All over

---

[70] A. A. Humphreys and H. L. Abbot, *Report upon the Physics and Hydraulics of the Mississippi River* (Philadelphia, 1861), p. 425

the world glaciers began a long process of retreat, and this shrinking has continued till the present day. Historical records show that all glaciers have been shrinking at least since classical times, and a good deal of research has gone into calculating the rate of shrinkage, plus the length of time taken for each glacier to have reached its present size. Following on from Velikovsky's thesis that a final series of cosmic catastrophes occurred as recently as the eighth century B.C., we might expect many glaciers to have been shrinking steadily since that time. Indeed, knowing the rate at which each glacier retreats, we might expect to identify exactly when it formed, and this should, if Velikovsky is right, have been about three thousand years ago.

What then do the glaciers tell us?

The answer is simple: throughout the world, many or most of the glaciers, judging by their rates of retreat, must have formed about three to four thousand years ago. A detailed study of the Rhone Glacier was carried out early in the twentieth century by Frenchman A. Cochon de Lapparent. As was evident from the location of terminal moraines, it was clear that at the time of its greatest expansion, the Rhone Glacier reached from Valais to Lyons. By comparing the average figure of progression as seen today on larger glaciers, De Lapparent came to the conclusion that the Rhone Glacier would have needed only 2,475 years to form. Then, comparing the terminal moraines of several present-day glaciers with the moraines left by the Rhone Glacier at its maximum expansion, De Lapparent arrived at a figure of about 2,400 years. In short, from the time of its formation, little more than 4,800 years had passed. Yet if the glacier was formed in the wake of a catastrophe which caused a rapid fall in the earth's temperature, as Velikovsky's hypothesis presupposes, then that figure would need to be reduced substantially.

But even De Lapparent's estimate caused disquiet. He was criticized, in particular, by Albrecht Penck. Yet,

> His objection was based not on a disproval of ... [De Lapparent's] figures, but on a claim that great evolutionary changes took place during the consecutive interglacial periods. The divergence of opinion between them was so great that hundreds of thousands of years in Penck's scheme were reduced to mere thousands of years in De Lapparent's calculations. Penck estimated the duration of the Ice Age, with its four glacial and three interglacial periods, as one million years. Each of the four glaciations and deglaciations must have consumed one hundred thousand years and more. The argument for his estimate is this: How much time was necessary to produce the changes in nature, if no catastrophes intervened? And how long would it take to produce changes in animals by means of a process that in our own day is so slow as to be almost imperceptible?

More recent field work in the Alps fully confirmed De Lapparent's findings. Numerous glaciers were found to be no older than 4,000 years, a startling discovery that made the following statement necessary:

> A large number of the present glaciers of the Alps are not survivors of the last glacial maximum, as was formerly universally believed, but are glaciers newly created within roughly the last 4,000 years.

Radiocarbon results, it might be imagined, would be an easy way of settling the date of the Pleistocene's end. After all, vast numbers of the creatures alive at the time are wholly or partly preserved in the Arctic ice. As a matter of fact, it is freely admitted that the last of the mammoths, found on Wrangel Island in the Arctic Ocean, did not die until circa 2000 BC.[71] Until the late 1990s it was claimed that these creatures were of a dwarf species and therefore perhaps better suited to survival on an isolated and immensely barren island of the Arctic Sea — the implication being that they were remnant survivors of a species which had elsewhere died out millennia earlier. However, this is now admitted to be untrue, and the mammoths of Wrangel were full-sized Siberian mammoths — and they were there until around 4,000 years ago. (This of course raises the shocking problem of how mammoths, which require huge calorie intake per day, could survive on the meager mosses and lichens afforded by this remote and desolate location). The Wrangel Island pachyderms were dated according to radiocarbon analysis, and the figure arrived at agrees very closely with multitudinous evidence, summarized above, marshalled by Velikovsky and others to the same effect.[72]

All of this material, which constitutes only a tiny proportion of what is available, is now routinely ignored in mainstream publications. Be that as it may, as new scientific techniques are developed, so appears new kinds of evidence, all pointing in the same direction. And so for example analysis of DNA has added yet another dimension of proof. Thus, over the past twenty years, it has been discovered that in relatively recent times several species of animals went through what is termed a "genetic bottleneck," a near-extinction catastrophe which left only a handful of survivors and which severely undermined the genetic health of that species. The most frequently-

---

[71] S. L. Vartanyan, "Radiocarbon Dating Evidence for Mammoths on Wrangel Island, Arctic Ocean, until 2000 BC." *Radiocarbon.* 37 (1) (2000), pp. 1–6. See also, Kh. A. Arslanov et al. "Consensus Dating of Remains from Wrangel Island." *Radiocarbon.* 40 (1) (1998), pp. 289–294.

[72] The radiocarbon dates from Wrangel stand in marked contrast to radiocarbon dates from other parts of the world, which often point to a much more ancient demise for the mammoths. This could possibly be explained, in part at least, by the fact that in warmer regions water washes radioactivity from samples – making them appear much older.

cited example is that of the cheetah, an animal whose genetic diversity is so limited that scientists have to conclude that all members of the species are descended from only a handful of ancestors alive just a few thousand years ago.[73] But as research has continued more and more species display similar traits. And so, for example, it was recently discovered that American bison too went through a near-extinction episode at the end of the Pleistocene, and their modern descendants display much reduced genetic diversity as compared to those of the Pleistocene.[74] Lions too display a marked lack of genetic diversity, indicating a near-extinction episode in the not too distant past. We are told that "Asiatic lions went through an event (most likely towards the end of the Pleistocene era) which drastically reduced the size of the population (i.e., a population bottleneck), followed by inbreeding."[75]

It is generally agreed that the "bottlenecks" experienced by surviving species were contemporary with the extinction of the vast number of Pleistocene species which did not survive. The horse, for example, originated in America; yet every last member of the horse family disappeared from the American continent at the end of the Pleistocene. When the Spaniards arrived in the sixteenth century, the native Mexicans were astonished to see these creatures, which they regarded as large deer. Spanish horses soon became feral and flourished in the American wilderness; so it is evident that the environment of the continent was eminently suitable for them.

But it was not only in America that the horse needed to be reintroduced. We know from Magdalenian cave paintings that wild horses roamed freely throughout Western Europe during the Paleolithic Age; yet here too, it would seem, they had to be reintroduced: For there is no evidence of the horse in Western Europe during the Mesolithic or Neolithic Ages, and they only reappear in the Late Bronze period.

The same can be said of the Middle East. Here the horse, which seems to have been brought from high steppes of central Asia, only appears in the time of the Assyrians — in the eighth century B.C.[76]

---

[73]See e.g., "Cheetahs: On the Brink of Extinction, Again," National Geographic Society, June 4, 2020. www.nationalgeographic.org

[74]See Kory C. Douglas, "Comparing the Genetic Diversity of Late Pleistocene Bison with Modern Bison bison using Ancient DNA Techniques and the Mitochondrial DNA Control Region," www.baylor-ir.tdl.org According to Douglas, "There is a measurable loss of genetic diversity in Bison bison [modern bison] compared to Pleistocene bison."

[75]See, "Lion Genetics," January 8, 2020. www.lionalert.org

[76]The horse and chariot are commonly believed to have spread throughout the Near East during the Hyksos epoch, which is conventionally placed around the sixteenth century BC. However, it can be shown that the Hyksos were one and the same as the Old Assyrians, who are rightly placed in the late ninth and eighth centuries BC. See Emmet Sweeney, *The Pyramid Age* (2007)

The genetic bottlenecks and extinctions, which we find throughout the globe, all occurred sometime near 2000 B.C., and were caused by the Deluge.

If the Pleistocene, the age of the mammoths, only came to an end around 2000 B.C., as we say, then we might expect the strange and often very large creatures of the time to have left a mark of their existence in human tradition. Is this the case? As a matter of fact, many of the Pleistocene megafauna seem to have found a prominent place in myth and legend. The Book of Genesis itself perchance makes a passing reference to these animals when it says of the pre-Flood times: "There were giants on the earth in those days."

Traditions current among the Native Americans apparently recalled the mammoth and mastodon. One story among the Delawares of the east, as recounted by Thomas Jefferson, spoke of a great creature which persecuted mankind, trampling and ruining crops in the fields, until the Supreme God rained down thunderbolts which destroyed them all. Another tradition spoke of how this enormous beast had an extra arm which appeared to grow out of its shoulder — clearly a reference to an elephant's trunk.

A rhinoceros-type creature with a single horn growing from its forehead named elasmotherium, which inhabited central Asia, is now recognized as being a contemporary of Paleolithic man, and the likely inspiration behind the legend of the unicorn.

Paleolithic man shared the earth with Neanderthals, as well as with various now-extinct species of hominids, and these seem to be recalled in the classical stories of satyrs and troglodytes, as well as in folk-legends from central Asia about the ape-like *almas*. The priapic reputation of the satyrs is perhaps explained by the fact that apes, like all animals, mate openly. If satyrs were Neanderthals, it could be that they displayed similar behavior.

During the Pleistocene a species of giant ape named gigantopithecus inhabited most of south-east Asia including India as far as the Himalayas, and it seems highly likely that the legend of the Yeti is a folk-memory of this enormous beast.

We could go on. Indeed, as mentioned earlier, it would be possible to fill many volumes with the evidence available. The fact that this data is rarely if ever treated in modern textbooks, particularly in books aimed at the general public, should not delude one into believing it does not exist. On the contrary, the amount of material just keeps growing. It is excluded from the popular accounts because it disagrees so radically with the prevailing hypothesis, a hypothesis predicated on the Darwinian and Lyellist notion that vast eons were necessary to both produce new species and make extinct old ones. Yet these eons, it appears, never existed. The last great mass extinction, accompanied by an enormous world-wide upheaval of nature, occurred little more than four thousand years ago. This event was witnessed by human beings, human beings who, in many parts of the world, had already attained a high level of culture and were on the way to producing civilized societies. The cataclysm, when it came, had a major impact upon human culture and on the shape taken by the rising civilizations. And the extreme recentness of the Flood cataclysm has profound consequences for human history. In 2000 BC, we are told, Egypt and Mesopotamia were already advanced cultures with over a thousand years of literate civilization behind them. But a Pleistocene terminated in a cataclysm around that time means that that cannot have been the case, and there is something seriously amiss with regard to the chronology of the early civilizations.

Chapter 2. The Legend of the Tower

The Tower, a Bridge to Heaven

According to Genesis, immediately after the Flood God sent the rainbow, allegedly as a sign that He would never again destroy the world by water. This is somewhat incongruous, since rainbows must have existed as long as the earth existed. Could it be that in the Genesis story the rainbow represents something else?

In every corner of the globe, from Lapland to southern Africa, and from Mexico to China, there is a tradition which states that after the Deluge terminated, a paradisal age of innocence, mankind — or in many cases a race of giants or titans — attempted to reopen communication with heaven by erecting a tower that reached the sky.[77] Sometimes this tower is described as a bridge or a ladder. Westerners are most familiar with the biblical version of the story, the Tower of Babel. In this, a very late and obviously amended account, it is the ambition of humans that leads them to attempt the raising of a tower to the heavens; but mankind's plans are frustrated when God confuses their speech. In the tradition of the Greeks, a much more primeval narrative, the tower-building is connected with a cataclysmic battle between the Olympians and a race of giants or titans, who attempt to storm heaven by piling mountains on top of each other. The resulting tower is smashed when Zeus strikes it with his thunderbolt. In the Norse myth, the Frost Giants attempt to reach Asgard by piling up a huge mound of clay, in the shape of a man. This tower is destroyed by Thor, the god of thunder, who strikes it

---

[77]Frazer (Folklore in the Old Testament) compiled several dozen of the Tower stories from various parts of the world, a few of which shall be mentioned presently.

with his hammer. From Africa there is an abundance of similar traditions, all of them of great antiquity, which are discussed at some length by a little-known writer named Brendan Stannard.

In his encyclopedic *The Origins of Israel and Mankind*. Stannard notes that,

> In many versions of the separation myth, the departure of Heaven [after the Flood] brought to an end a previously paradisal age, during which man and the gods were in close communication. Sickness, death, and the necessity of labour now entered man's domain. Man found himself abandoned and destitute of the necessities of life — fire, animals, food, etc., and in some myths mankind attempted to renew communication by building a bridge to heaven. In the Ashanti (Ghana, Ivory Coast) version, the woman who hit the sky with her pestle tried to build a pillar by stacking mortars one on top of the other. But this collapsed and caused the deaths of many people ... the Wapare of East Africa narrate how mankind built a tower so that they could attack heaven. When the supreme god saw what they were up to, the earth quaked and the tower broke in two and buried its builders.[78]

The very universality of the Tower motif convinces us that this was not a man-made structure, but some kind of natural phenomenon. But what kind of phenomenon? A clue lies in several traditions which describe the appearance of the Tower, as well as in the fact that Tower is often destroyed by an earthquake, or by a terrible wind. Legends from Britain and Ireland are here instructive: In British tradition Merlin, a child-prodigy, is destined for sacrifice by the tyrant Vortigern, whose tower is being continually destroyed by earthquakes.[79] Merlin of course evades sacrifice, but it is evident that the myth relates very clearly to the origins of the blood sacrifice ritual, and therefore to the origins of civilization. Merlin, with his magic wand, is clearly cognate with Lugos/Lugh, the Celtic Mercury, and a tradition from Ireland concerning the latter deity supplies us with crucial information. According to this, Lugh's mother Ethne was locked in a crystal tower by her monstrous father Balor, who feared a prophesy which told that his daughter would give birth to a son who would kill him. The prophesy is of course eventually fulfilled and Lugh duly slays his grandfather at the Battle of Magh Tuireadh ('Plain of the Tower').[80] The latter battle is fought between the Celtic gods — the Tuatha De Danann — and a race of monstrous giants, the Fomorians; and this is clearly the Celtic version of the Battle of the Tower as found in the Greek and Norse myth.

---

[78]Brendan Stannard, *The Origins of Israel and Mankind* (Lancashire, 1983), p. 761
[79]See e.g., Geoffrey of Monmouth, *History of the Kings of Britain* Bk. VI, Chapters xvii-xix.
[80]The story of the battle is told in the *Lebor Gabala Eren*, or Book of Invasions, and occurs also in a large number of early medieval Irish manuscripts.

4. The Tower of Babel, as imagined by Athanasius Kircher.

Aside from the obvious cosmogonic and cataclysmic imagery, it is striking that the Tower is described in the above myth (as well as in many others) as of a crystal appearance. In another Irish account, preserved in the *Lebor Gabala* ('Book of Invasions') it is described as being of gold, and located in the ocean.[81] Several other accounts place the structure in the middle of the ocean, as well as at the North Pole.

Over the past few decades, a kind of consensus has been arrived at among students of Velikovsky that the Tower or Pillar was some form of plasma or charged particle feature that became visible at the Poles after the earth's

---

[81] This golden tower is seen by the hero-deity Nemed as he sails north from Spain to Ireland. The story first appears in the Book of Invasions.

devastating encounter during the Deluge with the giant comet Typhon/ Tiamat/Ishtar.[82] Our planet was, as it were, electromagnetically "recharged" by this encounter, with the effects visible at the Poles. As such, the Tower or Pillar would, like the aurora borealis, have continually changed color and shape, sometimes appearing crystalline, otherwise golden in color and occasionally sporting many of the hues of the spectrum. If this were the case, then the rainbow mentioned in Genesis was not the normal rainbow but the Tower, a feature which, we recall, was seen by the inhabitants of the earth as a sign of renewed contact with heaven — as a sort of bridge to heaven, no less. Such an interpretation is confirmed by the fact that in Norse mythology we hear of a magical rainbow bridge, known as Bifrost, which connects Midgard, the world of men, with Asgard, the home of the gods. In the same mythology, the mystical bridge is destroyed by the Frost Giants during the Ragnarok, the Twilight of the Gods.[83] This circumstance strongly suggests that the post-Flood rainbow, or rainbow-bridge, is one and the same as the Tower.

Even more explicit clues come in Greek and Mesopotamian tradition. In Greek myth the rainbow is personified by the goddess Iris, who is seen as a messenger between gods and men. Importantly, she carries a caduceus or winged staff — the traditional symbol of the god Hermes, who is himself, as we shall see, intimately connected with the cosmic pillar or tower.

In early Mesopotamia the rainbow was explicitly connected to the Tower or World Tree. From the Epic of Gilgamesh, we hear that King Izdubar, one of the legendary rulers of Sumer, sees "a mass of colors like the rainbow's hues" that are "linked to divine sanction for war." Later in the epic, Izdubar sees the "glistening colors of the rainbow rise" in the fountain of life next to Elam's Tree of Immortality.[84]

The Tree of Life, or World Tree, is yet another manifestation of the Cosmic Pillar or Tower.

---

[82]The idea that the Tower was a polar plasma feature seems to have developed simultaneously among several of Velikovsky's followers. In the 1970s Dwardu Cardona and others concluded that the Tower had in some way been viewed as at the Pole, though they imagined that it was actually an optical illusion resulting from a series of planets lined up together, during the pre-Flood era. A theoretical turning-point was reached in 1982 when James E. Strickling concluded that the confusion of languages, often associated with the Tower story, was the result of an electro-magnetically induced dysphasia, which produced a temporary loss of speech amongst many of the earth's inhabitants. See Strickling, "The Tower of Babel and the Confusion of Tongues," Kronos, Vol. VIII, No. 1 (1982). See also Rense van der Sluijs, *The Mythology of the World Axis* (All-Round Publications, 2007), also, Anthony L. Peratt, *Physics of the Plasma Universe* (Springer, 2014).
[83]Mentioned in the *Eddas* of the 13th century composed by Snorri Sturluson.
[84]From the *Epic of Gilgamesh*.

The titanic battle in which the Tower or Tree of Life is "destroyed" or after which it, at any rate, disappears, makes us wonder whether this was some new cataclysm of the type which had brought the Flood in an earlier time. Though all the gods, or the majority, are credited with involvement in the Tower Battle, the god Mercury, in his various forms and names, takes center stage.

Destruction of the Tower

In all traditions relating to the Battle of the Tower a dragon or Gorgon-type monster is the leader of the forces of chaos which threaten to overturn creation. This is made very specific in the Greek retellings, the Titanomachy and the Gigantomachy, which portray the giants/titans as hideous and serpent-like, often with human upper bodies and reptile tails. As a matter of fact, the Greeks are said to have distinguished between two great wars involving gods and giants or titans, but these are clearly little more than different versions of the same myth. The Latin poet Ovid gives a brief account of the Gigantomachy in his poem *Metamorphoses*. Ovid has the Giants attempt to seize "the throne of Heaven" by piling "mountain on mountain to the lofty stars," an attempt that is foiled when Jupiter (Zeus) overwhelms the Giants with his thunderbolts, overturning "from Ossa huge, enormous Pelion." Later in the *Metamorphoses*, Ovid refers to the Gigantomachy as: "The time when serpent footed giants strove / to fix their hundred arms on captive Heaven."[85]

A far earlier account of this titanic struggle is provided by Hesiod, in his *Theogony*. Although the battle between gods and titans described by Hesiod is commonly identified with the Titanomachy and differentiated from the Gigantomachy of Ovid, it is evident that these are two retellings of the same story. Hesiod has the monster Typhon lead the assault upon Olympus. He is described thus:[86]

> Strength was with his hands in all that he did and the feet of the strong god were untiring. From his shoulders grew a hundred heads of a snake, a fearful dragon, with dark, flickering tongues, and from under the brows of his eyes in his marvellous heads flashed fire, and fire burned from his heads as he glared. And there were voices in all his dreadful heads which uttered every kind of sound unspeakable; for at one time they made sounds such that the gods understood, but at another, the noise of a bull bellowing aloud in proud ungovernable fury; and at another, the sound of a lion, relentless of heart; and at

---

[85]Ovid, *Metamorphoses*, I, 163
[86]Hesiod, *Theogony*, 820-835

another, sounds like whelps, wonderful to hear; and again, at another, he would hiss, so that the high mountains re-echoed.

From the above, it is fairly evident that Typhon represents the archetypal dragon or Cosmic Serpent; in short (in the Velikovsky interpretation), the great comet that had brought the Flood. In the Greek story, Typhon is a major participant in the titans' or giants' assault, but is struck by the thunderbolt of Zeus, after which he is either confined to Tartarus or has Mount Etna thrown on top of him. The encounter is clearly cataclysmic. Hesiod writes:

> [Zeus] thundered hard and mightily: and the earth around resounded terribly and the wide heaven above, and the sea and Ocean's streams and the nether parts of the earth. Great Olympus reeled beneath the divine feet of the king as he arose and earth groaned thereat. And through the two of them heat took hold on the dark-blue sea, through the thunder and lightning, and through the fire from the monster, and the scorching winds and blazing thunderbolt. The whole earth seethed, and sky and sea: and the long waves raged along the beaches round and about at the rush of the deathless gods: and there arose an endless shaking. Hades trembled where he rules over the dead below, and the Titans under Tartarus who live with Cronos, because of the unending clamor and the fearful strife.[87]

The monster is defeated and chained under the earth,

> So when Zeus had raised up his might and seized his arms, thunder and lightning and lurid thunderbolt, he leaped from Olympus and struck him, and burned all the marvellous heads of the monster about him. But when Zeus had conquered him and lashed him with strokes, Typhoeus was hurled down, a maimed wreck, so that the huge earth groaned. And flame shot forth from the thunderstricken lord in the dim rugged glens of the mount, when he was smitten. A great part of huge earth was scorched by the terrible vapor and melted as tin melts when heated by men's art in channelled crucibles; or as iron, which is hardest of all things, is shortened by glowing fire in mountain glens and melts in the divine earth through the strength of Hephaestus. Even so, then, the earth melted in the glow of the blazing fire.

The defeat of the Titans would imply that the threat posed by the comet was removed.

Now, in Velikovsky's reconstruction of the cosmic events of the time, the great comet/cosmic serpent remained a grave danger to humanity for many centuries until, about 700 years after its first appearance, it again came on a collision course with the Earth. This time, however, it was "intercepted" by

---

[87]*Theogony*, 835-850

the god Mars, and a celestial battle ensued. The end result was that comet lost much of its angular momentum, and its tail of debris. It then assumed an almost circular, planet-like solar orbit, and was removed as a threat to the world. These events Velikovsky placed in the eighth century BC., long after the Flood and the Tower catastrophes. Yet the Greek and Irish (and other) traditions would seem to place the "decapitation" of the comet/dragon at the time of the Tower. Furthermore, as we shall now see, it was neither Zeus (Jupiter) nor Mars but the god Mercury that was most often credited with delivering the death-blow to the monster.

We saw above how the Irish myth has Lugh/Lugos lead the gods in the war against the giants at the Plain of the Tower. It is he who actually destroys and decapitates the monster. Lugos was honored above all other deities throughout the Celtic lands, his title forming a component of numerous Gallic and British place-names. Yet Caesar stated specifically that Mercury was the major god of the Celts, and indeed it is not doubted that the deity he had in mind was Lugos. This is in accordance with tradition from throughout the world, which links the whole story of the Tower with Mercury. In Norse myth too it is Odin — Mercury — who leads the battle against the Frost Giants.[88]

It is interesting to note, at this stage, that in Greek myth, the decapitator of dragons *par excellence*, was Herakles (as for example in his destruction of the hydra). Velikovsky identified Herakles/Hercules with Mars on the strength of a statement by Macrobius which reads: "Tertia est stella Martis, quam alii Hercules dixerunt." ('The third star is Mars, whom others call Hercules') However, aside from this one statement in a lesser-known Roman author, there is little to recommend the fit. As a matter of fact, Herakles has far more features in common with Mercury, something plainly seen in the character of Perseus, a dragon-slaying hero who is widely viewed as a Herakles alter-ego. When he slays the dragon-monster Medusa, Perseus is equipped with the winged sandals (or helmet) of Mercury and images of him very much resemble those of the latter deity. But when we compare Perseus to the Celtic Mercury, Lugos, the parallels become too obvious to ignore. Like Lugos, Perseus is destined to slay his grandfather, King Acrisius of Argos, a prediction which prompts the latter to imprison his daughter Danae in a bronze chamber in his palace. When however Danae is impregnated by Zeus, who comes to her in a shower of gold, Acrisius casts both Danae and her infant into the sea in a sealed chest. In this, Lugos and Perseus are identical. Reaching adulthood, both heroes fulfil their destiny and kill

---

[88] As told in the Eddas.

their grandfather; in Lugos' case, the latter being the Gorgon-like giant Balor, whom he — like Perseus — decapitates.

Before Lugos' birth, his mother Ethne is imprisoned in a great tower after Balor finds her still alive. This tower, the World Tower itself, is evidently the origin of all medieval stories of a maiden imprisoned in a tower, such as Rapunzel.

In Greek myth, just as in Celtic, it is Herakles who plays the decisive role in the Battle of the Tower, and it seems clear that, if Velikovsky's cosmogonic interpretation of these myths is correct, then it was the god and planet Mercury, not Mars, which was mainly responsible for the "decapitation" of the great dragon-monster, the comet/protoplanet associated with the Flood. And this event happened during the destruction of the Tower, not some later time.

Mercury, the Tower, and the Confusion of Languages

The Greek Hermes (Mercury) was linked to the Tower in his fundamental symbol, the *Kerykeion* (*Caduceus*), the staff or pole — the original magic wand — which gives him access to the realm of the gods. The Caduceus is also, significantly enough, connected to the cult of the phallic menhirs, or *herma*, found throughout the Greek world. Phallic deities, wherever they occur, are all versions of Mercury. This will be seen, for example, in the case of the Egyptian phallic god Min (prominent during the Early Dynastic epoch) as well as in that of Abraham, the founding father of Israel, whose abortive sacrifice of Isaac (on a mountain top) takes place shortly after the fall of the Tower of Babel. In Greek tradition, Hermes is equally the source of high civilization and blood sacrifice.[89]

The phallus of Hermes/Mercury and Min is clearly a stylized version of the Tower itself.

Mercury's staff is the origin and source of the whole idea of the magic wand, as well as the royal scepter; and fittingly enough, the same deity was accredited with the origins of literate civilization as well as the idea of royal kingship — the two being intimately connected. As the heavenly messenger and ambassador, Mercury conferred eloquence upon his devotees. He was the inventor of writing and of language. Curiously enough, many of the traditions relating to the Tower and its destruction tell of a confusion of languages and the appearance of new languages at the time. This is found, of course, in the biblical account, where we read,

---

[89] Apollodorus, iii, 10, 2; *Homeric Hymn to Hermes*, 1-543.

[T]he whole land was of one language and of one speech. . . . And they said, Go to, let us build us a city and a tower whose top may reach unto heaven. . . . And the Lord said, behold, the people is one, and they have all one language. . . . Go to, let us go down, and there confound their language that they may not understand one another's speech. So the Lord scattered them abroad from thence upon the face of all the earth.

The Babylonian account, as reported by Abydenus, tells that once men "built a high tower where now is Babylon, and when it was already close to heaven, the gods sent winds and ruined the entire scheme. . . . and men, having till then been all of the same speech, received [now] from the gods many languages." Similarly, the Sibyl in Rome prophesied:

When are fulfilled the threats of the great God/With which he threatened men, when formerly/In the Assyrian land they built a tower/And all were of one speech, and wished to rise/Even till they climbed unto the starry heaven/Then the Immortal raised a mighty wind/And laid upon them strong necessity/For when the wind threw down the mighty tower/Then rose among mankind fierce strife and hate/One speech was changed into many dialects/And earth was filled with divers tribes and kings.[90]

The ideas recorded by Abydenus and uttered by the Sibyl emanated from the same part of the world as the Bible, but an almost identical tradition is found in many lands, as Velikovsky observed. Consider for example the account reported by the Mexican writer Ixtlilxochitl. After narrating the story of the Deluge which brought to an end the first world age, that of Atonatiuh, and killed most of mankind, Ixtlilxochitl describes the catastrophe which ended the second age, or Ehecatonatiuh— named "the sun of wind."

And as men were thereafter multiplying they constructed a very high and strong Zacualli, which means "a very high tower" in order to protect themselves when again the second world should be destroyed. At the crucial moment their languages were changed, and as they did not understand one another, they went into different parts of the world.[91]

Another Mexican tradition, recorded by Diego Duran in 1579, tells of giants who built a tower that almost reached the heavens, when it was destroyed by a thunderbolt. Again, a legend recorded by Pedro de los Rios concerned the foundation of the pyramid of Cholula in Mexico. After the waters of the Deluge had receded, one of the survivors came to Cholula, where

---

[90]Quoted by Theophilus of Antioch, To Autolycus II. xxxi, transl. by M. Dods in *The Ante-Nicene Fathers*, Vol. II (Grand Rapids, 1962); Cf. Josephus, *Antiquities* I. 109-121
[91]Don Fernando de Alvara, "Ixtlilxochitl," *Obras Historicas* Vol. 1 (Mexico, 1891), p. 12

he began to build a large structure. "It was his purpose to raise the mighty edifice to the clouds, but the gods, offended at his presumption, hurled the fire of heaven down on the pyramid, many of the workmen perished, and the building remained unfinished." Frazer, the source of this information, adds that "It is said that at the time of the Spanish conquest the inhabitants of Cholula preserved with great veneration a large aerolite [meteorite], which according to them was the very thunderbolt that fell on the pyramid and set it on fire."[92]

The *Popol Vuh*, the sacred book of the Quiche Mayas, narrates that the language of all the families that were gathered at Tulan was confused and none could understand the speech of the others. In North America, the Kaska, an Athabascan tribe, relate how "a great darkness came on, and high winds which drove the vessels hither and thither. The people became separated. Some were driven away. . . . Long afterwards, when in their wanderings they met people from another place, they spoke different languages, and could not understand one another."[93]

The same curious idea occurs everywhere a genuinely ancient tradition survives. Another example Velikovsky cites is from the island of Hao, part of the Puamotu (or Tuamotu) islands in Polynesia. Here the people recounted that after a great flood the sons of Rata, who survived, made an attempt to erect a building by which they could reach the sky and see the creator god Vatea (or Atea). "But the god in anger chased the builders away, broke down the building, and changed their language, so that they spoke divers tongues."[94]

Velikovsky notes that, "The question of Biblical influence was discussed by the folklorist: 'They [the natives of Hao] declared that this tradition existed already with their ancestors, before the arrival of the Europeans. I leave to them the responsibility for this declaration. All I can certify is that this tradition contains many ancient words which today are no longer understood by the natives.'"

What can such stories possibly mean? Velikovsky himself was of the opinion that they "give the impression that a strong electrical discharge," which could have come from an "overcharged ionosphere," after it "found a contact body in the high structure." He notes also a tradition recorded by the twelfth century traveler Benjamin of Tudela that "fire from heaven fell in the midst of the tower and broke it asunder." Certainly this could be interpreted as some form of lightning discharge. But if the Tower was itself some form

---

[92]Frazer, op cit., p. 149
[93]"Kaska Tales," collected by James A. Teit, *Journal of American Folklore*, no. 30 (1917), p. 442.
[94] R. W. Williamson, *Religious and Cosmic Beliefs of Central Polynesia* Vol. I (Cambridge, 1933), p. 94.

of electromagnetic phenomenon, the catastrophe which saw its destruction or disappearance might possibly have produced an electrical event that was felt over the entire globe.

In a 2007 article, English engineer David Salkeld revived an idea first mooted in 1982 by James E. Strickling; namely that the "confusion of languages" was a form of dysphasia, or loss of the power of speech, caused by exposure to a powerful electrical current. Having himself recently suffered a stroke along with temporary loss of speech, Salkeld noted that "when specific areas of the brain are targeted by an electrical current (using electrodes) it results in a partial loss of memory." Furthermore, "if a group of mountaineers are caught in an electrical storm and a bolt of lightning strikes, the group could temporarily suffer a partial dysphasia." "Could a huge electrical current," he asks, "have struck the tower of Babel ... and the builders of the tower have suffered dysphasia, so that they could not understand one another's speech?"[95] Although Salkeld, like Velikovsky, assumed the Tower to have been a man-made structure (or many man-made structures in different parts of the world), his argument is nonetheless valid if lightning bolts of immense energy struck the entire planet during the "destruction" of the Polar Tower. Such a solution could also help to explain, in part at least, why Mercury, the god of the staff or tower, was regarded as the inventor of new languages.

Archaeology finds evidence throughout the world of an immense catastrophe terminating the Neolithic/Chalcolithic cultures and directly preceding the rise of literate civilization in Mesopotamia, Egypt, India and China. New forms of worship, of ritual, of architecture, of metal and stoneworking and of pottery-making appear with great rapidity in the direct aftermath of this catastrophe. In addition, the worship of the tower (often portrayed with intertwining serpents, as well as the phallus and phallic-deities, now becomes supremely important. This was, to all intents and purposes, the Age of Mercury.

The Pillar and the Tree of Life

The Tower, in its various forms, became an integral part of mankind's religious symbolism in the centuries which followed the Tower Catastrophe. It was found, as we saw, in the caduceus of Mercury, as well as in the magician's wand and the royal scepter. The characteristic intertwined serpents of the caduceus are explained by the proposition that the Tower was an

---

[95] D. Salkeld, "Old Testament Tale XI: Dysphasia in Genesis?" Society for Interdisciplinary Studies, Chronology and Catastrophism Workshop, No. 1 (2007), pp. 9-10

electro-magnetic phenomenon, one that changed color and shape regularly. At times, filaments of charged energy, serpentine in appearance, seem to have flickered up and down the Pillar. These were interpreted by the ancients as dragons or serpents. Images of these intertwined serpents are found with great regularity in Egypt and Mesopotamia at the very beginning of the Early Dynastic period. And indeed, as we shall see, the Tower Catastrophe is intimately connected with the rise of the first literate civilizations in those areas.

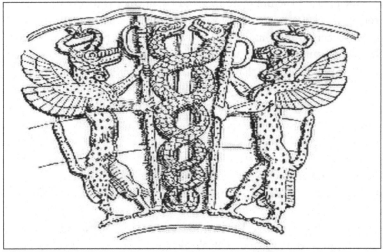

5. Early Mesopotamian image of serpents intertwined around the World Axis.

The theme of a tower with intertwined or "battling" serpents survived well into the historical age, and in regions far removed from the Middle East. In the British legend of Merlin, for example, we hear how a tower which the tyrant king Vortigern is attempting to construct, continually destroyed by earthquakes. Informed by a druid that, for his plan to succeed, Vortigern must sacrifice a flawless child (one born without a father) and sprinkle his blood at the base of the tower. The child Merlin is rumored to be such a one and is selected as victim. When brought before the king, Merlin reveals that below the foundation of the tower is a lake containing two dragons battling each other, and it is this that is creating the earthquakes.

The Merlin story is a late and much amended version of an evidently primeval myth, containing elements found repeatedly in the most archaic traditions. The tower wrecked by earthquakes is striking, as is the idea of sacrificing a child and burying the body under the foundations of a sacred structure. Human sacrifice is of course one of the markers of the earliest epoch of literate civilization, and is a feature we find again and again connected with the Tower myth, such as for example, the attempted sacrifice of Lugos and Perseus by their grandfathers.

As we saw, the Tower, being a plasma/electromagnetic phenomenon, changed shape and color regularly. At times it seemed to sprout arms and something like a head and took on the form of a human giant. Hence, the titan Atlas supporting the heavens on his shoulders. At other times it appeared to sprout branches, resembling a giant multi-colored tree. This was the World Tree, or the Tree of Life; a feature of virtually all the world's mythologies. The Tree of Life, like the Tower, had its own dragons which either guarded it or were entwined round it. In Greek myth, the Tree of Life was said to be planted in the Garden of the Hesperides (in the far West — the region of the dead), and to be guarded by the dragon Ladon. In the Welsh version of the myth, Lludd/Lud — evidently identical to the dragon Lotan/Ladon — is instructed to find the center, or axis, of the country (world axis), in his quest to locate the battling dragons underneath Vortigern's tower. In Norse mythology, the World Tree is named Yggdrasil, and it was upon it that Odin (Mercury) died. The dragon Nidhogg, it was believed, continually gnawed at the roots of Yggdrasil.

The whole concept of a world-axis, or pole (children to this day expect to see a physical pole at the North Pole), along with the various traditions linked to it, such as the European May Pole and the Mexican Pole Dance (*Danza de los Voladores*), thus ultimately derive from the visible pole anciently observed in the far north. Yet another clue comes in the testimony of Ovid, who describes how the catastrophe unleashed by Phaethon aroused the dragon of the north: "The serpent which lay close to the icy pole, and had till then been sluggish with the cold, no danger to anyone, now sweltered in the heat, and was roused to unprecedented fury."

So fundamental to subsequent history was the catastrophe which destroyed the Tower/Pole/World Tree, that the memory of this event was permanently engraved in human culture and consciousness.

Mythologically, the god Mercury is closely related to Min, the founder deity of Egyptian royalty, as well as to Abraham, the founding father of Israel. All three are strongly connected to phallicism and circumcision. The cult of Min was most important in Egypt in the Late Predynastic and Early Dynastic epochs, and it seems likely that he was identical to Menes, Egypt's semi-mythical first pharaoh. Herodotus actually calls the first pharaoh by the name "Min." Flinders Petrie discovered two large statues of Min at Koptos, dating probably from the early First Dynasty. These are the oldest examples of monumental sculpture ever discovered in Egypt, and it is almost certain that the custom of circumcision dates from this period. Min was, like all phallic deities, a symbol of fertility, and his black skin was evidently representative of Egypt's fertile black soil (the Egyptians actually called their country "The Black Land"). Osiris, with his green skin and erect penis, was obviously closely related to and virtually identical to Min. Like Min, he was regarded as the founder of Egypt's civilization.

6. Geb, God of the Earth, and father of Osiris, copulates with the sky-goddess Nut. This seems like a graphic illustration of the cosmic Pillar which stretched from the earth to the sky.

Osiris' myth, it would appear, is a retelling of the cosmic events that occurred from the Deluge to the Tower and its destruction. He reigns during a paradisal age of innocence — evidently before the Deluge — a paradisal age brought to an end by the bloody attack of Set, the god of chaos and destruction. In one version of the myth, Set dismembers Osiris, whose broken body is then reassembled by his wife/sister Isis. Another version relates how Set tricked Osiris into getting into a casket, which the former then cast into the Nile. This latter represents perhaps an echo of the ark in which a remnant of humanity is saved from the waters of the Flood — though its parallels with the birth/infanthood stories of Perseus and Lugos should not be overlooked. In any event, as the eldest child of the god of the earth, Geb, Osiris seems to represent the world in its idyllic pre-cataclysm state. His death and dismemberment represent the devastation wrought by the Flood, whilst the mummy bandages with which his wife Isis covers his body may perhaps be representative of the shroud of volcanic ash and debris which clouded the earth in the aftermath of the catastrophe.

Even after wrapping Osiris' corpse in a shroud of bandages, Isis cannot, to begin with, locate his penis. At last however it is recovered, and, after attaching it to Osiris' now mummified body, she succeeds in impregnating herself. The fruit of this strange union is the god Horus.

7. The Djed Pillar, the so-called "Spine of Osiris", was believed to be coated with natron salt and therefore crystalline in appearance. The Djed Pillar is another manifestation of the Cosmic Tower.

Osiris' penis is evidently another manifestation of the Tower reaching from the earth to the sky, though this Tower is also represented by the Djed Pillar, the so-called "Spine of Osiris." The latter was commonly portrayed as coated in natron salt, and was therefore a clear representation of the Tower as a crystal pillar — a common enough description of the plasma funnel. And we should note too, at this point, that Osiris' Spine may be mythically related to the Pillar of Salt into which the wife of Lot is transformed in the Genesis account of the destruction of Sodom and Gomorrah.[96] The name Lot, too, is significant, as it is

---

[96]The Arabah, the Valley enclosing the Dead Sea and the Jordan, from which region the Egyptians obtained bitumen and frankincense, two of the essentials of mummification, was anciently sacred to Osiris. See Chapter 3, "The 'Divine Land' of the Egyptians."

cognate with Lotan, Ladon, Latone, and Leviathan, the dragon-serpent which we have earlier noted wound itself round the Tree of Life.

An "Eruptive" Age

The destruction of the Tower was everywhere regarded as a cataclysmic event; and it was an event which left a very clear signature in the earth. Indeed, if ancient tradition is to be credited at all, the Tower's destruction was followed by a series of lesser catastrophes which continued for several centuries. This was the "eruptive age" spoken of by Percy Fawcett, and it left its mark.

If the Great Deluge marked the end of the Paleolithic (Old Stone) Age, then the centuries of human culture which followed were those now known to science as the Mesolithic (Middle) Stone Age, and the Neolithic (New) Stone Age. There is little evidence of major disruption in the natural order during these two epochs, which were, on the contrary, periods of rapid human progress. The Mesolithic saw the invention of many new techniques and technologies, among them the bow and the domestication of the dog, and later cattle. The Neolithic saw a plethora of new ideas, among which we might list the establishment of farming and settled communities (even small towns), pottery manufacture, and the first attempts at metal-working. Religious shrines now appear, as well as carving in stone and a host of artistic innovations. But the Neolithic was brought to a sudden and dramatic end: A great catastrophe, of fire and sometimes water, leveled the Neolithic villages and towns.

Evidence for this event was found everywhere archeologists looked, including in Egypt. Seaborne gravel occurs the length and breadth of the Nile Valley, sometimes at a considerable elevation above sea level. In Flinders Petrie's words, "The changes of sea-level, which occur alike all along the Mediterranean, formed an estuary up the valley to beyond Thebes. This filled up the whole valley with debris to the level of the plateau, leaving gravels on the top of present cliffs."[97]

The stratigraphy of the immediate Predynastic period reveals further clues. Petrie for example noted that the Badarian (Neolithic) epoch in Egypt seemed to be split into two distinct periods by some form of major natural disturbance. This event left a substantial layer of debris between the Early and Late Badarian strata.[98]

---

[97] F. Petrie, *The Making of Egypt* (London, 1939), p. 1.
[98] Ibid., p. 7. "That the Badarian age was a long period is shown by there being a thick bed of rock debris cemented together in the middle of the deposits, which seem indistinguishable in style above and below the interval."

Such is the situation in Egypt; yet it was other regions of the Near East, especially Anatolia and Mesopotamia that revealed the most dramatic evidence.

In 1922 an Englishman named Leonard Woolley began what was to become one of the most celebrated archeological digs of all time. The site he chose was Ur, the ancient Sumerian port named in the Bible as the home of Abraham, father of the Israelite nation. Digging down through the various levels of Bronze and Iron Age occupation and making some spectacular discoveries on the way, his work shed new and fascinating light on the brilliant and hitherto almost unsuspected civilization of ancient Sumeria. It was only when he went below the Bronze Age, however, that his most astonishing discovery came to light. At the bottom of the earliest level associated with a metal-using civilization, and delineating the transition from Late Neolithic to Early Bronze, Woolley came to a deep stratum of what appeared to be virgin clay. However, about three meters further down, the workmen again came upon evidence of human occupation. It was only then that Woolley realized the significance of the clay stratum: the clay was actually silt, waterborne silt — unequivocal evidence of a great flood.[99]

News that Woolley had discovered the "Flood of Noah" was flashed round the globe and caused great excitement at the time. Although this deluge could in no way be equated with the disaster which ended the Pleistocene, and which an earlier generation had equated with the biblical Flood, Woolley — coincidentally enough — dated his Flood at Ur to roughly 3200 BC., very close to the date postulated by the nineteenth century scholars (using the Bible) as the date for the termination of the Pleistocene and Noah's Deluge. This seemed to strengthen Woolley's claims and convinced many of the public. In the decade that followed, efforts were made to discover evidence of this "deluge" in other parts of Mesopotamia and further afield. If this was the event described so vividly in the Book of Genesis, then it should surely have left its mark throughout Mesopotamia and far beyond. But whilst clear signs of the flood of Ur could indeed be found in various parts of Iraq, no evidence of such an event, it was claimed, could be found beyond the Land of the Two Rivers. Eventually all talk of the Flood of Noah was discarded, and the Ur event was explained as a localized disaster caused by unusually heavy rainfall in the upper reaches of the Tigris and Euphrates rivers.

There the matter rested for many years, though indeed one or two dissenting voices were heard from time to time. It was pointed out, for example, that a silt deposit of three meters indicated flood waters of considerable depth, whilst the cultural discontinuity observed before and after the

---

[99]Leonard Woolley, *Ur of the Chaldees* (Pelican edition, 1950), p. 21.

flood stratum hinted at a catastrophe of greater magnitude than anything a normal river-flood could produce. Nevertheless, in spite of such factors, the Flood of Ur was decreed to be local to Mesopotamia. No evidence of a contemporary event outside the area, it was claimed, could be found. However, even as Woolley was completing his excavations at Ur, archeologists were discovering evidence of cataclysmic destruction in the Late Neolithic and Early Bronze Ages in site after site throughout the Near East. These destructions were often wrought by water, but also displayed the marks of earthquake and fire. Claude Schaeffer, for example, whose tireless work throughout the Near East made him one of the greatest authorities of his day on the archeology of the early civilizations, made it quite plain that he regarded the demise of the Stone, Copper and Bronze epochs as being the direct consequence of great upheavals of nature. Schaeffer's definitive work, *Stratigraphie comparée et Chronologie de l'Asie occidentale*, published in 1948, presented to the world the conclusions of a lifetime of excavation, cataloguing and research. Looking in detail at a number of very ancient sites in Anatolia, Syria, Palestine and Iran, he noted that in all these places human habitation had been repeatedly disrupted throughout the Bronze Ages.[100] In particular, he noted that the border between the Late Neolithic and the Early Bronze settlements was always marked by some form of catastrophic destruction, the agents of which were normally flood, earthquake and fire.[101] This destruction was by far the most violent of those identified by Schaeffer, and we shall have occasion to return to it at a later point.

Schaeffer did perhaps his most memorable work at Ugarit, the famous port in northern Syria. Here he noted that "the most ancient tombs of settlement 2 or Middle Ugarit 1 rest on a bed of shattered bricks covering a great accumulation of ashes, witness to a vast fire which had ravaged Early Ugarit 2."[102] He noted, however, that "The fire of Early Ugarit 2 is ... more than an episode of local history."[103] Ugarit's fate, he observed, was shared by settlements throughout Anatolia. At Tarsus, for example, a "brilliant" third-millennium culture was "destroyed by fire," whilst at Alaca Hüyük, Troy, and Alishar Hüyük, there were signs of a "general disturbance" which touched "vast areas."

---

[100]Les grandes perturbations ayant laissé leurs traces dans la stratigraphie des principaux sites du Bronze de l'Asie Occidentale sont au nombre du six. La plus ancienne d'entre elles a secoué entre 2400 et 2300 l'ensemble des pays s'étendant depuis le Caucase au Nord jusqu'à la vallée du Nil." *Stratigraphie comparée et Chronologie de l'Asie Occidentale*, 2me et 3me millénaires (Oxford, 1948), p. 563.

[101]Ibid.

[102]Ibid., p. 33

[103]Ibid., p. 36

Schaeffer eventually came to the conclusion that in all, six great catastrophes had at different epochs struck the entire Near East in early historical times. The first of these, and also by far the most violent, terminated the Early Bronze 2 epoch in Syria/Palestine.[104]

Since the publication of *Stratigraphie comparée* the evidence for these repeated catastrophes has grown more and more comprehensive. Orthodox scholarship, as enshrined for example in *The Cambridge Ancient History*, has by and large been compelled to accept the reality of these events. Thus we find J. Mellaart noting that Chalcolithic (Late Neolithic/Copper Age) Troy 1 was destroyed in a "violent upheaval"[105] and that "the burning of Emporio, the destruction of Thermi, Bayrakli, Helvaciköy-Hüyücek, Bozköy-Hüyücek, and every other Troy 1 site on the Aegean coast between Edremit and the Karaburun peninsula, in the Caicus Valley and the islands, suggests a catastrophe of some magnitude."[106]

Thus it would appear that the cataclysms described so vividly both in Genesis and other ancient traditions have left their mark very clearly in the archeological record. It is untrue to say that they were localized events. At the end of *Stratigraphie comparée*, Schaeffer considered all the evidence, including clear proof of similar disasters in areas much further afield than those he had personally visited and came to the conclusion that these upheavals were world-wide events, universal in the sense that they had simultaneously touched every part of the globe.[107] But if such be the case, which of these cataclysms was contemporary with the Flood of Ur, and how is it that it was never recognized as such?

The answer to that question lies in the contradictory and inconsistent dating techniques and stratigraphic terminologies employed by archeologists in the various regions of the Near East.

We recall at this point how Schaeffer discovered evidence of what he described as a vast conflagration at Ugarit in northern Syria. The Ugarit catastrophe left a layer of what appeared to be calcined or hardened ash almost four meters in depth, and it destroyed a settlement identified by Schaeffer as belonging to the Syrian Early Bronze 2. Neither Schaeffer himself, nor anyone else for that matter, could have been expected to see the fire of Ugarit as contemporary with the flood of Ur. Apart from the fact that the agents of destruction were apparently very different, the chronology also disagreed. After all, according to Woolley, the Flood of Ur had destroyed an

---

[104]Ibid.
[105]J. Mellaart, "Anatolia: c. 4000–2300 BC," in *The Cambridge Ancient History* Vol.2 part 2 (3rd ed.) p. 383.
[106]Ibid.
[107]Schaeffer, op. cit.

early Chalcolithic (Copper Age) settlement dated to circa 3300 BC, whereas the fire of Ugarit had destroyed a settlement which had already reached a fairly advanced state of the Early Bronze Age and was dated to circa 2300 BC.

Clearly then, the vast destruction observed by Schaeffer and others throughout Syria/Palestine and Anatolia could not be made to tie in with the great flood observed by Woolley in Mesopotamia. Such has remained the accepted wisdom for many years. However, there were always a great many clues that should have alerted scholars to the possibility that that view could be wrong. For in spite of the divergent terminologies, the pre-fire culture of Ugarit (Syrian E.B. 2) matches very closely the pre-flood culture of Ur (Mesopotamian Chalcolithic), whilst the post-catastrophe cultures of the two cities also match in detail. Most illuminating is the change in pottery styles. The pre-conflagration town of Ugarit employed 'Ubaid-type pottery of almost exactly the same kind as that used in pre-flood Ur. Similarly the immediate aftermath of the Ugarit fire saw the introduction of a new culture employing distinctive wheel-made pottery named Khirbet-Kerak. But the Khirbet-Kerak culture closely parallels the Jamdat Naşr culture of post-flood Mesopotamia. Again, pre-conflagration Ugarit was entirely illiterate, with early hieroglyphs only appearing afterwards — a situation precisely reflecting that of pre- and post-Flood Mesopotamia.

We could go on and on almost *ad infinitum* comparing the two stratigraphies, but the table below should illustrate the main points.

UGARIT	UR
Middle Bronze 2 (Hyksos) c. 1600 BC	Early Bronze 3 (Akkadian) c. 2300 BC
Middle Bronze 1	Early Bronze 2 (Early Dynastic 2 and 3)
Early Bronze-Middle Bronze (transitional)	Early Bronze 1 (Early Dynastic 1)
Early Bronze 3 (Khirbet Kerak) c. 2200 BC.	Jamdat Naşr (close parallels with Khirbet Kerak) c. 3200 BC.
GREAT FIRE (leaving 4 meters of hardened "ash")	GREAT FLOOD (leaving 3 meters of silt)
Early Bronze 2 ('Ubaid) c. 2400 BC.	Chalcolithic ('Ubaid) c. 3300 BC

8. Comparative stratigraphy: pre-conflagration Ugarit and pre-flood Ur

Apart from showing why no evidence for Woolley's Flood could be discovered outside Mesopotamia, the above table also helps to illustrate the need for a radical re-dating of absolute chronology. As we see, the compared stratigraphies reveal an enormous chronological discrepancy. Because archeologists still assume that the terms Early Bronze and Middle Bronze mean more or less the same thing in Syria and Mesopotamia, the Early Bronze 2 culture of Ugarit is dated to the same period (c. 2400 BC.) as the Sumerian Early Bronze 2 culture in Mesopotamia. Yet the table shows very clearly that the terms Early and Middle Bronze *do not* mean the same thing in the two regions. Entirely different systems of classification are followed, two systems out of sync. by between seven hundred and a thousand years. Thus we see that the Hyksos, who are generally dated to circa 1600 BC, were actually contemporary with the Mesopotamian Akkadians, who are generally dated around 2300 BC.

We shall presently return to this whole question, where we will find that the evidence requires a dramatic shortening of the whole of ancient chronology.

It is clear then that the Flood of Ur was an event of much greater magnitude than is now generally admitted, and that its effects were felt at least as far away as northern Syria — a region separated from Lower Mesopotamia by over 1000 miles and a substantial mountain range. The true extent of this cataclysm was disguised by the conflicting dating-systems employed by the archeologists in the various regions. However, as we shall see in Chapter 3, these inconsistencies followed a definite pattern, and were themselves but a reflection of confused and conflicting historiographies which formed round the great nations of the area, the Egyptians and Mesopotamians.

Dramatic Climate Change in the Age of Eruptions

The catastrophic events revealed in the archeology of the Near East had a major impact on the climate. Indeed it is well-known that the climate of the ancient Near East changed dramatically at the end of the Early Dynastic epoch, and it would appear that there were frequent and destructive alterations in climate right throughout and immediately preceding that era. This is demonstrated in numerous and often very obvious ways. It is known, for example, that during this period the Sahara was not a desert, but an enormous grassland supporting fauna typical of the African savannah. In Egypt and right across the whole of what is now the Sahara, vast numbers of rock-paintings and etchings show men, usually armed with bows, hunting various of these creatures, such as gazelle and ostrich. In fact, almost every animal of the African savannah occurs. In the midst of what is now sand and rock strewn wastelands, we find portrayals of elephants, rhino, lions, wildebeest and giraffe, to name but a few.

9. Image of giraffe and zebra, from central Sahara. Tassili-n-Ajjer, southern Algeria.

These etchings and paintings are known to be contemporaneous with Egypt's Protodynastic and Early Dynastic epoch. Thus we find, in the rock-art of Egypt's eastern desert, around the Wadi Hammamat and other places, symbols and iconography associated in the Nile Valley with the "Followers of Horus", who were closely associated with the kings of the First Dynasty. David Rohl has recently conducted a fairly exhaustive examination of this work, and has demonstrated beyond reasonable doubt the connection between these folk and the Early Dynastic Egyptians.[108]

The climate change which made almost the whole of northern Africa into one of the most arid regions on earth seems to have occurred in several stages from just before the beginning of the First Dynasty through to the end of the Third.[109] And the climatic perturbations of this period left their mark not only in Egypt, but all across the Near East. The evidence is found in Syria/Palestine as much as anywhere else. From what we have seen earlier, we would expect the strata in Syria/Palestine termed Early Bronze 3 and Middle Bronze 1 to be contemporary with Egypt's and Mesopotamia's Early

---

[108]David Rohl, *Legend: The Origins of Civilisation* (London, 1998)
[109]"Between the First and Fourth Dynasties, the second and major faunal break, characterised by the disappearance of the rhinoceros, elephant, giraffe, and gerenuk gazelle in Egypt, culminated in the modern aridity..." K. W. Butzer, "Physical Conditions in Eastern Europe, Western Asia and Egypt Before the Period of Agricultural and Urban Settlement," in *The Ancient History* Vol.1 part 1 (3rd ed.), p. 68.

Dynastic Age. Thus we should expect to find very clear evidence of climate disturbance in Early Bronze 3 and/or Middle Bronze 1 Palestine/Syria. Sure enough, disturbance there was. We are told that at the end of Early Bronze 3 there was "a complete and absolute break in Palestinian civilization."[110] This "break" was marked by the total destruction of all the inhabited sites in Palestine and Syria, and was accompanied by momentous climatic changes. We hear of an "absolute environmental break" with signs of a "lowering of the water-table [i.e., desertification], which in turn is associated with defor-estation and erosion."[111] These are the words of Kathleen Kenyon, one of the most respected Near Eastern archeologists of the twentieth century. Yet although a catastrophic change in climate is unequivocally indicated by the evidence, archeologists discuss the issue only with the greatest reluctance. For no mechanism, is it said, is known by which such an immense distur-bance in the climate could have been effected.

Archeologists tend only to comment upon the particular region or locality where they have experience and expertise. Nevertheless, they admit, in somewhat muted tones, that the climate disturbances of this time were by no means confined to one part of the world. These events were universal, as the utter devastation of the Saharan grasslands makes only too evident.

Over the past decade much debate has centered round the age of the Great Sphinx at Giza. To the annoyance (and consternation) of the academic establishment, a series of highly respected geologists and climatologists have nailed their colors to the mast in insisting that the Sphinx displays upon its back clear signs of water erosion.[112] It is unfortunate that the waters of the debate have been muddied by some of the outlandish claims made by writers who have seized upon this disclosure to claim that the Sphinx is a relic of a long-dead civilization, and that the water-erosion proves it to be 10,000 years old.[113] These authors seem unaware of the fact that the desertification of the Sahara occurred during Egypt's Early Dynastic period, and that condi-

---

[110] K. M. Kenyon, "Syria and Palestine c.2160-1780 BC: The Archeological Sites," in *The Cambridge Ancient History* Vol. 1 part 2 (3rd ed.), p. 567.

[111] Ibid., p. 574. In Egypt too there is very real evidence in the ground of this great desicca-tion. "The roots of acacias, tamarisks (?) and sycamores have been found in the low desert, well beyond the range of flood-waters or riverine ground water between Khawalid and deir Tasa, and also at Armant. These are dated between the Badarian Period and the Fourth Dynasty." See also Butzer, loc. cit., p. 67.

[112] Most famous in this regard is Professor Robert Schoch, a geologist of Boston University. Asked by John Anthony West to examine the erosion marks on the Sphinx, Professor Schoch expected to be able to issue a refutation, but was shocked to discover the oppo-site. His assertion that there are clear signs of water-erosion on the Sphinx has proved a major embarrassment to conventional scholarship for over a decade now.

[113] See, e.g., as one of a numerous genre, Graham Hancock and Robert Bauval, *Keeper of Genesis* (London, 1996).

tions in the Nile Valley were then very different from now. Nonetheless, one point made by some of them is perhaps worthy of consideration. The head of the Sphinx, which displays little or no erosion, appears in a very small scale, completely out of proportion to the rest of the body. The writers who suggested that the original head was re-carved in the Fourth Dynasty, in the likeness of the reigning pharaoh, may well be correct.[114]

Giza was a spot of immense sacredness and importance right from the beginning of the First Dynasty. Here was located the shrine of the *benben*, the sacred rock that fell from heaven, which was associated with the primeval hill, the first dry land to appear out of the watery abyss, the Nun. Much evidence of cult activity from Dynasties 1 and 2, including several key finds, has been discovered at Giza. The Sphinx may well date from the same period. It could be that originally the head was in the likeness of the lioness-goddess Sekhmet, who (often shown with serpent-like elongated neck) was of immense importance during the First Dynasty. By the end of Dynasty 3, the head may conceivably have been seriously eroded by water and unrecognizable. It was possibly then re-carved in anthropomorphic form, in the likeness of the reigning pharaoh (possibly Chephren). In the bone-dry climate of Egypt that has existed since then, little or no further erosion has occurred.

Sekhmet was one of the manifestations of the sphinx-god (or goddess), a being who personified the destructive power of the celestial deities, a power more commonly linked to Apop, the Cosmic Serpent (hence also her serpentine neck in early portrayals). Human sacrifices, it seems, were originally offered to the Giza Sphinx, a circumstance which probably finds an echo in the Greek legend of Oedipus, where the female sphinx devours those unable to answer her riddle.

Because the Early Dynastic epoch is conventionally located in the 4th/3rd millennium BC, most authorities place these climate alterations at that time. Yet we have seen that something is seriously amiss with regard to the chronologies and dating systems of the region. Similar climatic disturbances are noted outside the Near East, but here they are placed centuries later. In fact, the evidence shows that something of truly cosmic dimensions repeatedly plunged the climate of the entire planet into chaos between the fourteenth and tenth centuries BC. This was a phenomenon chronicled in great detail by Velikovsky.[115] In Europe, for example, he noted a dramatic *klimasturz*, or "climate plunge" in the early part of the first millennium BC. Temperatures

---

[114]It should pointed out, however, that the head of the Sphinx is carved from a harder stratum of limestone than that which lay beneath, from which the body of the Sphinx is fashioned, and this, by itself, could explain the erosion disparity without the need to postulate re-carving in the Fourth Dynasty.

[115]In his *Earth in Upheaval* (1956).

dropped by up to three degrees Celsius. Tree-lines retreated down mountainsides in the Alps, whilst in other areas oak forests were replaced by peat bogs. These changes were accompanied by massive seismic activity. The Bronze Age Lake Dwellings of central Europe were overwhelmed by massive inundations of water, as lake shorelines were suddenly and violently tilted.

Yet the true magnitude of what occurred is perhaps illustrated by another piece of evidence from Egypt. The Egyptians, we know, regarded the northern cardinal point as of immense religious significance. In the great age of pyramid-building, during the Fourth, Fifth and Sixth Dynasties, pyramids and temples are oriented very precisely with true north. The soul of the pharaoh had to ascend in that direction to attain immortality amongst the "imperishable" circumpolar stars. (Where, as we have seen, was located the Tower or Sacred Mountain, a veritable "stairway to heaven"). The astonishing fact however is that the pyramids and mastabas of the Early Dynastic Age are not oriented towards the north but towards a direction roughly corresponding to north by north-west, an alignment which is, as far as Egyptologists know, completely meaningless. Yet the alignment is not random; all the Early Dynastic monuments point in almost precisely the same NNW direction. Which then begs the question: Could it be that during the Predynastic or Early Dynastic Age the poles did not occupy their present positions?

The positions of the poles have, of course, changed repeatedly during the course of the earth's history. The magnetic poles move constantly and rather quickly. We should note too that the earth also "wobbles" slightly as it spins, so that over the centuries the position of the poles changes in relation to the fixed stars. Yet the Egyptians did not align monuments to the magnetic poles, nor to the fixed stars, but to the real axial poles, round which our planet revolves. These too change, but that change is normally believed to take vast stretches of time, as the drift of the continental plates alters the earth's topography. We know that since the erection of the Great Pyramid at least, virtually no such movement has taken place, for this tumulus is still aligned rather precisely to the present cardinal points. Yet between the end of the Second or Third Dynasty and the beginning of the Fourth, during which the Giza Pyramids were raised, a rather sudden and substantial shift may have occurred.

The explanation for such a sensational fact lies outside the scope of a history book, yet it is evident that the controversial hypothesis of Immanuel Velikovsky, who looked for answers to the skies, and particularly to the members of the solar system, is one that needs to be seriously examined.

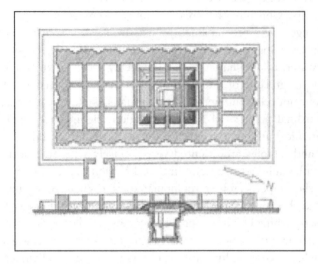

10. Mastaba of Dynasty 2, showing typical north-by-northwest orientation. (After I. E. S. Edwards)

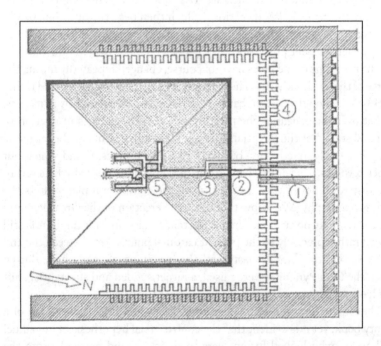

11. Pyramid of Sekhemkhet, Dynasty 3, showing north-by-northwest orientation. (After Edwards)

Priest-Kingship and the Rise of Blood Sacrifice

The catastrophic events experienced by humanity in the Late Neolithic and Early Bronze Ages had a profound impact. The continued threat of heaven-sent destruction scarred the minds of the earth's inhabitants, and they reacted everywhere in very similar ways. Professor Gunnar Heinsohn examined this topic in some detail in a 1992 article entitled "The rise of blood sacrifice and priest-kingship in Mesopotamia: A 'cosmic decree'?"[116] In the paper, Heinsohn argued that all early monarchs were simultaneously priest-kings, whose function was to offer propitiary blood — including human — sacrifices to the celestial gods. These sacrifices often took the form of a ritual re-enactment of a cosmic drama or dramas — or "battles" — recently witnessed in the heavens. In these re-enactments the priest-king would take the role of the "good" god, whilst the victim would take the role (and be dressed as) of the "bad" deity — Set, Tiamat, Loki, etc. The latter would, of course, invariably lose the battle and his life.[117] But thus taking the life of an innocent victim incurred a huge amount of guilt, for the individual and for the community as a whole. The priest-king took upon himself the burden of that guilt, thereby exonerating the rest of the community, which in turn rewarded him with virtually absolute power and authority.

Whether or not Heinsohn's interpretation of the psychology behind priest-kingship and blood sacrifice is correct (and the present writers feels that it is), there is absolutely no question that the earliest stages of high civilization, wherever we look, are marked by the practice of blood sacrifice — often on an enormous scale. In addition, we find everywhere an obsessive interest in the movements of the heavenly bodies, as well as an associated worship of these bodies. This star and planet-worship is furthermore associated everywhere we look — in both the Old World and the New, as well as in both hemispheres — with the raising of artificial hills or mounds or pyramids, which are themselves associated with the custom of human sacrifice. And this is a point worth stressing: Egyptologists tend to view pyramid-building as something unique to Egypt and routinely ignore the fact that it was a world-wide phenomenon. One "explanation", found repeatedly in textbooks, is that the pyramid-shape developed by accident in Egypt when the seer Imhotep — King Djoser's vizier — had the idea of placing a series of progressively smaller mastabas on top of a larger foundational one until

---

[116] G. Heinsohn, "The rise of blood sacrifice and priest-kingship in Mesopotamia: A 'cosmic decree'?" *Religion*, Vol. 22 No. 2 (April, 1992).

[117] Remnants of these primeval forms of blood-sacrifice persisted into the sixteenth century in Mexico with the so-called Mayan "Ball Game," whilst the gladiatorial contests of Rome were survivals of this ancient form of human sacrifice.

he achieved, by chance, the aesthetically pleasing shape of a step pyramid. Having thus stumbled upon the pyramid-shape, the Egyptians then went on to develop it to perfection.

But this "explanation" ignores two key pieces of evidence: First and foremost, pyramid- and mound-building is found almost everywhere on the planet in the first stages of civilization; and secondly, the pyramid and pyramid-shape existed in Egypt long before the time of Djoser and Imhotep. Indeed, both textual and architectural discoveries prove that the pyramid, in Egypt as elsewhere, represented the Sacred Mountain, or Tower, and that it is encountered from the beginning of the First Dynasty. As one author says: "There was no fixed form [in Egypt] for the Primeval Hill ... the mound was soon formalized into an eminence with sloping or battered sides or a platform surrounded by steps on each side. This became the most usual symbol. It is probably what the step pyramids represent."[118]

That the construction of these sacred mounds or platforms commenced at the start of the First Dynasty is an established fact: an inscription from Sakkara informs us that king Djet of Dynasty 1 built a pyramid there — presumably of mud-brick,[119] whilst it has been demonstrated that the "mastaba" tombs of Dynasties. 1 and 2 were constructed over mounds of earth that were sometimes given a stepped appearance.[120] Reisner was convinced that the superstructures of the tombs of Djer and Djet rose by two and three steps respectively to a level summit about eight and twelve meters in height.[121] These diminutive stepped pyramids are clearly the forerunners of Djoser's much larger stone structure. Indeed, in a sense, the Sakkara pyramid, inside its enormous enclosing wall, is, taken all together, little more than a giant mastaba in stone. All of these mud-brick stepped pyramids, occurring at the start of pharaonic times, undoubtedly represent the Primeval Hill, for, as we saw above, the hieroglyphic symbol employed was a stepped pyramid. The symbol may have been significant even before the start of the First Dynasty, for in Hierakonpolis (Nekhen), home of the first Horus kings, archeologists discovered quite possibly the earliest representation of the Sacred Hill. In the words of David Rohl, the city's primitive reed temple sat, " on a mound of clean desert sand (enclosed in a sloping revetment wall of bricks) [and] was the first foundation of the Shebtiu [ruling elite] in the Nile valley. Here is a striking architectural feature which links us with both Bahrain and Mesopotamia. As Petrie noted in 1939, the temple of Barbar in

[118]   R.T. Rundle Clark, *Myth and Symbol* (London, 1959), pp.38-9.
[119]See *Egyptian Archeology* No.6 (1995), pp. 26-7.
[120]Michael Rice, *Egypt's Making* (London, 1990), p. 118.
[121]   I. E. S. Edwards, "The Early Dynastic Period in Egypt," in *The Cambridge Ancient History* Vol.1 part 2 (3rd ed.), p. 65.

Bahrain was constructed on top of a hill or platform of clean sand as were many of the holy sites in Sumer. Such sandy mounds represent the primeval hill upon which the first temple of creation at Eridu was constructed. The Egyptian religious texts mention another sacred mound of sand at Heliopolis upon which the Benben was erected. The Benben was the sacred stone onto which the mythological Benu-bird (the fabulous Phoenix) alighted to establish the temple of Atum at the city of the sun ... This was the most important center of Atum/Re worship in Egypt and its roots go back to the legendary era of the predynastic Horus kings."[122]

The sacrifices offered atop these man-made Primeval Hills were almost certainly human, for human sacrifice, on a fairly grandiose scale, is attested both in Egypt and in Mesopotamia throughout the Early Dynastic epoch. We may mention, for example, a large mastaba-tomb at Giza, Mastaba V, apparently dating from the reign of King Djet (First Dynasty), which was surrounded by the graves of 56 retainers.[123] At Abydos and Abu Rawash there is evidence of large-scale sacrifice of prisoners, whilst one eminent authority was moved to comment: "In spite of the insufficiency of evidence to show the extent of the practice of human sacrifice during the Early Dynastic Period, the fact of its existence cannot be questioned. If the number of subsidiary graves bear any relation, as is probable, to the number of persons sacrificed, the custom reached its peak under Djer [Dynasty 1], whose two 'tomb' complexes at Abydos contained more than 590 subsidiary graves."[124]

The situation in Mesopotamia offers a precise parallel with Egypt, and the ziggurats of that region are rather obviously high altars upon which were performed the bloody rituals necessary to ward off calamity. Although no ziggurats survive from the Early Dynastic period, it is agreed that the custom of ziggurat-building had its origins at that time. Cuneiform documents make it plain that the sacrifices dedicated atop the ziggurats — in the House of the God — were all that stood between creation and a renewed assault by the serpent monster Tiamat. The Creation Epic itself tells us how immediately after destroying Tiamat, Marduk orders the building of the first ziggurat:

> I shall make a house to be a luxurious dwelling for myself
> And shall found his [Marduk's] cult center within it ...

The bloody rituals of human sacrifice were performed atop these structures, and the enormous scale of Mesopotamian human sacrifice during

---

[122] D. Rohl, op cit., pp.349-50.

[123] I. Shaw and P. Nicholson, *British Museum Dictionary of Ancient Egypt* (London, 1997), pp. 109-10.

[124] I. E. S. Edwards, loc. cit. p. 58.

this epoch was brought to the world's attention when Sir Leonard Woolley opened the notorious Grave Pits at Ur, where the bodies of hundreds of servants who had been forced to accompany their masters to the Underworld were discovered. Scholars agree that in Mesopotamia the practice of human sacrifice commenced at the start of Early Dynastic II — contemporary with the first ziggurats — and ended towards the close of that same epoch (the end of the Early Dynastic period).[125] Here there is fairly precise correspondence with the situation in Egypt, for here too the custom of human sacrifice apparently came to a rather abrupt end with the close of the Early Dynastic Age.

Despite the evidence quoted above, establishment academia persists in claiming to not understand the symbol of the Primeval Hill or Mountain or Tower. Consider for example the words of Egyptologist Michael Rice; "For reasons that are still largely obscure peoples with no apparent contact with each other, separated by enormous distances and with totally unrelated cultural traditions began, early in the third millennium, to build more and more complex structures in which to house the remains of their chiefs and Kings and, increasingly, a substantial part of the community's moveable wealth. Often these monuments were enclosed in mounds, or were themselves mound-like in structure, though built of stone [i.e., pyramids]."[126] "In the history of human obsessions the practice represents a curious chapter," Rice continues, "from the Orkney islands in the most remote north-west, across Europe, through Egypt and Mesopotamia, down the coastlands and islands of the Arabian Gulf, in Oman, and away into the Indian subcontinent and beyond, elaborate tombs of this type were constructed at this time."

The writer of the above words did not include the pyramids of the New World, for there it is known that pyramid- and mound-building did not commence until the latter part of the second millennium BC — almost two thousand years, allegedly, after it began in the Old World. But were it to be demonstrated that the custom began simultaneously throughout the Old World and the New, say around 1300 BC, then the above author would have had to admit a mystery much more profound than even he was prepared to acknowledge. Yet pyramid-building did indeed begin simultaneously on both sides of the Atlantic. As we saw in Chapter 1, the Flood catastrophe, which terminated the Pleistocene, was a much more recent event than is admitted in mainstream publications, whilst the massive chronological discrepancies observed in Old World archaeology — as we saw between the

[125]Sir Max Mallowan, "The Early Dynastic Period in Mesopotamia," in *The Cambridge Ancient History* Vol.1 part 2 (3rd ed.), p. 286.
[126] M. Rice, op cit., p. 171

record in Mesopotamia and Syria in the present chapter — mean that the chronology of world history as presently understood is entirely disjointed, and has given rise to a wholly distorted view of the early civilizations and their development.

In the chapter to follow, we shall again meet the chronological problem head-on: For there we shall find that the archeological discrepancy which we noted with regard to Syria and Mesopotamia is also reflected in the historiography; meaning that characters and events of Hebrew/Israelite history are placed a thousand years after characters and events of Egyptian and Mesopotamian history — with whom they were however, in reality, contemporary. For the age of pyramid-building and human sacrifice in Egypt and Mesopotamia is placed around 3000 BC, whereas in the Bible it is placed around 2000 BC.

Chapter 3. The Dawn of History

The Foundation of Egypt's History

With the founding of the First Dynasties of Egypt and Mesopotamia we move, finally, from the age of myth, or rather the age in which human memory is concerned primarily with the works of the gods, or more properly, with the works of Nature, to the epoch during which the lives and even the names of real human beings are recorded and noted. It was the invention of writing, of course, that was responsible for this remarkable transformation; and writing only appears at the beginning of the Early Dynastic period. Yet even then the age of myth is not left wholly behind; for, leaving aside the few meager inscriptions actually left by the early kings, the great majority of information we have about them comes from accounts written many centuries later, and these display a pronounced tendency towards mythologization. And this tendency is made worse by the fact that the "eruptive" age, during which Nature and the gods acted powerfully to change the face of the earth, had not yet come to an end, nor would it do so for several centuries yet.

According to the traditions of Egypt, before the time of the pharaohs the land of the Nile had been divided into two hostile kingdoms, Upper and Lower Egypt. Then came a ruler of Upper Egypt named Menes (or, alternatively Mena or Min) who, in a long-celebrated war, conquered Lower Egypt and founded the First Dynasty. It was with Menes that Egyptian civilization, as we now know it, commenced. Although no pharaoh named Menes has been positively identified from the monuments, it is generally assumed that he is likely an alter-ego of one of the powerful Early Dynastic kings, probably either Narmer or Aha, whose tombs have been discovered at Hierakonpolis

(Egyptian Nekhen), just to the south of Thebes. Along with these monarchs archeologists discovered the tombs of various other pharaohs and dignitaries of the First Dynasty, men with names such as Djer, Den, Anedjib, Semerkhet and Kaa, some of whom can be positively identified with rulers known from Manetho and the hieroglyphic king-lists. It seems in fact that Hierakonpolis, rather than Thinis, was the real source of the First Dynasty, the "Followers of Horus", who were ever afterwards known as the Great Ones of Nekhen.[127]

At the start of the First Dynasty the Nile Valley experienced a remarkable and unprecedented flowering of civilization. This occurred with a speed, almost a suddenness, which has astonished historians. The art of writing appears, without any real signs of prior development, in an almost fully-developed state. Few major innovations occurred after this. The plastic arts too, most especially carving in stone, reached unprecedented levels of sophistication. Egyptian craftsmen began to produce vessels of stone so outstanding in quality that modern scholarship is still at a loss to explain the methods used. One point upon which there is no contention however is that Egypt's Early Dynastic epoch, this age of dramatic progress in civilization, was roughly contemporary with the Early Dynastic epoch of Mesopotamia, and in fact parallels between the first civilizations of these two great lands have long been noted. So obvious are the similarities, in terms of art, religion and culture in general, that some scholars have been prompted to view Egyptian dynastic culture as an offshoot of the Mesopotamian.

Mesopotamian influence arrived in the Nile Valley at a very precise point in time. In the centuries before the start of the historical age, Egypt was the home to a series of cultures, each clearly defined by the characteristic artwork, pottery and burial customs of its people. The first pottery-using culture, known to archeologists as Badarian, or Amratian, was entirely native to the Nile Valley, a fact displayed by the parallels with other groups throughout northern and eastern Africa. The same was true of Naqada I, which followed the Badarian Age. But the demise of Naqada I saw the arrival of a new culture, Naqada II (or Gerzean), with strong links to Mesopotamia. Naqada II represents a major (though not complete) break with the past. Many things change. New forms of pottery appear, as do new forms of religious iconography; burial customs are different; economy and farming practices are different. Most striking of all however is the sudden appearance of writing — writing at a fairly advanced level of development; writing which has already moved beyond the level of pictographs. Along with this writing

---

[127]Horus, the son of Osiris, was the ultimate destroyer of the evil Set, whose "war" against Osiris we have already interpreted as the "war" waged by the unleashed forces of nature during the Tower catastrophe. As such, the close identification of the early kings of Egypt with Horus, the destroyer of chaos, is significant.

is the appearance of the cylinder-seal, a peculiarly Mesopotamian invention originally designed for marking ownership by impressing on the wet clay used for so many functions in the ancient Land of the Two Rivers.

The Naqada II culture immediately preceded the rise of dynastic Egyptian civilization — a civilization which continued, for a short period at least, to display the striking Asiatic features introduced shortly before.

The first scholar to devote serious consideration to this topic was Flinders Petrie, and the conclusions he reached have been further verified by discoveries made since. Because of the predynastic eastern influences, most especially the cylinder-seals and writing, Petrie regarded Egyptian civilization as a hybrid phenomenon resulting from the intermingling of native Egyptians with immigrant culture-bearers from Mesopotamia.[128] Thus he spoke of a great migration from Mesopotamia to Egypt at the dawn of history.[129]

Since Petrie's time our knowledge of Early Dynastic civilization has expanded greatly, and indeed the Mesopotamian origin of many features of Egyptian civilization has now become part of accepted wisdom. In the 1971 edition of *The Cambridge Ancient History*, I. E. S. Edwards devoted considerable space to a discussion of the question. "Foremost among the indications of early contacts between Egypt and Mesopotamia," he says, "must be counted the occurrence in both countries of a small group of remarkably similar designs, mostly embodying animals."[130] The artistic parallels are detailed and striking: "Both on the Narmer palette and on the seals, the necks of the monsters are interlaced — a well-attested motif in Mesopotamian art, to which the interlaced serpents found on three protodynastic knife-handles may be an additional artistic parallel."[131] Some Egyptian work of the period looks as if it was actually produced in Mesopotamia. A famous ivory knife-handle, for example, found at Gebel el-Araq, "portrays in finely carved relief a bearded man clothed in Sumerian costume and holding apart two fierce lions."[132] In Edwards' words, "so close does the composition of this scene resemble the so-called Gilgamesh motif, frequently represented on Mesopotamian seals, that the source of the inspiration can hardly be questioned."[133]

Since these words were written, things have moved on substantially, and more recent studies have revealed in fairly dramatic detail the extent of Egypt's debt to Mesopotamia. An in-depth examination of the material presented by the various scholars would be beyond the scope of the present

---

[128]   F. Petrie, op cit., pp.77-8
[129]Ibid.
[130]   I. E. S. Edwards, loc cit., p. 41
[131]Ibid.
[132]Ibid., p. 42
[133]Ibid.

work, though a brief overview of what has been discovered so far will serve to illustrate to the reader just how all-pervasive the evidence has become. Before doing so, we should note an important point. These Mesopotamian influences did not arrive by way of trade but through a migration, a movement of population that did not last any great length of time but which had a profound influence on the course of future events. Edwards names these folk the "Dynastic Race" and notes that they "differed unmistakably from the predynastic Egyptians."[134] Whereas the latter were unusually small in stature and possessed long and narrow skulls, "the newcomers were more massively built and their skulls ... were appreciably broader than those of their predecessors." We are further informed that, "The quality and distribution of the skeletons hitherto found suggest that the 'Dynastic Race' entered Egypt in considerable numbers from the north, where the purest examples of their racial type have been discovered; this fact alone would suggest that the immigrants came from Asia...."

The Impact of Mesopotamia

In his *Egypt's Making* (1990) Michael Rice lists at least a dozen areas of Naqada II culture that display very specific Mesopotamian parallels. David Rohl (*Legend: The Genesis of Civilization*, 1998) looks at even more, going into such detail that he has quite possibly forever silenced whatever lingering doubts there may have been. Foremost among the Mesopotamian parallels examined by Rohl, constituting perhaps the most pervasive material evidence in the Near Eastern sites, is pottery. From Naqada I to II there was an almost complete break in Egyptian pottery manufacture. The old, very distinctive red-glazed work of Naqada I is largely (though not completely) replaced by new forms of very clear Asiatic provenance. The Naqada II/Gerzean pottery in fact is virtually identical to that of the Jamat Nasr period of Mesopotamia, so similar indeed that the two types could almost have been produced in the same workshops. Most obviously, lug-handled jars of eastern type now become very common in Egypt. Rohl has noted that whilst the lug-handled pot may just have been developed independently in both regions (the form is very utilitarian), the same cannot be said of the other pottery form now appearing in Egypt: jars with distinctive teapot-type spouts. This form is so peculiarly Mesopotamian that, in Rohl's estimate, it is extremely unlikely the Egyptians would have evolved it independently.[135]

---

[134]Ibid., p. 40
[135]Rohl, op cit., p. 311.

12. The Gebel el-Araq Knife Handle. This famous artefact displays pronounced Mesopotamian influence, and it may even have been made there. The hero-figure between two lions, dressed in long coat and turban-like headdress, finds his exact counterpart in Early Dynastic Mesopotamia and Elam. According to Petrie, the two dogs underneath belong to the Babylonian myth of Etana and the flying eagle. (Cf. Petrie, *The Making of Egypt* (19039))

It is perhaps above all the evidence of pottery which tells us that the Asiatic penetration of Egypt at this time was not simply the result of trade, but of a significant population movement. Highly-quality products, such as weaponry and jewelry, might be traded over great distances, but pottery had to be produced locally; and the Naqada II (Late Predynastic) pottery in Egypt precisely parallels that of Jamdat Nasr Mesopotamia.

Along with the pottery, a whole host of cultural innovations arrived in the Nile Valley. These included various types of weaponry, but most especially maces with peculiar pear-shaped heads, the semi-precious stone lapis-lazuli, high-prowed boats, building in mud-brick, royal insignia and iconography, cylinder-seals, writing and some vocabulary; even the names of a few of Egypt's most important gods appear to have entered the land with the newcomers.

Much has been written about the introduction of the pear-shaped mace-head into Egypt at this time. That this type of weapon originated in Mesopotamia is beyond question, a fact which has prompted speculation that the easterners came as invaders.[136] Certainly there is every likelihood that such was the case, and the weapon stands as an important indicator of one possible method by which the Mesopotamians imposed their culture so effectively on the inhabitants of the Nile Valley.

A great deal of debate has also centered round the appearance of lapis-lazuli in Egypt at the beginning of the period under discussion. This highly-valued stone is known to have originated in Badakhshan on the borders of Afghanistan and Pakistan, and to have reached Egypt via Mesopotamia.[137] It appears in the rich graves of the protodynastic epoch, and continues to occur in the early burials of Dynasty 1. But it disappears abruptly after the reign of King Djer, in the middle of the First Dynasty,[138] not occurring again in Egypt until the Fourth Dynasty, hundreds of years later. This fact alone suggests that the movement or migration from Mesopotamia to Egypt was a "one-off" and that the flow of newcomers dried up after only a short period of time.

Much ink has been used in the debate over the high-prowed boats introduced by the Mesopotamian migrants. Illustrations of these vessels occur in the most unlikely of places, including the now-arid Wadi Hammamat in the eastern desert between the Nile and Red Sea. We have already noted that these rock-etchings also show animals of the African savannah, including ostriches, elephants, gazelle and giraffe, demonstrating in the most graphic way possible that in this epoch the area was not a desert. Regarding the boats, a number of writers, beginning with Petrie, have seen in these proof that the Mesopotamian immigrants reached Egypt by sea, rounding the Arabian Peninsula to the south. Yet illustrations of these same boats are found throughout central Arabia, and no one would surely suggest that the migrants would have needed to use ships to get there from the Land of the Two Rivers. In any case, the evidence shows that the boats illustrated were primarily cult-objects, and not necessarily vessels used for travel.[139]

The influence of Mesopotamia is found in the minutiae of predynastic culture, but also in the greatest things. The first Egyptian architecture dated

---

[136]Ibid., pp. 314-5.
[137] M. Rice, op cit., p. 35.
[138]Ibid., p. 89
[139]Ibid., p. 46

from this time and, just as we might expect, it is entirely Mesopotamian in character. The mastaba tombs of Naqada II have an eastern antecedent, as noted in 1971 by Edwards: "... excavation in Mesopotamia has revealed the more primitive wooden construction from which this style of architecture was no doubt derived, and ... the earliest Mesopotamian examples in brick are considerably older than the first mastabas of the Naqada form found in Egypt, where they appear quite suddenly at the beginning of the First Dynasty."[140] Various scholars have in fact illustrated how the perimeter walls of the mastabas, with their regular buttresses and recesses (or niched facades), display a style of construction very peculiar to Mesopotamia. In the words of Henri Frankfort: "Under the First Dynasty [of Egypt], when brick architecture came into its own, this new and more permanent architecture was used, at first, for the royal tombs which were decorated with buttresses and recesses on all four sides. This ornamentation was achieved, in some cases, by the use of two kinds of bricks — large ones for the core of the building and smaller ones for the recessing. These small bricks are of a size and shape peculiar, in Mesopotamia, to the latter half of the Protoliterate Period and were used in an identical fashion, three rows of stretchers alternating as a rule with one row of headers. The recesses and buttresses duplicate exactly the recessing of [Mesopotamian] Protoliterate temples. Other technical details — the manner in which a plinth or platform is constructed, the use of short timbers inserted horizontally as the strengthening in the niches — likewise reflect Mesopotamian usage in the Protoliterate Period ... In view of this great variety of detailed resemblances there can be no reasonable doubt that the earliest monumental brick architecture of Egypt was inspired by that of Mesopotamia where it had a long previous history."[141]

The influence of Mesopotamia was not confined to material culture, but exerted itself even on the Egyptian belief-systems and language. Furthermore, that language could now be written down for the first time. Because the symbols used in the Egyptian script were not (for the most part) directly copied from those developed in Mesopotamia, it was decreed that though there were "certain affinities", the differences between the two were "too significant to be disregarded," and "it is probably correct to assess the Sumerian contribution to the Egyptian science of writing as mainly suggestive and limited to imparting a knowledge of the underlying principles."[142] Thus the opinion of I. E. S. Edwards; Henri Frankfort, however, was inclined to go much further:

---

[140]Edwards, loc. cit.

[141] Cf. Rohl, op. cit., p. 326.

[142]Edwards, loc. cit., p. 44.

It has been customary to postulate prehistoric antecedents for the Egyptian script, but this hypothesis has nothing in its favour ... the writing which first appeared without antecedents at the beginning of the First Dynasty was by no means primitive. It has, in fact, a complex structure. It includes three different classes of signs: ideograms, phonetic signs, and determinatives. This is precisely the same state of complexity as had been reached in Mesopotamia at an advanced stage of the Protoliterate Period. There, however, a more primitive stage is known in the earlier tablets, which used only ideograms. To deny, therefore, that Egyptian and Mesopotamian systems of writing are related amounts to maintaining that Egypt invented independently a complex and not very consistent system at the very moment of being influenced in its art and architecture by Mesopotamia where a precisely similar system had just been developed from a more primitive stage.[143]

Along with writing, the Mesopotamian migrants brought many words and technical terms. These, according to some authorities, include the words for hoe, spade, plough, corn, beer and carpenter, a series whose significance in terms of the development of agriculture is obvious enough.[144] Egyptian is distantly related to the Semitic languages of western Asia; but most of these words are derived from the non-Semitic Sumerian. One word which has attracted much attention is *maat*, which in Egyptian signified "truth" or "order". *Maat* is a feminine word carrying an unpronounced "t" at the end, and it was therefore an almost exact counterpart of the Sumerian term used to denote cosmic order, *me*. David Rohl argued that many of the Mesopotamian immigrants came from the Eridu region and noted that the sacred mound in Hierakonpolis was modeled on similar structures in southern Mesopotamia. He also regarded the Egyptian name for the Primeval Hill, Nun, to be derived from one of Eridu's ancient names, *Nun.ki* — the "Land of Nun".[145]

To all of these must be added the names of several of Egypt's most important gods. Thus Isis (Egyptian Aset) appears to be in origin exactly the same word as Ishtar, with whom she was in any case linked in ancient times. Isis' husband Osiris (Egyptian Asar) also has a Mesopotamian name, for Asar was an important deity in that region in primeval times.[146] Furthermore, the actual myth of Isis and Osiris bears remarkably close comparison with that of the Sumerian Innana (Ishtar) and Dummuzi (Tammuz). Isis' search

[143]Ibid., pp. 317-8
[144]Ibid., p. 63
[145]Rohl, op. cit., p. 347.
[146]Rice, op. cit. p. 54.

for Osiris after his murder is strikingly similar to Inanna's descent into the underworld in search of Dummuzi.

There is strong evidence too, noted both by Rice and Rohl, that some aspects of Egyptian divine and royal iconography, such as for example the white crown of Upper Egypt, had Mesopotamian origins.

This great migration touched large areas of the Near East. The immigrants settled not only in Egypt, but also, and even more so, in Syria/Palestine and Arabia. Now, we must ask ourselves, did this mass population movement, so momentous in its consequences, leave any trace in the traditions of the populations of the region? Or is it, as the archeologists seem to believe, totally lost in the mists of time?

The great migration was not lost to history. All the peoples of the region, the Arabs, the Syrians and the Jews, and even the Egyptians, recalled very clearly the journey of their ancestors from Mesopotamia.

The Abraham Migration

The Israelites or Hebrews, as they appear to have been known at an earlier stage, were for centuries in close contact with the people of Egypt. Almost all the most important events of early biblical history directly involved Egypt. This applied even to the first phase of Israelite history, when Abraham, the founder and father of the Israelite/Jewish people, was said to have entered the Land of the Nile in the course of his wanderings. For centuries scholars sought to "tie-in" the Egyptian and Hebrew histories, and repeated attempts were made to discover which pharaoh reigned during the lifetimes of Abraham, Joseph and Moses. Immediately prior to the decipherment of the hieroglyphs, it was hoped and expected that the native records of Egypt would provide definitive answers to these questions, and it was confidently believed, in some quarters, that the Bible was about to find unequivocal confirmation.

Yet no such thing happened. To the despair of both Egyptologists and biblical scholars, it was found that the hieroglyphs produced barely a single reference to the Israelites. Eventually it was admitted that the Patriarchs and other renowned figures of Genesis were not the great and important men that the scriptural sources implied. If they existed at all, they must have been the leaders of small bands of Semitic shepherds whom the scribes of Egypt did not consider important enough to mention. Thus it is now widely assumed, both in lay and scholarly circles, that the Old Testament deals solely with the history of the Israelite people, and that the great events of the past are largely ignored, or alluded to only insofar as they affected the Chosen People.

There is no doubt that the later parts of the Old Testament, as found in the books of the prophets, Kings and Chronicles, do generally conform to this pattern. Yet this is eminently not the case with regard to the Book of Genesis. Here the focus is upon events of truly cosmic dimensions. The Creation of Man can hardly be described as insignificant; nor was the Flood. Nor, as we have seen, was the Tower of Babel episode. Genesis, it would appear, in its earlier parts, deals with happenings whose very magnitude impressed themselves upon the minds of subsequent generations. Knowledge of the past was in those days transmitted by word of mouth, a restriction, it seems, which effectively filtered out the trivia.

Bearing this in mind, we must now re-examine the story of Abraham, an episode which both the Bible and extra-scriptural Jewish tradition viewed as being of immense significance.

Abraham, famously, a native of southern Mesopotamia,[147] was the founder and original patriarch of the Jewish people. Instructed by God, his father Terah quit his home in southern Mesopotamia (Ur of the Chaldeans) in search of a land that God would show him. The migration was completed by Abraham, who, after a brief sojourn in Egypt, reached and settled in the Promised Land of Canaan. Yet Abraham was the progenitor not only of the Jews. Other peoples, most particularly the numerous tribes of Arabia, were said to have been descended from him. His very name means "father of many".

The great migration from southern Mesopotamia, which archeology places at the beginning of Egypt's First Dynasty, displays many remarkable parallels with the Abraham migration. Were it not for chronology scholars would probably have looked at the possibility of linking the two events. Such a possibility however was never explored, or even considered, because the accepted chronology placed Abraham around 2100 BC and the founding of Egypt under Menes around 3200 BC. Yet, as we shall see, neither the date provided for Abraham nor for Menes has any firm scientific foundation. If scholars had been more careful, if they had considered the fundamentals and set aside "traditional" chronological schemes, they would have discovered astonishing parallels between the Mesopotamian migration told in the Book of Genesis and that discovered by archeology.

---

[147]Abraham's home, "Ur of the Chaldees," is normally identified with Ur in Lower Mesopotamia. However, a significant number of voices have been raised over the years arguing that Abraham's home was a region of northern Mesopotamia.

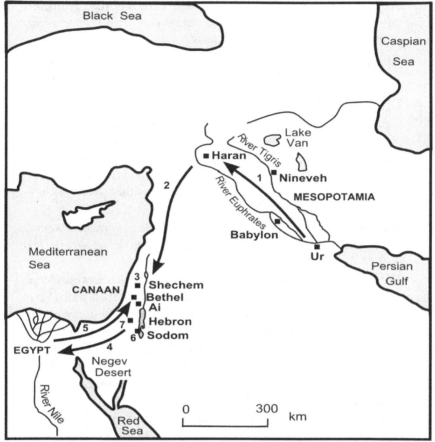

13. Route of Abraham's migration from Mesopotamia to Egypt and Canaan.

According to Josephus, Abraham's tribe entered Egypt at the dawn of that country's history. This is in striking agreement with the archeological record, which shows a distinct Mesopotamian influence on the First Dynasty.

We shall shortly demonstrate how the entire Patriarch epoch should have been located in the Early Dynastic Age. Numerous clues in Genesis, either misunderstood or ignored by the majority of scholars, point in this direction. Most importantly, we may note here and now that Jewish tradition states very explicitly that in the time of Abraham the Egyptians were virtual barbarians, and that it was the Patriarch himself who taught them the rudiments of civilization. Upon entering Egypt the father of the Jews, according to Josephus Flavius, was given leave by pharaoh to,

... enter into conversation with the most learned of the Egyptians: from which conversation his virtue and his reputation became more conspicuous than they had been before.

For whereas the Egyptians were formally addicted to different customs, and despised one another's sacred and accustomed rites, and were very angry with one another on that account; Abram conferred with each of them, and confuting the reasonings they made use of, every one for their own practices, he demonstrated that such reasonings were vain and void of truth; whereupon he was admired by them in these great conferences as a very wise man, and one of great sagacity. He communicated to them arithmetic, and delivered to them the science of astronomy; for, before Abram came into Egypt they were unaccustomed with these parts of learning.[148]

Other Jewish tradition, as compiled for example in Ginzberg's *Legends*, states very clearly that Abraham entered Egypt during the reign of the first pharaoh.[149]

We saw earlier how the great migratory wave which left southern Mesopotamia and the Persian Gulf at the dawn of the literate age penetrated Egypt and settled in strength on the western parts of Arabia and in Syria/Palestine. Here there is precise agreement with the picture painted in Genesis. As well as entering Egypt and teaching the natives the essentials of civilized life, Abraham is said to have peopled Arabia through Ishmael, his son by the Egyptian Hagar.[150] Intermarriage with the Egyptians is also suggested in the temporary liaison of Sarai with the pharaoh. (Gen. 11:15)

It would appear then that Hebrew tradition concurs with archeology in claiming a Mesopotamian origin for Egyptian civilization and that the story of Abraham recalls that culture-bearing migration. Could it be then that the experts have got it wrong? That no gap of 1,100 years exists between Menes and Abraham; and that the chronological disagreement here exposed is merely a reflection of the stratigraphic and archeological discrepancies already noted in the previous chapter? Or could it be that the archeological disagreement is not the cause but the result of an already chaotic chronology?

Before making a final judgment on this, and before looking at some of the truly astounding similarities between Menes and Abraham, it needs to be stressed that neither the Egyptian nor the biblical dates are reliable. Before seeking to find which may be wrong, we have to emphasize that in

---

[148]Josephus, *Jewish Antiquities* (trans. Whiston) Bk.1 155-7.
[149] L. Ginzberg, *Legends of the Jews* Vol. 1 (Philadelphia, 1909), p. 225. "The Egyptian ruler, whose meeting with Abraham had proved so untoward an event, was the first to bear the name pharaoh."
[150]Genesis 16: 1-5.

all probability both are. The biblical date of Abraham was established via a fundamentalist interpretation of the genealogies and life spans provided in Genesis. Characters such as Abraham, Isaac and Jacob were treated as real people, and their life spans added together to reach Abraham's supposed epoch. Yet scholarship has proved fairly conclusively that all of these were founder-deities, not people; hence it was quite wrong to use them to establish chronologies. Nevertheless, dates derived from these characters are still published, without comment, in textbooks. With Egyptian time-scales things are no better. Elsewhere I have demonstrated how the chronology still provided for Egypt is ultimately dependent on the early Christian writer Eusebius, who, seeking to prove the authenticity of Genesis, made Egyptian civilization commence with the Creation of the World, as recounted in Genesis.[151] Eusebius therefore, echoing early Jewish chroniclers working in Alexandria, who identified Menes the first pharaoh with Adam the first man, provided a date of circa 3700 to 4000 BC for Menes, a date which has formed the cornerstone of Egyptian chronology for centuries, and which has been subject to only minor amendments by modern scholarship.

In the Time of the Patriarchs

The question as to where the Patriarchs should be placed historically is one that has long exercised the minds of historians and theologians. Whilst it is readily admitted that many features of the Patriarch narratives seem to belong to the remotest antiquity, the tyranny of accepted chronology, which places Abraham around 2000 or 2100 BC, has forced the belief that the archaic elements are anachronisms, and that the biblical Patriarchs inhabited a world of long-established empires and civilizations which had already reached an advanced stage of the Middle Bronze Age.

Yet, as we shall shortly see, other evidence points in the opposite direction. Thus the occurrence of camels (dromedaries) in the narrative, has convinced not a few scholars that the entire story is a fiction composed in the sixth or even fifth century BC, for it was only then that camels were domesticated.

How to make sense of such radically contradictory data?

When looking at the Patriarch chapters of Genesis we must bear in mind first and foremost that the established chronology is in error. We must understand that the Patriarch epoch has been misplaced by a thousand years and uprooted from its true location. The evidence for placing Abraham in the Early Dynastic epoch, at the very dawn of civilization, should not have

---

[151] In my *Pyramid Age* (2207)

been ignored. Yet we must also bear in mind the fact that these stories were handed down by word of mouth for many generations and centuries before being committed to writing. When they were finally thus recorded the world had changed beyond recognition, and the scribes who committed them to the parchment or papyrus implanted many of the social and cultural norms of their own epoch into the narrative. Nonetheless, enough genuinely ancient material remained to put the true location and context of these stories beyond question.

Consider the facts. Right throughout the Patriarch narratives there are details which strongly suggest we are in very primitive times. Abraham and his followers travel apparently uninterruptedly throughout the Fertile Crescent. There appear to be no formal international boundaries or control of movement. His people engage in a war (The "War of the Four Kings") where the outcome is decided by the intervention of a few hundred men (Genesis 14:14-17). When Abraham initiates the custom of circumcision (a custom attested in Egypt from the very start of Dynasty 1), he appears to use a flint knife to perform the operation. Certainly Moses, after the Exodus, orders the operation to be performed with such implements (Exodus 4:24), a circumstance strongly suggesting that these were the traditional tools used.

We have already seen that human sacrifice was a defining characteristic of the Early Dynastic epoch, both in Mesopotamia and in Egypt. These rituals, we recall, were performed atop raised, stepped platforms — the earliest pyramids. Now there is abundant evidence to show that both human sacrifice and the raised altars upon which the ritual was performed were of central importance in the epoch under discussion. Most famous in this regard is Abraham's abortive sacrifice of Isaac. In the account that has come down to us, Abraham does not sacrifice his son, but instead offers a ram caught in a nearby thicket. Because of this, some commentators have argued that Abraham is here abolishing human sacrifice. This was not, however, the opinion shared by the great Eduard Meyer, who held that the legend originated in the sacrifice of children to a god named *pachad yitzchak*, or "Fear of Isaac".[152]

It may be, therefore, that Abraham was originally cast in the role of initiator of flesh sacrifices, and that his true nature was altered — in order to be more palatable — at a comparatively late date.

Irrespective of whether Abraham initiated or ended human sacrifice, the custom is hinted at throughout the Patriarch epoch. Thus in Jewish legend astrologers of the tyrant king Nimrod see a comet in the east which swallows four stars in different quarters of the heavens. This they interpret as a

[152] E. Meyer and B. Luther, *Die Israeliten und ihre Nachbarstämme* (Halle, 1906), pp.254ff.

prophecy concerning Terah's son Abram, whom they predict will grow to be a peerless leader whose own descendants will inherit the earth.[153] To fore-stall such an outcome, Nimrod is advised to kill the child, but is thwarted in his designs when Terah substitutes a slave-woman's infant. His own son he conceals in a cave, in the care of a foster-mother, for ten years. It is said that this was the event which led to Terah's migration from Ur. Thus Abraham is saved from sacrifice by the sacrifice of another infant. Human sacrifice is fundamental to his entire story.

In the story of Moses, the killing of the Hebrew boys by pharaoh is almost certainly another oblique reference to human sacrifice. Jewish tradi-tion makes the connection more specific, for it is said that the blood of the murdered babies was mixed with the mud and straw employed by the slaves in their brick-making. Ancient tradition from various regions tells us that the body of a sacrificed child was frequently placed in the foundation of a sacred building. The legend of the baby Moses being consigned to a basket in the Nile is quite likely a reflection of ancient beliefs about the fate of sacri-ficed children. The basket is a barque which conveys the dead child through the waters of the Underworld to the home of the gods. In the Hebrew Bible the word used for this basket is *tebhah* — exactly the same word as is used for Noah's Ark.

It is surely significant that the same story was told of the mighty Meso-potamian king Sargon I, who was, moreover, supposed to be the child of a temple prostitute (which in effect made him a child of the creator-god). Children of temple prostitutes were perhaps, at this stage, especially marked out for sacrifice. But to be a victim of human sacrifice was to share in the divine nature. These children were god-like. Hercules and Perseus too, as well as a myriad of other hero-founders from almost every culture, were also placed in peril whilst in their cradle-baskets (as for example Lugh/Lugos of the Celts). For Moses and Sargon to be linked to such a story was a mark of their divine natures.[154]

In addition to human sacrifice, the Patriarch legends are full of hints that high places were then viewed as meeting points with the gods. There is also direct evidence of links with Mesopotamian ziggurat-worship.

---

[153]Ginzberg, op. cit., pp. 186-7

[154]We should not overlook the parallels here with the story of Osiris. According to this legend, the Lord of the Underworld was locked in a chest by his evil brother Set (i.e., he was sacrificed) and cast adrift on the Nile. Eventually, it was said, he was washed ashore in Byblos. And the myth has a wide distribution, occurring for example in the story of Perseus, cast into the sea in a chest, and in the Celtic myth of Lugh (Lugos), also cast into the ocean in a chest.

We have already seen how Abraham's sacrifice of Isaac occurred at the top of a mountain, and the long biblical tradition which viewed mountain-tops as meeting-points with the divine evidently has a very ancient pedi-gree. As we saw in the previous chapter, during the Early Dynastic epoch (in Mesopotamia and Egypt), pyramids and ziggurats were in some way or other viewed as representations of the universal concept of the Sacred Mountain, and the Egyptian festival of Min, chief god of the First Dynasty, known as the Festival of the Coming Forth of Min, showed the deity standing atop a stepped throne or stairway. Michael Rice notes how in Early Dynastic times, "the ladder ... played some part in the earlier rituals associated with the divine Kingship."[155] It is evident too that the pyramid was itself seen as a symbolic "stairway to heaven".

The same concept appears in Genesis. Jacob, the grandson of Abraham, came to "a holy place" on his way from Beersheba to Harran. There, "He lay down to sleep, resting his head on a stone. He dreamed that he saw a stairway reaching from earth to heaven, with angels going up and coming down on it" (Gen. 28:12). He named the place *Bethel* ("house of God"). Upon waking, the Patriarch is said to have exclaimed, "What a terrifying place this is! It must be the house of God; it must be the gate that opens into heaven" (Gen. 28:17).

Now, the term "House of God" is precisely that used by the Sumerians to describe the shrine at the top of the ziggurats — which of course was also reached by a great stairway. Could we have a more clear-cut statement of context?

It should be remarked also that on another occasion Jacob is embroiled in a wrestling bout with God (Gen. 32:22-30). This again seems to recall very clearly the ritual combats of the Early Bronze Age, where the partici-pants played the role of deities, and which ended in the sacrifice of one of the combatants.[156]

Thus the theme of priest-kingship, which in the previous chapter we have identified as marking the earliest phase of literate civilization, runs right through the Abraham narrative. And the most striking illustration of this comes when Abraham meets the archetypal priest-king himself, Melchizedek, the "king of Salem", who is priest of the "most high God". (Genesis 14: 18-20). The encounter between the Father of the Hebrews and the priest-king of Canaan has been the occasion of endless commentary throughout the centuries. Who was this mysterious and godlike being, a man who briefly comes into the story of Abraham only to disappear again

---

[155] M. Rice, op. cit., p. 181
[156] The gladiatorial contests of Rome were a late survival of these early forms of human sacrifice, as were the various ball-games etc. of Central America.

without trace? What he is and what he represents is an infallible historical marker: He is the archetype of the priest-king, the character who, more than anyone else, tells us that we are in that epoch which, as the Sumerian tradition tells us, priest-kingship first descended from heaven to earth.[157]

Finally, it cannot be overlooked that the Patriarchs, even the most historical of them (whom we shall argue was Joseph), display many of the characteristics of gods. This was a point emphasized by Albright.[158] When we are dealing with the Patriarchs we are not in the historical era proper but in what might be called the era of "proto-history": a primitive epoch predating the appearance of historical consciousness. This is evident enough even in the Book of Genesis, where editors of the Hellenistic age have clearly made efforts to make the characters as human as possible. But it is beyond question when we consider extra-biblical Jewish tradition. Thus for example in the various Talmudic and Midrashic traditions we learn that even the story of Joseph is replete with cosmogenic imagery. When Judah confronts his brother Joseph over the detention of Benjamin, the combatants become possessed of fearsome powers. We are told that "Manasseh stamped his foot on the ground and the whole palace shook."[159] Later, we are told how Judah broke into sobs and cried aloud,

> and when Hushim the son of Dan heard it in Canaan, he jumped into Egypt with a single leap and joined his voice with Judah's, and the whole land was on the point of collapsing from the great noise they produced. Judah's radiant men lost their teeth, and the cities of Pithom and Raamses were destroyed, and they remained in ruins until the Israelites built them up again under taskmasters.[160]

In addition to these and various other examples of prodigious, inhuman power, the Patriarchs are routinely associated in the legends with celestial beings. Thus Judah is, famously, "the Lion" (i.e., Leo), whilst Joseph, with whom he contends, is "the Bull" (Taurus).

These characters are, in some ways at least, celestial deities. Only one, Jacob's son Joseph, may be regarded as at least partly historical. But, living in the Age of Myths, when the gods interacted on an everyday basis with mortals, even he underwent a process of deification. The Patriarch Age is therefore without question one that must be placed in the remote past, at

---

[157]As intermediaries between gods and men the priest-kings took on the personality of gods themselves, and this is evident in the character of Melchizedek, whose divine nature is made rather explicit in the narrative.

[158]William F. Albright, *Yahweh and the Gods of Canaan: An Historical Analysis of Two Contrasting Faiths* (New York, 1968).

[159]Ginzberg, op. cit., p. 104

[160]Ibid., p. 106

the very dawn, perhaps, of historical consciousness. As we shall now demonstrate, Abraham himself, the founding father of the Jewish Patriarchs, is no more to be regarded as a real human being than his children and grandchildren. In all essentials, in fact, Abraham is identical to the god whom the ancients believed had bequeathed the arts of civilization to mankind.[161]

Menes and Abraham

If the Age of the Patriarchs begins right at the start of the epoch known to historians as the Early Dynastic Age, we are on much stronger grounds when we declare that the biblical story of Abraham is, in part at least, a traditional account of the epic population movement disclosed by archeology right at the beginning of the literate age. The Jewish chroniclers, it would appear, were right to have Abraham teach the Egyptians the essentials of civilization and make him a contemporary of the first pharaoh. However, it is worth repeating, and cannot be emphasized too strongly, that we cannot regard Abraham, or even Menes, as historical characters. Both are essentially founder-deities, though presumably the Mesopotamian migrants would have had some leader or leaders, upon whom no doubt the attributes of the great deity of the age would have been placed in the popular imagination. The same may be said of Menes. That there was, at some point, a king who actually united the country and made himself master of Upper and Lower Egypt is beyond question. But the other deeds credited to Menes, which we shall discuss presently, belong to the tutelary god of the epoch — Min.

Placing these two characters in the same cultural epoch we must therefore expect them to display strong similarities. Are these exhibited by them?

In fact, the parallels between Menes and Abraham are numerous and precise. The most obvious similarity being that the lives of both were reputedly marked by great upheavals of nature. Herodotus and Manetho, as well as other ancient authors, hinted strongly at such events in First Dynasty times.[162] Manetho says that Menes was eventually killed by a hippopotamus — a death almost certainly referring to upheavals of nature, as the hippopotamus deity must be linked to the crocodile god Sebek, or the Double Crocodile Henti, who symbolized the universal destruction said to occur at the end of a world cycle.[163]

---

[161]In his *Folklore in the Old Testament*, Frazer demonstrated that virtually all of the characters and events of Genesis, as well as of later epochs of Jewish history, are typically mythic and find their exact counterparts in legend and tradition wherever we look in the world.
[162]Similar suggestions are found in Eratosthenes and Diodorus Siculus.
[163]See, e.g., Brendan Stannard, op. cit., p. 761.

Hebrew tradition is, if anything, even more explicit about natural catastrophes during the time of Abraham. Both Abraham and the later Patriarchs were uprooted from their homes by devastating famines on more than one occasion. Indeed, it was a famine that brought Abraham and the Hebrews into Egypt for the first time. We are told that a few years after this episode the twin cities of the Dead Sea plain, Sodom and Gomorrah, met a frightening fate. The story of this disaster is one of the most popular tales from the Old Testament. Lot, Abraham's bother, was advised to flee the city of Sodom before its merited destruction:

> The sun had risen on the earth when Lot entered Segor. The Lord poured down on Sodom and Gomorrah sulphur and fire from the Lord out of heaven. He overthrew those cities and the whole region, all the inhabitants of the cities and the plants of the soil. (Gen. 19: 23-5)

Other translations have the agents of destruction as "fire and brimstone", but whatever caused the damage, it clearly came from the sky. The region in which Sodom and Gomorrah stood, near the shores of the Dead Sea, is described as a fertile plain prior to the catastrophe. Afterwards, it was a barren waste. What manner of disaster could pour "sulphur and fire" on a city? Being unable to answer this question, commentators throughout the centuries have doubted the existence of the two cities of sin. According to the biblical account, they were situated just to the south of the Dead Sea, an area that is now a wasteland. Not a single trace of any settlement that may have been either of the towns has been discovered.[164]

As an answer to this question, some historians have postulated an immense and extremely powerful series of volcanic eruptions, as proof of which they point to the volcanic nature of the region, and to the fact that the entire Dead Sea/Jordan Valley depression is but a branch of the highly active Great Rift Valley that separates Asia from Africa.[165] All around the northern shores of the Dead Sea there is ample evidence, in the large deposits of pumice, of recent and severe volcanic activity. However, attempts to explain the cataclysms of the Abraham epoch in terms of the types of natural calamities ordinarily inflicted upon the planet by nature, can only be sustained by ignoring a great deal of the evidence. As we saw in the previous chapter, the catastrophes which affected the earth in the first epoch of civilization were of a magnitude and severity far beyond anything in the experience of modern

---

[164]However, it may be that Sodom and Gomorrah were situated in an area that was subsequently flooded by the Dead Sea. See, e.g., Werner Keller, *The Bible as History* (London, 1980), pp. 90-2.

[165]The Great Rift Valley forms the Red Sea and runs as far south as Lake Victoria in Africa.

man. This is a fact insisted upon both by the traditions of the ancients and by the discoveries of science.

If we wish to understand this epoch, and to comprehend the nature and character of the figure we know as Abraham, we will need to look seriously at those traditions.

As well as living during the "eruptive" age at the dawn of civilization, both Menes and Abraham were linked (in terms of character and personality) to Thoth, the god — or one of the gods — who bequeathed civilization to mankind. Thus for example Egyptian tradition told how the art of writing, along with the science of medicine, dated from Menes' time.[166] More specifically, Manetho associated the invention of medicine with Menes' son and successor Athothis. This king's name, rendered as Teta or Teti (*dhwty*) in the hieroglyphics, honors the god Thoth, and indeed Thoth held a prominent position throughout the early period. In Manetho's testimony at least two kings of Dynasty 1 were named in his honor. Now Thoth, the Egyptian equivalent of Hermes/Mercury, was universally regarded as the patron of learning. He was, as we saw in the previous chapter, intimately associated with the Tower legend and thereby linked to the earliest phase of high civilization. And in keeping with the Tower's connection with the whole concept of language diversity and indeed confusion, it should come as no surprise to find that the Egyptians regarded Theth as the inventor languages,[167] as well as writing and medicine. The Greeks, who were very insistent that Thoth was identical to their own Hermes, regarded the latter as one of the oldest of the gods. He had a frivolous and impetuous nature, and, it was suggested, could be destructive. It was said that he assisted the Three Fates in the invention of writing, astronomy, the musical scale, the arts of boxing and gymnastics, weights and measures and the cultivation of the olive tree.[168] In addition, he invented divination and was made the herald of Zeus. As such, his duties included the making of treaties and the promotion of commerce.

As noted in Chapter 2, the symbol of Hermes/Thoth — a staff entwined with coiled serpents — was a frequently encountered motif in Early Dynastic Egypt and Mesopotamia. We saw too that in the classical world Hermes/Mercury was worshipped in orgiastic rituals around a standing phallic stone, or *herme*. Again, this ties him to Menes, whose name (Mena, Mina) clearly links him to the phallic Min, as well as to the ritual of circumcision. Egyptian tradition never specifically states that the custom of circumcision was inaugurated by Menes, but in view of the fact that Min's cult was of

---

[166]Diodorus Siculus, i, 45, 1 and i, 94, 1.

[167]The invention of languages links Thoth with the Tower of Babel story and thus also with Abraham.

[168]Diodorus Siculus, v, 75; Hyginus, *Fabula* 277.

immense importance during the First Dynasty, and in view of the other inno-vations attributed to the first pharaoh, we can scarcely doubt that the ritual dates from this period.[169]

Here of course we have a direct link with Abraham, whose phallic nature is clearly expressed in his inauguration of circumcision, his name ("father of a multitude"), and in his association with the probably ritual homosexuality of Sodom.[170]

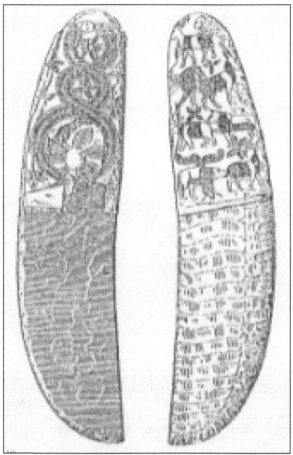

14. Flint Knife of the Early Dynastic or Late Predynastic epoch. The inter-linking serpents, characteristic of contemporary Mesopotamian art, are symbols of the god Thoth/Hermes. Weapons such as this would have been used for sacrifice and circumcision.

---

[169]Min was always portrayed with an erect penis, so our attributing circumcision to his cult and his epoch is hardly open to question.

[170]See G.R. Harvey, "Abraham and Phallicism," Society for Interdisciplinary Studies, Chronology and Catastrophism Workshop (1998) No.2 pp. 10-12.

It has already been shown how Hermes, or Thoth, was particularly linked by the Egyptians with Menes' epoch. The evidence linking Thoth/Hermes and Menes is quite comprehensive, but the link with Abraham is perhaps even more so. In Hebrew legend Abraham plays the role allocated to Thoth/Hermes in the traditions of other ancient peoples.

15. Victory Palette of King Narmer, often held to commemorate the union of Upper and Lower Egypt. Narmer seems also to have been known as Mena (Menes), a name which probably means "Min's Man"; Min being the phallic god in whose honor circumcision was first practiced and who was one of the most important deities of Late Predynastic/Early Dynastic times.

One of the most important innovations attributed to Hermes — and here the link with Abraham becomes even more clear — was that of flesh sacrifice. The Greeks told how Hermes, in his infancy, had stolen some cattle from Apollo (the sun). Upon being discovered and accused before Zeus, the newly born god admitted the charge, adding that he had already slaughtered two, cutting them into twelve equal portions as a sacrifice to the twelve gods. According to the Greek writers this was the first flesh sacrifice ever made.[171] We are immediately reminded here, of course, of Abraham's abortive sacrifice of Isaac, and the evidence presented in the previous section should convince most readers that the Abraham epoch was *par excellence* the age of flesh sacrifice. The practice of flesh (and more especially human) sacrifice, along with the construction of temples within which to perform these, was, as noted, one of the characteristic features of the first epoch of civilization. Flesh sacrifice had a propitiatory function, and if we remember that this was an era still afflicted by vast upheavals of nature, we can well understand the origin of this need.

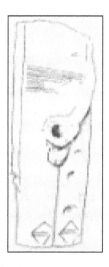

16. One of three Late Predynastic/Early Dynastic Statues of Min from Koptos. This image, like all others of Min, makes his connection with phallicism and circumcision all too apparent, and it is evident that the first pharaoh, Menes, was named in his honor.

In summary, then, Abraham and Menes share at least three very outstanding features:

- Both characters were credited with initiating civilized life and with being cultural innovators.
- Both were believed to have introduced new forms of religious worship, including, almost certainly, flesh sacrifice.
- Both were associated with circumcision and were linked to a phallic cult.

---

[171]Apollodorus, iii, 10, 2; *Homeric Hymn to Hermes*, 1-543.

Both share virtually all of the above features with the god Thoth (also Min)/Hermes, who in Egyptian and Greek tradition laid the foundations of civilized life.

Bringing Abraham into the same epoch as Menes means that the histories of Egypt and the Bible are out of sync by over a thousand years, and this historical misalignment is reflected in archeology. We have already seen how the archeology of Mesopotamia is out of sync with regard to that of Syria/Palestine by over a thousand years, so that the "Great Flood" of Ur, currently dated to circa 3300 BC, is actually contemporary with the "Great Fire" of Ugarit (in Syria), currently dated to 2200 BC. — an incongruity which has effectively disguised the scale and magnitude of the aforementioned catastrophe. Strange to relate then that the archeology of Egypt, which is properly aligned to that of Mesopotamia, is not aligned to that of Syria/Palestine, and we find the same discrepancy occurring once more. Thus in Egypt the protodynastic or Naqada II (also called Gerzean) culture, which is dated to the mid- or latter fourth millennium, and is evidently contemporary with the Jamdat Nasr culture of Mesopotamia, also displays striking parallels with the Palestinian Early Bronze 3 culture, which is however dated to the latter third millennium — a thousand years later! Figure 24 in the Appendix to the present volume illustrates the point. But how did it come about that not only the histories, but also the archaeologies of Egypt and Mesopotamia on the one hand and Syria/Palestine on the other are out of alignment in this way? This is a topic of great importance, and one that shall be further addressed towards the end of the present chapter.

We may perchance reconstruct the events which led to the culture-bearing migration from Mesopotamia just prior to the beginning of the Early Dynastic Age thus: Following the catastrophe known to myth as the Destruction of the Tower, and to the Bible as the Tower of Babel disaster (and marked by Woolley's "Flood of Ur"), many of the inhabitants of the region came to the conclusion that the place, though fertile and well-watered, was no longer safe to inhabit: Hence the great migration in search of a Promised Land. We are told that Abraham's father was instructed by God to quit Ur, and we can scarcely doubt that the religious leaders of the epoch, who were the spokesmen of the gods, did indeed instruct the people in such a way.

The pristine lands of Arabia and Egypt, through which the Mesopotamian wanderers passed, were not the parched and arid wildernesses of our time. Stretching before the travelers lay vast and seemingly endless savannahs, teeming with game. The Egypt which they entered was a richly fertile land inhabited by a race of Berber/Hamitic speech, who knew nothing of building in brick, though they had already mastered many of the finer arts of civilization, such as pottery manufacture, stone-carving and some metal-lurgy. In time, incomers and natives intermingled, and from that union arose the great and glorious Egypt known to us all.

The "Divine Land" of the Egyptians

The Egyptians did not forget the great migration which brought such major innovation to their land. As might be expected, the ancestors of the Mesopotamian culture-bearers formed an aristocracy closely associated with the pharaoh — much in the same way the Normans constituted an aris-tocracy after the Conquest of England. This aristocracy was known as the *Iry-Pat*, and were clearly differentiated from the rest of the Egyptian popula-tion. From the ranks of the Iry-Pat came the Horus Kings of Hierakonpolis who founded the First Dynasty. These Horus Kings always claimed that their ancestral home had been in the east, in a region which they named the "Land of the God", or "Divine Land" (*Ta Netjer*).

One of the most intriguing questions to emerge from ancient Egypt is the location of this "Divine Land", because on one level the term was clearly used to describe the land of Canaan, the area we now call Syria/Palestine.[172] For Christians and Jews, of course, Israel has been the Holy Land from time immemorial. Scholars did not however expect the Egyptians to call the same region by a similar name.

Explanation of this remarkable coincidence has proved elusive. Some see the Lebanese cedars as the source of the term, by reason of the fact that these plants were the source of some of the fragrant gums and resins used in the embalming process.[173] The Dead Sea/Jordan Valley also supplied many of the essentials of embalming, such as bitumen and aromatic herbs like frankincense, and these too would have linked the region with Osiris, the original mummy. But there may have been yet another reason for the land's sacredness.

In ancient texts the term Divine Land, *Ta Netjer*, although clearly used to denote Syria/Palestine, is usually also associated with Punt. In fact, the terms Punt and Divine Land are virtually interchangeable. Yet Punt, unlike the Divine Land, is not believed to be located in Syria/Palestine, but at the southern end of the Red Sea. This has caused profound confusion amongst Egyptologists. However, but for the illustrations in Queen Hatshepsut's

---

[172]See, e.g., Margaret S. Drower, "Syria Before 2200 BC," in *The Cambridge Ancient History* Vol.1 part 2 (3rd ed.), p. 346 "To the Egyptians, Byblos was the key to 'God's Land', the Lebanon on whose steep slopes grew the timber trees they coveted."

[173]Ibid., p. 349. "As a source of the material used in mummification and for coffins, 'God's Land' would have held a special and sacred significance for the Egyptians."

temple at Deir el Bahri, which portray what appears to be African fauna in Punt, there is little doubt that the region would always have been associated with Syria/Palestine. For example, an official of the Sixth Dynasty described how he had visited Punt and Byblos eleven times.[174] It is perfectly clear from this that the Egyptians regarded the two countries as adjacent. In actual fact, as Velikovsky pointed out, the name "Punt" may well be etymologically identical to "Phoenicia".[175] Classical sources inform us that the eponymous ancestor of the Phoenicians was called Pontus, and the word appears again in the "Punic" Wars waged between the Phoenician Carthaginians and the Romans. That the Phoenicians, like the Jews, originated in the Persian Gulf/ Lower Mesopotamia region is hinted at in a number of ancient writers; whilst, as David Rohl has pointed out, Christian Lebanese to this day regard themselves as having originated in the coastlands of the Persian Gulf.[176] Also, we need to consider the fact that two of the islands of Bahrain were originally called Aradus and Tylos (Tyros) — identical in name to two of the greatest Phoenician island cities.[177]

Punt and the Divine Land were thus either Canaan and Phoenicia, or interchangeable names for the whole region of Palestine/Phoenicia. Once this is accepted, it provides us with a startling clue to the origin of the term Divine Land. In his book *The Making of Egypt* (1939) Flinders Petrie emphasizes the symbolic importance of Punt for the Egyptians. The Land of Punt, he says, was "sacred to the Egyptians as the source of the race".[178] Right from the beginning, the Horus kings of the First Dynasty insisted that their ancestors had been natives of Punt. Yet Petrie, with equal certainty, derived the Punt people from Lower Mesopotamia. They had, he says, "certainly originated in Elam."[179] Of course, we now know that the decisive culture-bearing immigration into Egypt immediately preceding the start of Dynasty 1 was not quite from Elam but from the adjacent region of Lower Mesopotamia. The great "Abraham" migration, after touching on Egypt and giving birth to Egyptian civilization, eventually settled mainly in Palestine/Phoenicia and western Arabia — this, in the testimony of the archeologists. Genesis, we have seen, agrees with the archeology, for the Arabs were reputed to be descendants of Abraham's son Ishmael.

The Divine Land of the Egyptians was therefore identical to the Holy Land of the Jews, the Promised Land pledged by God as the home of Abra-

---

[174]   J. A. Montgomery, *Arabia and the Bible* (Philadelphia, 1934), p. 176 n.28.
[175]In his *Ages in Chaos* (1953)
[176]Rohl, op cit., p. 305.
[177]Ibid.
[178]Petrie, op cit., p. 77.
[179]Ibid.

ham's descendants. The pharaohs of Egypt's First Dynasty were of the same blood-line as the Hebrews (and this is almost certainly recalled in the story of Sarai's marriage to the pharaoh, as well as Abraham's marriage to the Egyptian Hagar), so it is little wonder that they too called Palestine by this name.

Truth is indeed stranger than fiction.

One possible objection to the above assertion may be raised. The term *ta netjer*, it might be argued, is more accurately translated as "Land of the God" (rather than "Divine Land"), and it is true that the word Netjer ("god") was peculiarly associated with Osiris,[180] a deity who was especially linked with Byblos and the Lebanon. According to Egyptian tradition, Osiris' body was floated down the Nile in a wooden casket and washed ashore at Byblos, where it became encased in the trunk of a tamarisk tree. This tree, according to the legend, was felled by the king of Byblos, who had it carved into a great pillar which he lodged in his palace. It was to this region that Osiris' wife Isis journeyed on her search for her lost husband. She retrieved the pillar containing Osiris' body and returned with it to Egypt. This Pillar became the sacred Djed Pillar, known as the "Spine of Osiris". Thus Byblos was sacred to Osiris and his cult. But mention of the Djed Pillar brings us to another intriguing clue: The Djed Pillar was ritually covered in natron salt, the material most essential to embalming. The word natron itself is related to the Egypt word *netjer*, "god", a term peculiarly associated with Osiris. Indeed, Osiris, the original mummy, was often named simply "Netjer". Now it so happens that most of the materials used in embalming came from Syria/Palestine. The Dead Sea supplied natron salt and bitumen,[181] whilst the cedars and other trees of Lebanon supplied various gums and resins. So, several clues point insistently to Syria/Palestine as the Land of the God, the Land of Osiris.

But Osiris' connection with Asia was not just by virtue of the aforementioned. As we saw, David Rohl has argued persuasively that Osiris himself was in origin an Asiatic deity, one of the gods brought to Egypt by the early Mesopotamian culture-bearing migration. If this is correct, and the evidence seems conclusive, it means that Osiris' links to Asia had more than one source.

There remains the problem of the Hatshepsut reliefs, which apparently place Punt and the Divine Land somewhere in Africa. I do not intend to go into this question in any detail here, for it is essentially outside the scope of

---

[180]See, e.g., S. Morenz, *Egyptian Religion* (Cornell University Press, 1973), p. 19.
[181]See e.g. Tine M. Niemi, Zvi Ben-Avraham, and Joel Gat (eds.) *The Dead Sea: The Lake and Its Setting* (Oxford, 1997), p. 251. Also, J. Rullkoetter and A. Nissenbaum, "Dead Sea asphalt in Egyptian mummies: Molecular evidence," *Naturwissenschaften* (December, 1980)

the present work, and, in any case, I have dealt with it extensively in another place.[182] Nonetheless, a brief examination of the problem is inevitable.

To begin with, it should be remarked that Velikovsky, for other reasons entirely, located the land of Punt in Palestine/Phoenicia. He also made Hatshepsut identical to the fabulous Queen of Sheba, who visited Solomon in Jerusalem, and regarded the bas-reliefs at Deir el Bahri as a commemoration of that visit. The present writer concurs entirely with Velikovsky on this issue, though the identification has been criticized even by some of Velikovsky's most loyal students. It has been pointed out, for example, that typical African animals (such as giraffe and hippopotamus) are shown inhabiting Punt, whilst many of the inhabitants appear to be negroes. Nevertheless, it is simply untrue to say that the natives are negroes. Most of the inhabitants of Punt, as portrayed at Deir el Bahri, appear to be Semitic or such like, and the men sport long pointed beards of a type worn in Egypt *only by the pharaoh* (we recall here the Puntite origins of the Egyptian ruling class). The African fauna can be equally easily explained. Giraffes and hippos lived in Egypt until Old Kingdom times, and, according to a number of sources, giraffes still inhabited the border regions of Syria and Arabia until Roman times.[183] As I have shown elsewhere, in antiquity, the Syria/Palestine region supported all of the creatures now more typically associated with the African savannah. These gradually became extinct through a combination of hunting and climate change. Yet in the time of Hatshepsut many of them survived, especially in more remote parts, such as the semi-desert regions surrounding the Jordan Valley and the Lebanese uplands. One didn't need to go as far as Somalia to find such creatures.

As for the negroes pictured in Hatshepsut's temple; we are all too aware of how Africa was plundered for slaves almost from time immemorial, and the Punt reliefs, as Velikovsky remarked, make it quite plain that the Africans portrayed were presented to the Egyptian travelers as gifts.

The Deir el Bahri inscriptions describe Punt as a source of *anti*, or incense, a plant which is said to grow on "the terraces." Since nowadays incense grows only to the south of Egypt, in southern Arabia and the Horn of Africa, this was seen as providing definitive proof of an African location. Yet the Jordan Valley, with its tropical climate, was a major source of frankincense and other exotic herbs and spices during antiquity, a fact well-recognized by modern botanists and confirmed for me by Yadin Roman, editor of the Israeli natural history journal *Eretz*.[184] Furthermore, it should be noted that in Greek

---

[182]See my *Theban Empire* (2020)
[183]Diodorus Siculus, ii, 50-1.
[184]Personal communication, 2nd October, 2009.

legend Adonis (a god recognized by the Hellenes as belonging to Lebanon — his name is identical to Hebrew *Adonai*, "the Lord," a title of Tammuz), was born out of a myrrh tree.[185] Since Adonis/Tammuz was another alter-ego of Osiris, it seems highly probable that the tree from which the body of Osiris' was cut was originally not a tamarisk but a frankincense one. And here we come to one of the most intriguing elements of Hatshepsut's journey to Punt and its reporting.

Hatshepsut, it is known, identified herself with the goddess Hathor, whom she saw as her tutelary deity. Actually, she went further, endlessly insinuating that she was nothing other than an incarnation of Hathor herself. The latter was described in Egyptian texts as the "Lady of Punt."[186] Yet Hathor was also known as the "Lady of Byblos," as was Isis, who traveled to Byblos to retrieve the body of her husband. This confirms what Egyptologists already know: that by the time of Hatshepsut, Hathor and Isis were virtually identical.

When we realize this, the journey to Punt, which Hatshepsut placed next to scenes of her divine birth on her great funerary monument, begins to make sense. As a woman wearing the crown of the pharaoh, Hatshepsut felt the need to justify her position. This she seems to have done by portraying herself as an incarnation of Hathor/Isis and, to underline that identification, she essentially retraced the journey of Isis to Punt/Byblos, who went there to claim the body of Osiris from the tamarisk (or more likely in the original, the frankincense) tree.[187] And sure enough, the pilgrimage to Punt is undertaken, in the Queen's own testimony, by a "divine command", which directed her to proceed to Punt in order to bring home the sacred living frankincense trees. A command she obeyed and commemorated most lavishly.

In short, the journey to Punt was a masterful piece of political/religious propaganda.

All in all then we can say that it looks as if Velikovsky got it exactly correct and that Punt or the Divine Land of the Egyptians was so called because it was the region peculiarly associated with Osiris, who was himself an Asiatic god (Adonai or Tammuz) and whose ultimate origin was Lower Mesopotamia, which region, as Flinders Petrie remarked, was the original Punt.

---

[185]Ovid, *Metamorphoses*, x.

[186]There thus seems little doubt that the expedition to Punt was for Hatshepsut a pilgrimage, a voyage home — even if she never, as is usually believed — took part in the journey.

[187]See e.g. Lewis M. Greenberg, "The Land of Punt, Redux," *Society for Interdisciplinary Studies, Review* No. 2 (2018)

Dates and Chronologies

The First Dynasty of Egypt, as we have demonstrated, must belong in the same epoch as the figure known to the Bible as Abraham, yet according to conventional ideas the first pharaoh reigned around 3300 or 3200 BC, whilst Abraham is dated to circa 2100 BC. If we are correct and these two charac-ters were indeed contemporary, then we are involved in a radical questioning of ancient chronology. Assuming that Abraham's epoch is correctly dated to 2100 BC, this means that Egyptian history must also commence at that point and that the thousand years separating Abraham and Menes in the textbooks are "ghost" centuries.

Yet the situation is made infinitely worse when we realize that Abraham's date is itself untrustworthy and that the nine or ten centuries separating the Patriarch from the founding of Solomon's temple are equally phantom. In fact, the date of 2100 BC, still accepted in most textbooks, is arrived at, as we saw, by accepting at face value the dates provided in the early books of the Old Testament for the various Patriarchs and Judges. These sources allot life spans of up to 175 years for the earlier Patriarchs; and it is on such a basis that the date of 2100 BC is reached!

As a matter of fact, the fundamental unreliability of virtually all the dates and figures provided in the Old Testament has been demonstrated repeat-edly over the past century and a half. The Old Testament was composed by scribes who followed a pious numerology, and very few of the dates and figures provided can be accepted at face value. The number 40, it has been shown, was regarded as especially sacred. So too were compounds of 40, as well as of 400. Thus the 400-plus years which separated Joseph from the Exodus, and the 480 years between the Exodus and the building of the temple in Jerusalem, are in no way to be taken as historical. On hindsight, it is astonishing that such sacred formulae could ever have been mistaken for anything else.

Before moving on, it is perhaps ironic to note that even a fundamentalist interpretation of the Old Testament could not support conventional dates. Thus in the Gospel of Matthew a genealogy is provided for Jesus aimed at demonstrating his descent both from Abraham and David. From Abraham to Jesus the evangelist lists 42 generations. Now, allowing 25 years to a generation (a generous figure for ancient times), this would place Abraham around 1050 BC! Although these generations cannot be regarded as historical (certainly those preceding David, at any rate), it so happens that this date is reasonably close — it has to be admitted, by pure accident — to the date which will be proposed by the present writer.

As we have seen, the discrepancies observed in the historiographies of Egypt and Israel are also reflected in the archeology. Strata which in Egypt and Mesopotamia are dated to the fourth and third millennia BC, are dated in Syria/Palestine to the beginning of the second millennium BC. The post-Flood strata of Egypt and Mesopotamia (that is, post-Tower of Babel), for example, dated in the latter two regions to between 3400 and 3200 BC, is dated in Syria/Palestine to around 2200 BC. Later strata are equally inconsistently dated. Thus the Syrian Middle Bronze 2 stratum, dated between 1700 and 1500 BC, and containing Hyksos material, corresponds both in culture and stratigraphy with the Mesopotamian Early Bronze 3, which is generally dated between 2300 and 2200 BC (the Akkadian epoch). We find then that the Hyksos of Syria/Palestine were actually contemporary with the Mesopotamian Akkadians, who are generally dated seven centuries earlier. This means that the Akkadians or the Hyksos (or both) have been grossly misplaced.

There are very good reasons why this — approximately — thousand year gap appears in both archeology and historiography. The archeologists in fact were working with a time-scale which was ultimately (though few modern archeologists are now aware of this) based upon the chronology provided in the Book of Genesis, and if we wish to discover exactly when the First Dynasty of Egypt reigned — and, by extension, when the epoch of Abraham should be placed — we must completely ignore the dates provided in the Bible as well as the dates provided by Egyptologists and Assyriologists, which are in fact also derived, one way or another, from the Bible. Having done that, we will find that an overwhelming body of evidence suggests that no literate civilization existed anywhere prior to the 12th or 13th century BC, and that the great cultures and peoples said by the textbooks to have flourished in the second and third millennia are "ghosts" or "phantoms"; cultures and peoples who only ever existed in textbooks.

In another place I have shown in some detail — following the work of Professor Gunnar Heinsohn — how the erroneous chronologies of Egypt and Mesopotamia were formulated.[188] There it is demonstrated how the chronology of the ancient Near East was put together using three quite separate dating blueprints, each a replica of the other, which produced in the end an actual triplication of ancient history. There was the history of the region known to the classical authors, covering the first millennium BC, which was in fact the true history of the region. A duplicate history, placed in the second millennium, was then supplied by applying material from Egypt, and another phantom history, this time placed in the third millennium, was supplied by

---

[188]In my *Pyramid Age*

cross-referencing with Mesopotamian material. Thus the Akkadians of the third millennium are in fact stratigraphically contemporary with (and identical to) the Hyksos of the second millennium, and both are one and the same as the Assyrians of the first millennium BC.

A great deal of evidence, from many fields (quite apart from the stratigraphic), would in any case suggest that early Egyptian and Mesopotamian culture could not possibly be dated to the third millennium BC. As a matter of fact, scholars are astonished at the achievements of the Egyptians during the earliest epoch of her civilization. The natives of the Nile Valley, it appears, performed feats of engineering and art far in advance of what should have been expected in the third and fourth millennia BC.

Trade relationships, it seems, had been established between Egypt and Europe during the Early Dynastic Age, and merchants travelled immense distances to bring luxury items to adorn the palaces and tombs of the pharaohs. We have noted too that even before the founding of the First Dynasty, lapis-lazuli from the borders of Pakistan had reached Egypt in considerable quantities. Thus also gold used in the jewelry of Khasekhemwy (Dynasty 2) was found to have originated in the Carpathian Mountains in Romania.[189] Such far-reaching links appear to be out of the question in the early third millennium BC (the date normally given for Khasekhemwy). The arrival in Egypt of gold from north of the Danube speaks of a highly developed system of international trade, some of it apparently conducted by sea. And this impression is further reinforced by the discovery in Early Bronze Age Troy, Troy II, the city destroyed in the great cataclysm, of artifacts made of tin-bronze.[190] The only sources of tin known to the ancient world were in Europe: Bohemia and the Atlantic west, southern Spain and Britain. It is generally assumed that the first tin to reach the Near East was from Bohemia, yet mineralogist John Dayton has argued persuasively for Britain as the primary source of the material, mainly due to the fact that in Britain, and here alone, tin and copper are found together in the ground, already mixed, in ore-form.[191] For Dayton, the evidence says that true bronze was invented in Britain, and nowhere else, which, if correct, means that the bronze of Troy II almost certainly reached Anatolia by sea trade.

We note, too, that Schliemann discovered a lump of nephrite, or white jade, in Troy II, a material that could only have come from the Kunlun Mountains on the borders of China.[192]

---

[189]See A. R. Burn, *Minoans, Philistines and Greeks* (London, 1930), p. 73.
[190] J. Mellaart, loc cit., p. 392.
[191]John Dayton, *Minerals, Metals, Glazing, and Man* (London, 1978).
[192] A. R. Burn, op. cit., p. 72

The idea then that the first phase of the Early Bronze Age (or, more accurately, the Early Dynastic Age) was an epoch of tiny, isolated, and entirely self-sufficient city-states and kingdoms needs to be abandoned. The civilizations of this time were highly-evolved, enterprising and largely literate. And this last is a point that needs to be stressed. With the discovery of the (unfortunately) little-known writing-system of the Vinca culture of Neolithic-Early Bronze Age Europe (the most famous example of whose script are the so-called Tartaria Tablets from Romania), we can now say that the art of writing was known from Mesopotamia through to Egypt, to (almost certainly) Anatolia and the Balkans, and very possibly throughout North Africa and western Europe — if certain ciphers on Neolithic pottery from Portugal are anything to go by.[193]

Yet how are such achievements to be explained if Menes and the Early Dynastic epoch be placed in the late fourth and early third millennia BC? The vast reach of trade, as far, apparently, as Britain and China, must be viewed too in tandem with the extraordinary levels reached by technology. Some of the most damning evidence here has come from the pen of mineralogist John Dayton. In his exhaustive *Minerals, Metals, Glazing, and Man* (1978), Dayton looked with a specialist's eye at the development of metallurgy and pottery manufacture and referred repeatedly to the advanced metallurgical and glazing techniques evident in finds of the Early Dynastic and Pyramid Ages. Iron, for example, appears to have been widely used from the Pyramid Age (supposedly commencing circa 2600 BC.) onwards,[194] and the Pyramid Texts are full of allusions to the metal. Dayton noted that glass was known in the Early Dynastic period, the first recorded instance being a set of beads from a First Dynasty tomb. Yet tradition stated that glass was first manufactured by the Phoenicians, who did not exist as a nation before the beginning of the first millennium BC.[195] Mention of the Phoenicians brings to mind the fact that these people were well-known to the Egyptians from the Pyramid Age onwards. Texts of the time refer to seagoing ships as *kbnwt* (Byblos boats),[196] whilst King Sneferu of the Fourth Dynasty records the import of 40 ship-loads of cedar from Lebanon.[197]

---

[193]According to T. Rice Holmes, "True writing is ... evident on a potsherd taken from a Neolithic settlement at Los Murcielagos in Portugal." *Ancient Britain and the Invasions of Julius Caesar* (Clarendon Press, 1907), pp. 99-100.

[194]See, e.g., H. Garland and C. O. Bannister, *Ancient Egyptian Metallurgy* (London, 1927), p. 5.

[195]Pliny, *Natural History* ii; John Dayton was very much concerned with the apparent contradictions in the whole account of glass-making as it is presented in the textbooks. op. cit.

[196]Margaret S. Drower, loc cit., p. 348.

[197] W. Stevenson Smith, "The Old Kingdom of Egypt and the Beginning of the First Intermediate Period," in *The Cambridge Ancient History* Vol.1 part 2 (3rd ed.), p. 167.

I could go on, but the above should suffice to illustrate the point. Not only is the millennium said to separate Abraham (circa 2100 BC) from Menes (3200 BC) a phantom; so too is the millennium said to separate Abraham from the founding of the world's other great civilizations (those of China, eastern India and the Americas), which are not dated with reference to the chronology of the Near East. These civilizations arose around 1300 BC or shortly beforehand, and it is regarded as remarkable that the Near Eastern civilizations had a two thousand year "head start" over them. Yet there was no head start. All the world's mound- and pyramid-building cultures arose around 1300 BC in direct response to the cosmic events then occurring

Chapter 4. King Djoser and His Time

Setting the Scene

Having placed the founding of Egyptian civilization in the same epoch as the biblical Abraham and therefore having fixed the start of Egypt's and Israel's semi-legendary histories at the same point in time (the 13th/12th century BC), we must now attempt a reconstruction of the two narratives along the new chronological lines. If we are on the right track, we might expect the histories of the two neighboring peoples, which have hitherto shown few signs of agreement, to match closely. Hebrew tradition tells us how for two centuries or so after Abraham, the patriarch's tribe was settled in Canaan, where his grandson Jacob was blessed with twelve sons. One of these, Joseph, the youngest and favorite, aroused his brothers' jealously, was sold as a slave and taken into Egypt. In Egypt his fortunes improved dramatically when his ability to interpret dreams came to the notice of the pharaoh. He soon became the king's most trusted advisor and brought the entire Israelite tribe into Egypt during a momentous famine. Joseph was thus an exceptional person whose life-story became a symbol of how God could raise the lowly from the dung-heap. No less than a quarter of the Book of Genesis is devoted to him.

Now we ask ourselves, did the Egyptians remember Joseph or does Egyptian tradition know of any character whom we could possibly identify with him? More specifically, does Egyptian tradition of the Early Dynastic period — the two or three centuries following the unification of Egypt by Menes — know of anyone identifiable with Joseph? Was there, around this time, a renowned wise man and interpreter of dreams, some kind of sage celebrated for his knowledge and highly regarded by the reigning pharaoh? The answer is a resounding yes! It so happens that two centuries or so after the establishment of the united kingdom under Menes there lived the greatest sage of Egypt's history: this was Imhotep, the godlike vizier of King Djoser.

Before looking at the truly remarkable parallels between Joseph and Imhotep, we need first to say something about Djoser, for he was accorded a place in Egyptian tradition almost as important as that of Imhotep himself.

Djoser, or Zoser, the second king of Manetho's Third Dynasty, occurs in the monuments under the title Netjerkhet. The name Djoser, which means 'The Splendid", was only conferred upon him long after his death. Much scholarly debate has centered round Djoser. He is, for example, commonly believed to have been the first pharaoh to erect a pyramid. As we have shown in Chapters 2 and 3, this notion is mistaken. Nevertheless, he was certainly the first pharaoh to erect a pyramid or large monument of stone. The design of the Sakkara Pyramid's adjacent temple complex, in particular, provides ample proof of this: columns are shaped in imitation of reed bundles and ceilings in imitation of palm logs; doors are provided with imitation hinges, and it is evident that the builders were translating directly into stone architectural forms that had previously been executed exclusively in wood and reed.

17. Pharaoh Djoser's Step Pyramid at Sakkara, the oldest surviving large stone monument anywhere in the world.

Yet, as with almost all other areas of Egyptian history, the Step Pyramid and temples of Sakkara present numerous difficulties for conventional chronology. It has long been observed, for example, that the temple complex seems to display a number of very modern-looking features,[198] and to this day visitors are immediately struck by the so-called 'proto-Doric' columns of the temple hall.[199] Furthermore, mineralogist John Dayton argued convincingly that the glazing work found in these monuments is unlikely to have predated by any great stretch of time the eighth or seventh century BC; he accordingly

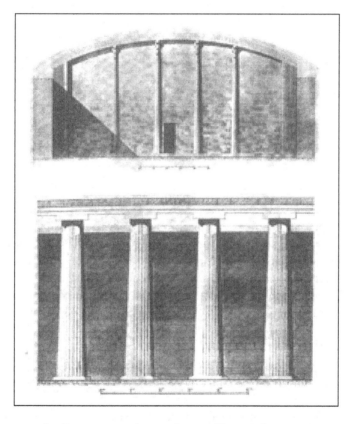

18. Details of Djoser's Temple-complex at Sakkara. (After Petrie)

dated the entire complex to the eighth century.[200] We need to remember too the enormous body of evidence, briefly alluded to at the close of the previous chapter, suggesting that Egypt's First Dynasty could not have commenced

[198]Petrie, *A History of Egypt* Vol. 3 (London, 1901), pp. 58-61
[199]Leonard Cottrell, *The Mountains of Pharaoh* (London, 1956), pp. 152-3.
[200]Dayton, op. cit.

much before 1200 or 1300 BC. If this is correct, it suggests a date of circa 1100 BC for the commencement of the Third Dynasty.

As it transpires, this estimate concurs reasonably well with the evidence of the well-known Khnumibre genealogy. In the inscription, Khnumibre, an architect under one of the earlier Persian kings, listed his ancestors, father to son, stretching back twenty-five generations. The second earliest name on the list is given as Imhotep, with Djoser as the reigning king. It is clear then that the genealogy separates Khnumibre, who must be dated around 450 BC, from Imhotep by twenty-four generations. Allowing twenty to twenty-five years per generation, which, given the habitually early marriages and deaths of ancient peoples, is rather generous, we would be obliged to locate Djoser and Imhotep sometime between 1075 and 930 BC — not far removed from the date suggested by Dayton on the evidence of Third Dynasty technology and precisely in agreement with the chronology proposed by us.

Early scholarship was nonplussed by the evidence of Khnumibre's genealogy but because it clashed so decisively with the "established" chronology, it was soon dismissed as "symbolic" and "lacking historical substance".[201]

Who Was King Djoser?

Egyptians of later years came to regard Djoser's reign as something of a golden age, and the pharaoh himself was accredited with almost godlike powers. Above all, he was regarded as a paragon of wisdom (as evinced by the name Djoser). His cult grew and grew, and by the Saite period (Twenty-Sixth Dynasty) he was already deified. He was, in the words of one commentator, viewed: "both as a patron of literature and a physician of such eminence that he came to be identified with Asklepios, the Greek god of medicine.... In after years he was remembered with reverence as one of the greatest of the early Pharaohs ... on one of the votive tablets of the Apis worshippers of the Twenty-Second Dynasty, reverence is done to his name; we read of a priest of his spirit named Sonbf, and another, Ahmose, in the Twenty-Sixth Dynasty."[202]

Djoser then had a priesthood dedicated to him and was invoked as a god centuries after his death. What could have prompted such adulation? The explanation normally given is that as the first pharaoh to leave great monuments of stone, later generations would naturally have been impressed by him. His monuments guaranteed his immortality. There is no doubt a certain amount of the truth in this explanation, but it does not cover everything. For

---

[201]See Jesse E. Lasken, "Towards a New Chronology of Ancient Egypt," *Discussions in Egyptology*, 17 (1990).
[202]Arthur Weigall, *A History of the Pharaohs* Vol.1 (London, 1952), p. 147.

Djoser's reputation was enhanced by that of his vizier, the godlike Imhotep. This man was, as we shall see, regarded as Egypt's greatest ever seer and interpreter of dreams. He is also normally accredited with designing the great structures at Sakkara. Acting together, these two exceptional figures were believed to have shaped the course of Egyptian civilization in a unique way, and, it was said, they saved the country from a well-remembered and potentially devastating famine.

19. Djoser performing the ritual Heb-Sed run.

Thus the legend, of which more shall be said in due course. But of the man Djoser there is precious little that can be ascertained. He is usually regarded as first pharaoh of the Third Dynasty, but why this should be so is viewed as most mysterious. He "Is connected with Khasekhemwy, the last king of the Second Dynasty, through Queen Nymaathap who has generally been accepted as the wife of Khasekhemwy and the mother of Djoser",[203] which means, in effect, that Djoser was the son of Khasekhemwy. Why then is he

203 W. Stevenson Smith, loc cit., p. 146.

considered the founder of a new line? The same author continues, "It must be admitted that here and in other cases later in the Old Kingdom we do not understand clearly the facts governing a change of dynasty, although we follow the division into groups of kings which is indicated in the dynastic lists of the Ptolemaic writer Manetho." Attempting to answer the puzzle, he notes that, "It now seems likely that Neterykhet Djoser was preceded by Sanakhte as the first king of the Third Dynasty," and that "Sanakhte may have been an elder brother of Neterykhet [Djoser]..." But this hardly solves the problem. The undeniable fact appears to be that Djoser was a son of Khasekhemwy of Dynasty 2 and that he should not, therefore, be regarded as representing a new dynasty.

Yet from the perspective adopted in the present volume an answer is perhaps forthcoming. Djoser did not represent a new dynasty so much as a New Age. The clue comes in evidence already alluded to, suggestive of severe disturbances in the cosmic order right throughout the period of the Second Dynasty. In 1973 Professor William Mullen of New York remarked on the strange obsession during the time of the battle between Seth and Horus, a battle which later Egyptian tradition insisted left the country a devastated wasteland. It is remarkable that the fourth king of the Second Dynasty ceased to identify himself with Horus (the "good" god) and championed the cause of Seth instead; he changed his name from Sekhemib to Peribsen. In Mullen's words, "In the first of the three names in standard Old Kingdom titulary where a drawing of the hawk of Horus should appear he substituted the dog-like animal of Seth (a species now extinct). Seth also appears on a seal found in his tomb which reads 'the god of Ombos [Seth's cult center] to his son Perabsen....'" Mullen remarked too on how the final two kings of the period, Khasekhem and Khasekhemwy, named themselves "Appearance of the power" and "Appearance of the two powers", and how these names as said to designate the re-establishment of order. Khasekhemwy also added a title meaning "the two gods in him are at peace". Mullen called attention too to the fact that all the royal tombs of the period were badly damaged by fire.[204]

That this strange nomenclature was indicative of unusual natural events is confirmed by two quite separate pieces of evidence. On the one hand, archeology has identified, as we saw, a dramatic change in climate, or rather series of changes in climate, right throughout the Early Dynastic period. This evidence has been dealt with in detail above and needs no further elaboration here. Essentially, the Early Dynastic Age saw the Sahara transformed from

---

[204]William Mullen, loc cit.

a well-watered savannah into a barren wasteland.[205] Secondly, Manetho, accessing Egyptian records and traditions now lost, clearly describes major disturbances in the natural order at the time. Again, we need not go into the details as they have already been examined. What needs to be stressed here is that right at the start of the Third Dynasty, Manetho speaks of a strange "waxing" of the sun which so frightened the Libyans, with whom the Egyptians were then at war, that they capitulated.[206] From the evidence cited in the previous chapter, it would appear that this "waxing" of the sun cannot be separated from the cosmic events which afflicted the world during this epoch, the very events which rendered the Sahara a desert.

It would appear then that Djoser's reign was regarded as marking the inception of a new dynasty because of these events. The order of the cosmos had been disturbed yet again in the time of Khasekhemwy, Djoser's father, in the midst of which the young prince seized the reins of power and restored order. That such an event actually occurred is confirmed by the evidence of an inscription near the First Cataract, where he is said to have rescued Egypt from a devastating famine. In this enterprise he was assisted by one of the most extraordinary characters ever to appear in Egyptian history.

Djoser and the Seven Years' Famine

Egyptian tradition recorded a great famine lasting seven years. This disaster was said to have occurred during the reign of Djoser, and from the story of this event we may come to understand exactly why pharaoh Netjerkhet was called *djoser*, "The Splendid".

The only account of the seven years' famine to survive is on a rock-cut inscription at Elephantine, which dates from a very late period — possibly from the reign of Ptolemy V (Epiphanes), who lived in the second century BC.[207] The inscription records the famine as an historical fact, placing it in the eighteenth year of Djoser. More than one authority has interpreted the text as a forgery perpetrated either by the priests attached to the nearby temple of Khnum, or, more unusually, by Jewish or pro-Jewish propagandists of the Ptolemaic age, intended to give credence to the biblical tradition of Joseph.[208]

There is no question that the famine inscription is of late date. The language used places it very clearly in the Ptolemaic Age, and various other

---

[205] K. W. Butzer, loc. cit.

[206] See e.g., www.tertullian.org/rpearse/syncellus/index.htm.

[207] See H. K. Brugsch, *Die biblischen sieben Jahre der Hungersnoth* (Leipzig, 1891) and J. Vandier, *La Famine dans l'Égypte ancienne* (Cairo, 1936).

[208] See e.g. P. Barguet, *La stèle de la famine à Séhel*, Institut français d'archéologie orientale — Bibliothéque d'étude Paris, volume 34. Cairo 1953; also Miriam Lichtheim: *Ancient Egyptian Literature: The Late Period*. (Berkeley 2006), pp. 94-100

---

clues suggest the reign of Ptolemy V. Those who see it as a forgery point to the late language, and to the fact that the text justifies the ownership of the region by the priesthood of Khnum.

Neither of these objections carry a great deal of weight. As we have said, famines and climate disturbances really did occur during the Second and Third Dynasties — especially at the interregnum between these two epochs — which makes it likely that the inscription records a real tradition about Djoser and Imhotep. The story seems therefore to have been genuinely ancient, and the priests merely retold it in the language and vocabulary of their own time. The land round Khnum's temple must have been granted to the priesthood at some period by some pharaoh. Why invent a fiction when they could simply have retold the true story of how the territory was acquired?

The second argument against the story — that it was a Jewish or biblically-inspired forgery — carries even less weight, and is given little credence by Egyptologists. Nevertheless, it is appropriate to answer the charge.

There is no question that a Jewish military colony existed at Elephantine in Persian times, though it seems to have disappeared before the end of the Persian epoch. The inscription on the other hand is fairly reliably dated to the second century BC, a hundred-and-fifty years after the end of the Persian age. But apart from the fact, noted above, that Imhotep's era really was a period of major climate disturbance, the idea of it being a Jewish-inspired propaganda piece seems highly unlikely for several other reasons:

First and foremost, monotheistic Jews of the Ptolemaic epoch would hardly have been likely to identify Joseph with an Egyptian seer and soothsayer (popular Egyptian tradition even described Imhotep as a "magician") who interpreted dreams sent by the ram-headed god Khnum. For Jews, such an identification would have been blasphemous.

Secondly, and following on from the first point, the details of the Egyptian story are very different to those of the biblical. In the Egyptian account the famine occurs first, and only then does the king have his dream. Furthermore, in this version there is no mention of fat or lean cows. Imhotep's interpretation of the dream involves the building of a shrine to Khnum, not the building of store-houses. If the inscription had been written by Jewish exiles, these details must cause us to wonder. The inscription, after all, purports to come from the time of Djoser and therefore to be a contemporary account, which would imply, in effect, that the Egyptian version of the story is true and the biblical one a fiction. If Jewish exiles had concocted the story, it would surely have conformed more closely to the Genesis narrative.

Finally, the Jews of the Ptolemaic Age had a very definite chronology which linked their own history with that of Egypt, and in that chronology Imhotep lived many centuries before Joseph. If they were going to create a forgery, they would have picked an Egyptian vizier probably of the Hyksos Age or just slightly earlier, one who lived in an age closer to what they imagined was Joseph's epoch.

It is highly likely then that the famine text at Elephantine records a genuinely Egyptian tradition of some antiquity, and is therefore, for us, of great interest. We are told that in Djoser's eighteenth year Egypt found itself in a crisis. The pharaoh bewails his lot:

> I was in distress on the Great Throne, and those who are in the palace were in heart's affliction from a very great evil, since the Nile had not come in my time for a space of seven years. Grain was scant, fruits were dried up, and everything which they eat was short.[209]

In his distress, the king asks Imhotep, described as the "Chief Lector Priest", for advice. He wishes to know the secrets of the river: "What is the birthplace of the Nile? Who is ... the god there? Who is the god?" At this Imhotep departs and returns with a strange tale about the island of Elephantine in the upper Nile:

> There is a city in the midst of the waters [from which] the Nile rises, named Elephantine. It is the Beginning of the Beginning, the Beginning Nome, [facing] toward Wawat. It is the joining of the land, the primeval hillock of earth, the throne of Re, when he reckons to cast life beside everybody.[210]

Elephantine, says the wise priest, is the home of the ram-headed Khnum, and it is he who sends the life-giving waters of the Nile thence. He goes on to recite Khnum's divine powers, and mentions some of the other gods of the region. Pharaoh then performs a number of services to Khnum and the other divinities as an act of repentance. Next, we hear how Khnum appears to the king in a dream:

> As I slept in life and satisfaction, I discovered the god standing over against me. I propitiated him with praise; I prayed to him in his presence. He revealed himself to me, his face being fresh. His words were:

> "I am Khnum, thy fashioner ... I know the Nile. When he is introduced into the fields, his introduction gives life to every nostril, like the introduction [of life] into the fields ... the Nile will pour forth for thee, without a year of cessation or laxness for any land. Plants will grow,

---

[209] Ed. and trans. John A. Wilson in Pritchard (ed.), op cit., p. 32.
[210] Ibid.

bowing under the fruit. Renenut will be at the head of everything .... Dependents will fulfil the purpose of their hearts, as well as the master. The starvation year will have gone, and [people's] borrowing from their granaries will have departed. Egypt will come into the fields, the banks will sparkle ... and contentment will be in their hearts more than that which was formerly."[211]

On awakening, pharaoh ordered that a large tract of land stretching from Elephantine to Tacompso should be dedicated to Khnum, and that a temple should be erected on the island in his honor. In addition, various other pious decrees were enacted in gratitude to the god.[212]

Bearing in mind that Djoser reigned near the close of the Early Dynastic Age, we must wonder whether this "famine", which could only be brought to an end by raising a temple to one of the celestial deities, refers to another of the cosmic disturbances which periodically afflicted the Earth throughout this epoch. In fact, we shall argue that this is precisely what it was, and that, as an event, it must be placed contemporaneous with the penultimate flood layer observed in the stratigraphies of Lower Mesopotamia.

Djoser's famine, of course, closely resembles the other from ancient tradition, that of Joseph the Hebrew. Virtually all the elements in the Egyptian account are there, though in a different order. In Joseph's tale, the pharaoh's dream comes first, although both legends agree that the dream's interpretation provided the key to alleviating the famine. Again the Egyptian story has the wise seer Imhotep assist the king in dealing with the famine, and it is obvious that Imhotep's role closely resembles that of Joseph in the Genesis story. In addition, the nature of the god Khnum is here significant. In early times, the ram-headed divinity had been one of the foremost in Egypt. He was regarded as the creator god and was portrayed, in biblical style, fashioning mankind upon the potter's wheel.[213] Khnum was indeed viewed very much as the Old Testament Spirit of God, a fact that induced some scholars to regard the whole cult of Khnum as influential in the development of Hebrew religious ideas.[214]

Scholars were not slow to associate Djoser's famine of seven years with that of Joseph, and they would undoubtedly have made the connection between Imhotep and Joseph, Djoser and Joseph's pharaoh, had it not been for the chronological discrepancy. Djoser was supposed to have reigned

---

[211]Ibid.
[212]Ibid.
[213] J. G. Wilkinson, *The Ancient Egyptians* Vol.3 (London, 1878), pp. 1-4.
[214]Ibid., p. 4 "Kneph, or more properly Chnoumis, was retained as the idea of the 'Spirit of God', which moved upon the face of the waters'." The same writer notes that classical writers identified Khnum with Jupiter, the father of the gods.

around 2600 BC, whereas according to biblical chronology, Joseph would have lived around 1700 BC — yet again, that gap of 1000 years. Scholars had therefore to content themselves with vague "connections" between the two legends. Some argued that the story of Joseph had influenced the Egyptian tale, whilst others argued that the Genesis account was influenced by the Egyptian story. The best-known proponent of the latter argument was Brugsch.[215]

Such ideas held good only if the conventional chronology was correct. However, we now see that such is not the case, and that Djoser, as well as Joseph, must both belong, in terms of cultural context, in the final years of the second millennium or the early part of the first millennium. Could it be then that Djoser is indeed Joseph's pharaoh, and that Imhotep, the great seer who advised Djoser on the seven years' famine, is none other than Joseph himself? Before making a final pronouncement, let us briefly take a closer look at the life and character of Joseph as they are revealed in the Genesis account.

The Story of Joseph

The story of Joseph, one of the best-known and best-loved of the Old Testament, occupies almost a quarter of the Book of Genesis. That fact alone illustrates the importance of Joseph to Israel's early history. He it was who brought the Twelve Tribes to Egypt, where in time they would grow to nationhood. Yet the story outlined in Genesis reveals the importance of Joseph not only to the history of Israel but also to the history of Egypt and furthermore illustrates the thoroughly Egyptian background to the entire episode.

Joseph was portrayed as the classic underdog, the maltreated younger brother, who rose to power and eventually returned good for evil. As such, there seems little doubt that the story we now have — in the form that we have it — dates from a comparatively recent time. The idea of returning good for evil was essentially alien to the early peoples. No one who knows anything of how ancient man thought would dare to date the story of Joseph, as it now stands, before the eighth or seventh century BC. Fully confirming this conclusion is the fact that the Egypt portrayed in the Joseph narrative is a highly civilized, imperial state. The pharaoh rides on a chariot and issues written decrees. The ceremony in which Joseph is made vizier/prime minister is an accurate portrayal of New Kingdom/Late Period ritual.[216] The

---

[215] H. K. Brugsch, *Steininschrift und Bibelwort* (1898), pp.88-97.

[216] See J. Vergote, *Joseph en Egypte* (1959); also Werner Keller, *The Bible as History* p. 101.

Egyptian names given in the narrative, i.e., Potiphar (Pedephre) and Asenath (Nasneith), are names of the Late Period, popular in the mid-first millennium BC.[217]

In harmony with all this, though puzzling in its own way, is the astonishing amount of Egyptian influence now recognized as present in the Joseph narrative. The terms and idioms used are Egyptian through and through. Indeed such is the resemblance to Egyptian phraseology and custom that that some scholars now regard these chapters of Genesis as based on an Egyptian record. One such commentator is the Israeli Egyptologist A. S. Yahuda, a man whose work we shall examine in greater detail at a later stage. Yahuda wondered at the superabundance of Egyptian terms, phrases, metaphors and loan-words present throughout Genesis, remarking on their comparative absence from later books of the Old Testament. Some examples provided by Yahuda are as follows: Joseph's appointment as vizier was the "kernel" of the story, according to Yahuda. For this office, a Hebrew word with a root which has the meaning "to do twice, to repeat, to double" is used. Yahuda explained that in the same way the Egyptian word sn.nw ("deputy") was formed from sn, the word for "two".[218] In the same verse, pharaoh commands all to "bow the knee" before Joseph. The Hebrew word for "bow" is agreed by most authorities to have been taken from the Egyptian.

Joseph was titled "father to pharaoh," and, as Yahuda says, the Hebrew expression corresponds with the Egyptian itf, "father," a common priestly title, and one borne by viziers.[219] At the start of his conversation with Joseph, pharaoh says: "I have had a dream ... I have heard that you understand a dream to interpret it" (Gen.41:15). For "understand" the Hebrew uses the verb "to hear." This term has proved very difficult for commentators, but, according to Yahuda, it corresponds entirely with the Egyptian use of sdm meaning "to hear" or "to understand".[220] Another problem for commentators has been the sentence of Gen. 41:40, where pharaoh says literally to Joseph: "According to your mouth shall my people kiss." The verb "to kiss" here has always seemed completely out of place. However, when we compare it with the Egyptian, "kiss" proves to be "a correct and thoroughly exact reproduction of what the narrator really meant to convey. Here an expression is rendered in Hebrew from a metaphorical one used in polished speech among the Egyptians."[221] In polished speech the Egyptians spoke of sn, "kissing" the food, rather than the ordinary, colloquial wnrn, which meant "eating."

---

[217]Ibid.
[218] A. S. Yahuda, *The Language of the Pentateuch in its Relation to Egyptian* (Oxford, 1933).
[219]Ibid., p. 23
[220]Ibid., p. 7
[221]Ibid.

In the Joseph story, pharaoh is addressed in the third person, e.g., Gen. 41:34, "Let Pharaoh do this." According to Yahuda this corresponds precisely to the court etiquette of Egypt. A characteristic term recurring in several passages of Genesis is "in the face of Pharaoh", or "from the face of Pharaoh", meaning "before pharaoh". This, says Yahuda, corresponds with Egyptian court custom, where one might not speak to his majesty "to his face", but only "in the face of his majesty" (*m hr hm-f*).[222] Again, in the Joseph narrative, the word "lord", in reference either to pharaoh or Joseph, is given in the plural. This corresponds exactly with Egyptian usage where pharaoh, as well as being referred to as *nb* ("lord"), is spoken of as *nb.wy*, in the plural.

These instances are only a small sample of the evidence mustered by Yahuda, but they illustrate very clearly the profoundly Egyptian background to the whole story. Indeed, as we have said, so strong is the evidence that some commentators have suggested an Egyptian original of the narrative which Hebrew scribes more or less copied. In short, when the Israelites came to write down the story of Joseph, they borrowed heavily on what the Egyptians themselves had written about him. Indeed, they went further; they added details which they borrowed directly from other, unrelated Egyptian popular traditions. Thus for example the attempt by Potiphar's wife to seduce Joseph is taken directly from the Egyptian Story of the Two Brothers.[223] None of this should surprise us: Genesis tells us quite clearly that Joseph was a major personality; he became the king's vizier; he brought Asiatics into Egypt; he presided over a social/political revolution. According to Genesis (47:22), the land of Egypt changed hands during his lifetime: Pharaoh became absolute master of the kingdom. But on top of all that Joseph was — most extraordinarily — a seer, a prophet, a visionary. Such a man, we would imagine, could not have been forgotten by the Egyptians.

Having stated all this, we now find that Joseph, coming just a few generations after the time of the Abraham migration, would have lived in roughly the same era as "The Splendid" King Djoser and the wise seer Imhotep. It thus begins to look more and more clear that Joseph and Imhotep, the two great sages, were identical persons and that Joseph's wise king was Djoser. But the evidence is not yet exhausted. If we examine the personalities of Joseph and Imhotep in detail, we shall find even more clues to their identity.

---

[222]Ibid., p. 13

[223]"The Tale of the Two Brothers," preserved in the British Museum Papyrus d'Orbinay. See, e.g., Gaston Maspero, *Les contes populaires de l'Egypte ancienne* (Paris, 1900), pp. 1-20

Joseph and the Seer Imhotep

Imhotep, the sage and prophet of King Djoser's time, was long remembered and honored by the Egyptians, who regarded him as the greatest seer who ever lived. He was ranked, along with King Menes and the god Thoth, as the founder of civilization. Indeed, Imhotep was like a second founder; with him, Egypt entered into an entirely new phase of her history. His reputation was immense and the powers accredited to him godlike. James Baikie provides a fairly typical assessment of the man:

"Age by age the reputation of [Imhotep] the great architect and statesman grew. By the time of the rise of the Middle Kingdom his words were being quoted in songs as the ultimate expression of human wisdom; he became the typical wise man, philosopher, coiner of wise sayings, and physician; the scribe caste of Egypt looked upon him as its patron saint, and the scribe poured out a libation to Imhotep before beginning any piece of writing. A temple was reared in his honor near the Serapeum at Saqqara, not far from the site of his greatest achievement, the pyramid of King Zoser. Finally, the process of making a man into a god was accomplished by the acceptance of Memphite belief that he was indeed the Son of God, being the offspring of Ptah, the Creator-God of Memphis, by a mortal mother.... When the priests of Edfu, in the Ptolemaic period, thirty centuries after his death, were describing the origin of the great temple which is the most complete extant example of an Egyptian house of God, they believed they could give it no higher recommendation that to say that the building was a reproduction of the plan which 'descended to Imhotep from heaven to the north of Memphis' in the days of King Zoser. The Greeks, who cherished a kind of awed reverence for the mysterious sort of impracticable wisdom which they imagined they discerned in the teaching of ancient Egypt, took over Imhotep with the rest, calling him Imouthes, and identified him, as his master had been identified, with Asklepios, as the patron god of learning. Stranger destiny has been reserved for no man than for this faithful servant of a great king."[224]

There is little that can be added to the above assessment. Imhotep, plainly and simply, was the greatest of all Egypt's wise men. As we have said, the close correlations between Imhotep and the biblical Joseph have not gone unnoticed by scholars. In recent years, English historian Tom Chetwynd revived the whole debate and argued strongly for identifying the two men. Chetwynd held to the conventional view that Imhotep belonged in an "Old Kingdom" dated to the third millennium BC and did not attempt to resolve the chronological difficulties inherent in this. Nevertheless, he demonstrated

---

[224]James Baikie, *A History of Egypt* Vol.1 (London, 1929), p. 97.

that the parallels between the two were sufficiently compelling to overrule the chronological problems. In short, so powerful was the evidence that irrespective of what the chronology apparently said, the two men simply had to be one and the same.

Some of the points raised by Chetwynd have already been referred to. He takes a detailed look, for example, at the two accounts of the seven years' famine.[225] Next, he points to the very similar roles allocated to pharaoh's counselors in the biblical and Egyptian accounts of the famine. Quoting from Budge's translation of the Egyptian story, he illustrates the parallels: "The nobles are destitute of counsel," says the Egyptian scribe, and, "He [a counselor] would like to go to the temple of Thoth to enquire of that god, to go to the College of Magicians and search through the sacred books."[226] In the parallel text from Genesis, Chetwynd finds, "[Pharaoh] sent and called for all the magicians of Egypt and all its wise men, and told them his dream, but there was none could interpret it to Pharaoh" (Gen. 41:8).

Regarding the pharaoh's dream, Chetwynd remarks: "In both stories the Pharaoh dreams of a time of plenty, when the granaries are full, and in both, the dreams are fulfilled so that there is abundance throughout the land; but in the Egyptian account the abundance follows upon the famine, whereas in the Joseph story this is reversed."[227]

Next, Chetwynd points to the grants of land and the levy of tithes in both accounts. From the Egyptian story we hear that, "The King endowed Khnum — and his priesthood — with 20 shoinoi, or measures, of land, on each bank of the river." This is compared with the biblical "And Pharaoh said to Joseph: I will give you the best of the land of Egypt and you shall eat the fat of the land" (Gen. 47:22). The whole question of social reforms under Joseph's administration, including land ownership and tithes, is of course of the utmost importance and ties in with reforms and rituals traditionally associated with Imhotep.

Chetwynd also emphasizes parallels between the cult of Imhotep and the enduring reputation of Joseph, as well as the role of magic, dreams and oracles in the traditions surrounding both men. But perhaps his strongest point is the evidence he brings to light concerning the names Joseph and Imhotep. Imhotep, he notes, means "Im is content" or "Im is satisfied". Chetwynd quotes Albert Clay, who affirms that Im "is a Syrian god, probably identifiable with Baal Adan or Baal Saphon."[228] But, "Saphon or Zaphen

---

[225]Tom Chetwynd, "A Seven Year Famine in the Reign of King Djoser with other Parallels between Imhotep and Joseph," *Catastrophism and Ancient History* IX:1 (January, 1987).
[226]Ibid., p. 50
[227]Ibid., p. 51
[228]Ibid, p. 55

also occurs again in the Egyptian name given to Joseph by the Pharaoh: 'Zaphenath Paneah'."[229] Further emphasizing the link, he notes that "Later editors of the Bible took a dim view of personal names with Baal in them and sometimes substituted the shortened form of Yahweh: Je — Jehu — Jeho — Jo."

Could "Joseph" have been derived from Baal Saphon, as "Jehu-saph(on)"? For Chetwynd, such a solution seemed very plausible, and it was further strengthened by the fact that on their departure from Egypt, the Israelites encamped opposite Baal-Zaphen on the shores of the Red Sea.

Chetwynd argued therefore that Joseph was named for the Syrian/ Canaanite god Saphon and that Imhotep was named for precisely the same deity, Im/Saphon. In view of this, and despite the fact that he could not reconcile the apparent chronological discrepancy — which placed Joseph a thousand years removed from Imhotep — Chetwynd came to the conclusion that Joseph and Imhotep must have been one and the same person; and that, furthermore, Imhotep was an Asiatic, just as Genesis claims. Yet here there is a problem, one not mentioned by Chetwynd; for the Egyptians regarded Imhotep as a native of their own land.

Imhotep the Man

According to the genealogy of Khnumibre, Imhotep was the son of a native Egyptian named Ka-Nefer, described as "the director of works". Whilst it is probable that the earlier part of Khnumibre's list is not to be taken as historical in the strict sense of the word, it is nevertheless true to say that the Egyptians of later times very definitely regarded Imhotep as a native Egyptian. The titles, or some of the titles, of the great seer have been found inscribed on a statue base from the great court of Djoser's complex at Sakkara. They read:

> The chancellor of the King of Lower Egypt; the first after the King of Upper Egypt; administrator of the great palace, hereditary lord, the high priest of Heliopolis, Imhotep — the builder, the sculptor, the maker of stone vases.[230]

Two points immediately strike us here. Imhotep is described as a "hereditary lord" and as the "high priest of Heliopolis". Both titles strongly suggest that he was a native Egyptian and not some foreigner appointed to high office. The term "hereditary lord" is a translation of the Egyptian, *Iry-pat*, a group or class of people whom we may broadly define as the Egyptian nobility, a

---

[229]Ibid.
[230]Rohl, op cit., p. 360

group which appeared to be linked by blood to the pharaoh. In the words of David Rohl, "These iry-pat were an elite nobility which surrounded the pharaoh — they were effectively the courtiers of the royal palace. They also had ancestral links back to the Followers of Horus. The ancient texts make a clear distinction between the Patu and the two other population groups in the Nile valley — the *Henemmet* and the *Rekhyt* ... The most famous iry-pat was none other than the great architect, magician and sage, Imhotep — the genius who built the magnificent Step Pyramid complex at Sakkara for his king, Djoser."[231]

20. Late Period portrayal of Imhotep. By that time the great seer was regarded as divine and associated by the Greeks with their god of healing, Asclepius.

[231] Ibid., p. 352

On the face of it therefore it does appear that, in spite of everything, Joseph and Imhotep cannot have been the same person. What then is the solution? There are, in the present writer's opinion, two possibilities. First and foremost, it could be that the Iry-pat, or hereditary nobility, were identified by both Egyptians and early Hebrews with the Asiatic culture-bearers who entered Egypt just prior to the founding of the First Dynasty. We have already suggested that these were blood-relations of the Hebrews, Canaanites, and Syrians. Intermarriage between Egyptians and Asiatic newcomers is suggested in the story of Abraham's Egyptian wife Hagar and in the brief marriage of the pharaoh to Sarai. We saw too that in all probability one of the reasons why the Egyptians named Canaan (or at least the Jordan Valley) the "Divine Land" was because they were aware that many of the tribe from which their ruling class, the Iry-pat, were descended, originated in that part of the world. Egyptian texts make it clear that Punt (also called the "Divine Land") was regarded as the ancestral home of their nobility, whilst other evidence (such as the custom of circumcision and tracing descent through the female line), strongly suggest an extremely close link between the Hebrews and the Egyptian ruling class. Could it be then that Imhotep's identification with the Iry-pat alludes to his Puntite/Canaanite blood? That is certainly one possibility, though there is another, and far more likely answer; one that will make uncomfortable reading for those taking a literalist interpretation of these passages in Genesis.

We recall here that Asiatic migrants seem to have entered Egypt on a fairly regular basis throughout the Early Dynastic epoch. This is certainly the impression conveyed by the archaeological evidence. We may surmise that, towards the end of the Second Dynasty, a major disturbance in the natural order, leading to climate disruption and hunger, once again propelled a substantial movement of Asiatic refugees into the Nile Delta. Egypt, as it turned out, was able and willing to provide food for these groups and fodder for their flocks, probably in exchange for labor and other kinds of tribute. Under the wise rule of Djoser and the clever management of his vizier Imhotep, the Land of the Nile became a place of refuge for many desperate people; and, as a benefactor of humanity, Imhotep would perchance have been regarded by the nomads almost as one of their own. Thus, to the question: "Were Joseph and Imhotep the same person?" we can provide a qualified Yes. Qualified because the question itself is an over-simplification. We can discount, for example, the idea that Imhotep began his career as a Hebrew slave, and we can be fairly certain that he was an Egyptian by blood as well as by reputation. A far more likely solution is that Imhotep was the historical personage upon whom was based the largely fictional or legendary character of Joseph. And the evidence for this is overwhelming. We have already examined the thoroughly Egyptian background to all the details of Joseph's story. Indeed, so pervasive is the Egyptian influence that it leads the biblical authors to an admission they would surely not have made had the character and identity of Joseph not been thoroughly Egyptian: We hear that Joseph's wife Asenath was the daughter of the "pagan" Egyptian High Priest of Heliopolis; the implication being that Joseph too became (or was) a pagan High Priest. And, sure enough, we find that Imhotep was indeed the High Priest of Heliopolis (On).

It is impossible that the biblical authors — who loathed the "gods of the peoples" — would have made this admission had not Joseph been an Egyptian and their knowledge of him not been derived directly from Egyptian sources.

It seems that the Jewish editors of Genesis, working perhaps in the late Persian or early Ptolemaic epoch, balked at the idea of a foreigner rescuing their ancestors from death by hunger, and accordingly transformed the legendary Joseph ("Yahweh will provide") into a Hebrew of the lineage of Abraham.

CHAPTER 5. EXODUS

The Plagues of Egypt

The Exodus of the Israelites from Egypt has already been thoroughly covered by Velikovsky, and the exhaustive investigation found in *Ages in Chaos* (1952) deserves much more credit than it has hitherto received. Velikovsky showed in great detail how the Book of Exodus portrayed a land and a whole world in the grip of some tremendous upheaval of nature. This upheaval manifests itself firstly in the Ten Plagues, and then, as the children of Israel flee Egypt, the forces of nature, in the form of great tidal waves or some such phenomenon, are released with terrifying violence against the pharaoh and his army:

> The biblical story does not present the departure from Egypt as an everyday occurrence, but rather as an event accompanied by great upheavals of nature. Grave and ominous signs preceded the Exodus: clouds of dust and smoke darkened the sky and colored the water they fell upon with a bloody hue. The dust tore wounds in the skin of man and beast; in the torrid glow vermin and reptiles bred and filled the earth; wild beasts, plagued by sand and ashes, came from the ravines of the wasteland to the abodes of men. A terrible torrent of hailstones fell, and a wild fire ran upon the ground; a gust of wind brought swarms of locusts, which obscured the light; blasts of cinders blew in wave after wave, day and night, night and day, and the gloom grew to a prolonged night, and blackness extinguished every ray of light. Then came the tenth and most mysterious plague: the Angel of the Lord 'passed over the houses of the children of Israel ... when he smote the Egyptian, and delivered our houses' (Exodus 12:27). The slaves, spared by the angel

of destruction, were implored amid groaning and weeping to leave the land that same night. In the ash-grey dawn the multitude moved, leaving behind the scorched fields and ruins where a few hours before there had been urban and rural habitations.[232]

Thus Velikovsky sets the scene for the greatest event of Israel's history. More than any other single episode, the Exodus shaped the character of the Hebrew nation. So sacred is the memory that each year at the Passover, the greatest festival of Judaism, the eldest son of every Jewish family is enjoined by tradition to ask his father to recite from the Haggadah some of the wonderful events that occurred when their ancestors were delivered from the Angel of Death, and from Egypt.

The Exodus, in short, was *the* event of Hebrew history. A natural catastrophe of almost unparalleled dimensions had apparently dissolved royal authority, allowing the Israelites to escape their bondage. But modern scholarship here stands in total disagreement with tradition. According to conventional ideas, the Exodus was not a notable event; there were no extraordinary happenings; the country was not beset by plagues; there was no unnatural darkness; pharaoh and his army were not drowned in the Red Sea. Indeed, historians now hold that the Egyptians were so unimpressed by the Exodus that they didn't even bother to mention it. If the Exodus occurred at all, conventional scholarship believes, it was merely the departure from Egypt of a minor band of Semitic shepherds.

Common sense alone would suggest that there is something seriously amiss here. Could an event that made such a profound impression on a people be totally fabulous? What could possibly have been the motive for inventing such a story, and how could such a lie be promoted as truth? As Velikovsky himself stressed, ancient peoples commonly regarded their ancestors as heroes and demigods. Why invent a story making your ancestors into help-less slaves? And even mainstream scholars have to admit that this presents a problem. Thus in the pages of *The Cambridge Ancient History*, O. Eissfeldt remarks that "It is quite inconceivable that a people could have obstinately preserved traditions about a dishonorable bondage of their ancestors in a foreign land, and passed them on from generation to generation, unless it had actually passed through such an experience."[233] And yet, having admitted that, the same writer remarks, "There is no evidence outside the Old Testament for the sojourn of Israel in Egypt or for the exodus."

---

[232]Velikovsky, *Ages in Chaos* (London, 1952), pp. 12-3.
[233] O. Eissfeldt, "Palestine in the Time of the Nineteenth Dynasty: (a) The Exodus and Wanderings," in *The Cambridge Ancient History*, Vol. 2 part 2 (3rd ed.), p. 321.

We have already identified the reason for scholarship's abject failure to solve the Exodus enigma: Searching in the records and events of the Eighteenth and Nineteenth Dynasties, they were unlikely to find evidence of an event that actually occurred many generations earlier. The Exodus, we shall find, did happen, and it happened much as it is recorded in the Torah. The Egyptians also recorded it, though the records they left of the event have been misdated and misinterpreted.

At some stage early in Egypt's history, a great natural disaster plunged the country into chaos. This occurred when the Kingdom of the Nile was already, and had been for some time, a highly civilized and fully literate society. But during this event royal authority disappeared, slaves rose in rebellion, Asiatics invaded from the east, and famine stalked the land. A whole series, or rather *genre*, of documents dealing with these occurrences — now known as the Pessimistic Literature — clearly tell how the primary cause of these calamities was a great natural disaster, a disaster that blotted out the light of the sun and disrupted the flow of the Nile.

Virtually all of the Pessimistic treatises are dated to the First Intermediate Period, an epoch of anarchy that supposedly followed the collapse of the Old Kingdom towards the end of the Sixth Dynasty. According to one Egyptologist, most of these texts "can be dated within a period of no more than 50 years."[234]

It is evident, even to the most conservative Egyptologists, that the Pessimistic writers are not pessimists in the sense that they are inventing misfortunes or exaggerating the unpleasant side of life. Quite clearly they are describing disturbing events that have shaken the entire kingdom. Royal authority has collapsed. The dead are everywhere. Banditry and rapine are rife. Even worse, the forces of nature, it seems, have been unleashed in a most violent manner. One text from this era, popularly known as "A Man Dispute with his Soul over Suicide," provides important clues. This document speaks of a flood-storm gathering in the north and the sun disappearing. The narrator's wife and children are lost in the Lake of the Crocodile, a lake which commentators have surmised corresponds with the cosmic waters, the Nun, that surround the Primeval Island or Hill.[235] Later in the story we hear of the children being "crushed in the egg", apparently because they had "looked into the face of the Double Crocodile before they had lived." The Double

---

[234]Barbara Bell, "The Dark Ages in Ancient History: The First Dark Age in Egypt," *American Journal of Archeology* 75, (1971) 24.
[235]Stannard, op. cit., p. 761

Crocodile appears to be Henti, a cosmic monster who symbolizes the final destruction at the end of a World Cycle.[236]

What the exact significance of this cosmic crocodile, or serpent, is, should be apparent from what we have said in Chapter 1.

Perhaps the most important of the Pessimistic writers are Neferty, apparently a contemporary of the Fourth Dynasty pharaoh Sneferu, and Ipuwer, whose long and fragmentary Lamentations, have been the subject of much scholarly conjecture over the years. Without question, and this is a fact conceded by even the most skeptical of commentators, the Ipuwer Papyrus recounts events almost identical to those described in the Book of Exodus. Throughout the text, the scribe bewails the fate of his country, reduced as it is by some natural calamity to complete anarchy and lawlessness. Velikovsky recognized in the Papyrus Ipuwer in particular one of the missing Egyptian accounts of the Exodus, and he illustrated the biblical parallels by the simple method of juxtaposition. Here we shall follow his lead, and provide a small example of the two texts:

1. Plague is throughout the land. Blood is everywhere (The Papyrus 2:6).

... and there was blood throughout all the land of Egypt (Exodus 2:6).

2. Why, really, all animals, their hearts weep. Cattle moan because of the state of the land (The Papyrus 5:5).

... behold the hand of the Lord is upon thy cattle which is in the field, upon the horses, upon the asses, upon the camels, upon the oxen, and upon the sheep: there shall be a very grievous murrain (Exodus 9:3).

3. Why really, gates, columns and walls are consumed by fire (The Papyrus 2:10).

... and the Lord sent thunder and hail and fire ran along the upon the ground; and the Lord rained hail upon the land of Egypt. So there was hail, and fire mingled with the hail, very grievous ... (Exodus 9:23-24).

4. Why really, trees are destroyed (The Papyrus 4:14).

Why really, that has perished which yesterday was seen, and the land is left over to its weakness like the cutting of flax (The Papyrus 5:12-13).

... and the hail smote every herb in the field, and brake every tree in the field (Exodus 9:25).

5. No fruit nor herbs are found for the birds (The Papyrus 6:1).

Why really, grain has perished on every side.... Everybody says: There is nothing! The storehouse is stripped bare (The Papyrus 6:3).

---

[236]Ibid. As it happens, I am not the first person to place the Exodus at such an early date in Egypt's history. In his *Exodus Problem and Its Ramifications* (Crest Challenge Books, 1987), Donovan Courville likewise dated the event to the end of the Early Bronze Age.

And the locusts went up over the land of Egypt ... very grievous were they; before them there were no such locusts as they, neither after them shall be such. For they covered the face of the whole earth, so that the land was darkened; and they ate every herb of the land and all the fruit of the trees which the hail had left: and there remained not any green thing in the trees, or in the herbs of the field, through all the land of Egypt (Exodus 10:14-15).

6. ... fear ... Poor men ... the land is not light because of it (The Papyrus, fragments 9:11).

And Moses stretched forth his hand toward heaven; and there was a thick darkness in all the land of Egypt for three days (Exodus 10:22).

7. Why really, the children of princes are dashed against the walls. The [once] prayed-for children are [now] laid out on the high ground (The Papyrus 4:3).

And it came to pass, that at midnight the Lord smote all of the firstborn in the land of Egypt, from the firstborn of Pharaoh that sat on his throne unto the firstborn of the captive that was in the dungeon (Exodus 12:29).

8. It is groaning that is throughout the land, mingled with lamentations (The Papyrus 3:14).

... and there was a very great cry in Egypt. (Exodus 12:30).

9. He who places his brother in the land is everywhere (The Papyrus 2:13).

For there was not a house where there was not one dead (Exodus 12:30).

10. Behold now, the fire has mounted up on high. Its flame goes forth against the enemies of the land (The Papyrus 7:1).

And it came to pass, when Pharaoh had let the people go ... the Lord went before them by day in a pillar of cloud, to lead them that way; and by night in a pillar of fire, to give them light (Exodus 13:17).

Even a skeptic would admit that, to all intents and purposes, the Papyrus Ipuwer appears to contain a graphic, blow by blow account of the disastrous Ten Plagues that struck Egypt at the time of the Exodus. It is untrue that the Egyptians did not remember it. The disaster, if Ipuwer and the others are to be believed, was as great a watershed in the history of Egypt as it was in the history of Israel. Yet the Exodus is not connected with these Pessimistic Texts because once again chronology gets in the way. The Pessimistic treatises, it is said, notwithstanding their similarities to the contents of the Book of Exodus, could not possibly be referring to the same events, because the Pessimistic literature was composed almost a thousand years before the accepted date of the Exodus. We have encountered that span of time before, that thousand years. So, one more time, scholars have had to content themselves with surmising the "influence" of the Pessimistic writers on the authors of Exodus.

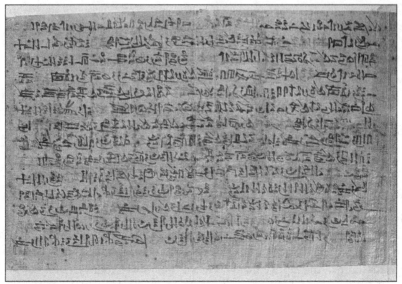

21. The Ipuwer Papyrus, which records a catastrophe very similar to that described in the Book of Exodus.

Before moving on, we should note that some of the Pessimistic writers, though generally believed to be contemporary with Ipuwer and Neferty, seem actually to belong to a later period. Among these must be placed the works of various dignitaries associated with the Tenth and Eleventh Dynasty kings Achthoes III and Inyotef II. It is easy to see why scholars would place these along with the better known Pessimistic authors. Consider for example the famous inscription of inscription of Ankhtifi:

> I fed/kept alive [the towns of] Hefat, Hormer and ... at a time when the sky was [in] clouds/storm and the land was on the wind [and when everyone was dying] of hunger on this sandbank of Hell ... All of Upper Egypt was dying of hunger to such a degree that everyone had come to eating his children.[237]

We have here, apparently, all the elements which concerned Ipuwer and Neferty. In the midst of some great natural catastrophe, it seems, cannibalism had broken out. A primeval chaos enveloped the land. In a number of accounts Inyotef III himself speaks of what he describes as the "Day of Shed-yetshya" or "Day of Misery" that brought devastation to the whole land.[238] A text from the same period written by a dignitary named Kay records how

---

[237]Barbara Bell, loc. cit.
[238] W. C. Hayes, "The Middle Kingdom in Egypt: Internal History from the Rise of the Heracleopolitans to the Death of Ammenemes III," in *The Cambridge Ancient History* Vol.1 part 2 (3rd ed.), p. 471.

he "made a gateway for all who came frightened on the day of tumult."[239] But alongside natural calamities, these documents also mention warfare. The chaos here lamented is partly the result of human activity. Such being the case, it is evident that these latter-day "Pessimistic" writers describe events during the Hyksos epoch, when the Herakleopolitan Achthoes rulers, allies and clients of the Hyksos, battled against the Inyotef rulers of Thebes, who styled themselves as patriotic freedom fighters. Though clearly in the style of Ipuwer and Neferty, it is clear that Egyptian scribes of the Hyksos epoch modelled their work on the earlier texts which described a land in the throes of a natural rather than man-made calamity. According to the chronology proposed by the present author, the Hyksos Conquest would have occurred about 160 years after the Exodus.

The Drowning of Pharaoh and His Army

In Exodus we read how pharaoh repented of letting the Hebrews go, then set out in pursuit of them with his soldiers, intent on cutting them to pieces. However, as he neared his prey, a most incredible phenomenon occurred. The sea, which the slaves had to cross, opened, forming "walls of water." When the Egyptians attempted to follow, the water returned to its normal state, drowning the pharaoh and his men.

Such an event, so extraordinary in all its elements, must have made a deep impression on the people of the time. If it occurred at all (which of course conventional academia denies), it would surely not have been forgotten by the Egyptians. As a matter of fact, the story now told in the textbooks is that the Egyptians remembered no such thing and that the supposed cataclysm of the Red Sea is a fiction partly resulting from a mistranslation of the Hebrew *Yam Suf*, which, it is held, should properly be read as Sea of Reeds. During the dry season, it is surmised, one of the Bitter Lakes that now lie along the course of the Suez Canal probably evaporated sufficiently for the Hebrews to cross over it. Yet had the Israelites fled over the dried bed of a shallow lake, we must wonder how tradition could possibly have translated this into a miracle of awe-inspiring dimensions, a work of the Deity so extraordinary that it became one of the foundation stones of an entire religion.

But there is another, more probable, translation of *Yam Suf* — "Sea of the Hurricane", from Hebrew *suf, sufa*, a great storm. This interpretation, though rarely mentioned in textbooks, far more readily agrees with the account recorded in the Book of Exodus and agrees furthermore with the Egyptian name for the Red Sea, *Shari*, implying Sea of Thundering, or Hammering.

[239] Ibid.

The very term Red Sea itself is also probably of significance, for it reminds us of various ancient traditions – among them the Egyptian story of Mankind's Destruction by Hathor – which spoke of the world turning red and rivers running red, as with blood.[240] The Book of Exodus, of course, records the same story. The Book of Exodus, of course, records the same story.

From the point of view of the interpretation offered in the present study, it will be obvious that we view the momentous events at the Sea of Passage as a direct consequence of the cosmic disturbances of the period. Whether the Red Sea, or part of it, actually parted, or whether, in response to a massive submarine earthquake, the sea temporarily retreated only to return in a great wall of water, is a question that will have to be posed at a later stage. Suffice for the moment to state that historians and archeologists have sought a "Sea of Reeds" explanation because they have misunderstood the whole nature of the catastrophic events described throughout Genesis and Exodus. We of course would place the disaster at the Sea of Passage contemporary with the Pessimistic Texts, so we must wonder whether any hint of catastrophe involving the drowning of a pharaoh is mentioned in this literature.

In fact, at least a couple of the Pessimistic writers specifically tell us that the pharaoh has been killed in the disaster they deplore, and in all of them this is implied. Ipuwer, we have seen, refers to the "children of princes dashed against the walls," whilst in his Prophecy, Neferty goes much further when he says, "Behold, the great one [pharaoh] is fallen in the land whence thou art sprung.... Behold, princes [nomarchs] hold sway in the land, things are made as though they had never been made."[241] Various non-hieroglyphic sources also refer to the death of a king (usually in water) at some early stage in Egypt's history. Thus Manetho mentioned a pharaoh Akhthoes, "who was more dreadful than all who went before him, who did evil throughout Egypt, and being seized with madness was destroyed by a crocodile."[242] We have already encountered the crocodile god, the primeval monster Henti or Sebek,

---

[240] As for example in the story of the Destruction of Mankind, recorded in the Book of the Divine Cow, where the Nile and the entire world is colored red, as with blood. Another parallel comes in a ritual text from the Libyan period which identifies one of seven demons of the goddess Bastet (in this case a manifestation of the lioness goddess Sekhmet) as "The one who is in the Nile-flood who makes blood." Thomas Schneider observes: "This could be understood as a demon who creates carnage in the Nile, and thus turns the Nile into blood (Exod. 7: 17-20)." T. Schneider, "Modern Scholarship versus the Demon of Passover: An Outlook on Exodus Research and Egyptology through the Lens of Exodus 12," in *Israel's Exodus in Transdisciplinary Perspective* (Springer, New York, 2015), pp. 537-553

[241] A. H. Gardiner, "New Literary Works from Egypt," *Journal of Egyptian Archeology* 1, (1914) 100-16.

[242] Petrie, *A History of Egypt* Vol. 1, p. 112.

who symbolized the general dissolution of all things at the end of a world age. It is therefore apparent that the story of Akhthoes' destruction by the crocodile belongs to the same epoch as the Pessimistic Literature, and this is seemingly confirmed by the fact that Manetho's Akhthoes is generally identified with the Akhety kings who formed the Herakleopolitan Tenth Dynasty. These rulers of course reigned right through the Intermediate Period from which the Pessimistic Texts are dated, though they were not, I shall argue, contemporaries of the Exodus.

Another tradition recorded in classical literature told of an Egyptian king named Typhon who, engaging in some cosmic battle with the elements, was buried beneath the waters of Lake Serbonis on the northern shores of the Sinai Peninsula.[243]

Reflecting these late accounts is an obscure inscription on an old shrine from el Arish in the eastern Sinai Peninsula. The shrine, apparently of Ptolemaic date, was being used as a water trough by shepherds before being rescued archeologists in 1890. Two separate translations of the text were made, and the subject has been the center of fairly extensive debate. The shrine, which originally stood in a temple marking Egypt's eastern boundary, is inscribed with a long paean to the gods, describing, among other things, how they defended the land against the depredations of the Asiatics in times long past. These latter are clearly named as the "companions of Apopi," who can only be the Hyksos. However, as well as the human enemies of Egypt, the shrine seems to commemorate some form of cosmic battle of the elements, reminiscent of scenes from the Pyramid Texts. We are told how the god Atum, who is nevertheless described in terms identical to those used for the pharaoh, follows his enemies, or the enemies of Egypt, into a whirlpool. In *Ages in Chaos*, Velikovsky identified this episode as an Egyptian account of the drowning of pharaoh at the Sea of Passage and followed the French translator Georges Goyon in naming the drowned pharaoh as Tom or Thoum. He took things a stage further when he proposed linking "pharaoh" Thoum to the king Tutimaeus who, according to Manetho, reigned during the Hyksos Conquest.

Yet the el Arish shrine does not name the pharaoh who entered the "place of the Whirlpool." Indeed, it is not a pharaoh at all, but the sun-god Ra-Atum (the name can be written variously as Atum, Tum, Tumi etc.). Velikovsky seems to have been aware of this, for he emphasizes that the name "Thoum" is encased within a royal cartouche, as if to stress that "Atum" in this case

---

[243]Herodotus, iii, 5. However, Typhon was the name of a dragon-monster or cosmic serpent (comet?) who had, according to numerous classical sources, visited great destruction upon the earth in an early age.

was a human being. However, the names of deities could also, on occasion, be written within a cartouche.

Notwithstanding this mistake (an error his critics made much of),[244] Velikovsky was clearly onto something of great importance. In spite of the fact that the inscription is badly mutilated and the order of events by no means clear, it is evident that some form of catastrophe is being described, in part of the text at least. We are told how,

> The land was in great affliction. Evil fell on this earth ... It was a great upheaval in the residence ... Nobody left the palace during nine days, and during these nine days of upheaval there was such a tempest that neither the men nor the gods could see the faces of their next.[245]

Impenetrable darkness was of course one of the most terrifying of the Ten Plagues visited upon Egypt. Velikovsky explained it as the result of a combination of volcanic ash and cinders combined with hurricane force winds which disturbed the desert sands. Next we are told how, in the midst of this, Asiatics moved against Egypt. The pharaoh, it is said, went forth to meet them, " his majesty of Shou went forth to battle against the companions of Apopi."[246] Thus the Egyptians explained the god's actions as representing a defense of the country. The outcome however was a disaster:

> Now when the majesty of Ra-Harmachis (Harakhti?) fought with the evil-doers in this pool, the Place of the Whirlpool, the evil-doers prevailed not over his majesty. His majesty leapt into the so-called Place of the Whirlpool.[247]

In Velikovsky's interpretation, the "god" here (Ra-Harmachis) was actually pharaoh, and he did not survive his encounter with the whirlpool. He was raised high in the air, according to the shrine, he ascended to the gods. In other words, he died. But what are we to make of the lines immediately following those quoted above?

> His legs became those of a crocodile, his head that of a hawk with bull's horns upon it: he smote the evil-doers in the Place of the Whirlpool? In the Place of the Sycamore.

Velikovsky's critics pointed to these words as proof that the "god" here referred to was indeed a god and not a pharaoh. How else to explain his shape-shifting? How else could his legs become those of a crocodile and his head that of a hawk with bull's horns upon it? In answer to that, Velikovsky

---

[244]See e.g. Sean Mewhinney, "El-Arish Revisited," *Kronos* XI: 2 (Winter, 1986)

[245] F. L. Griffith, *The Antiquities of Tell el Yahudiyeh and Miscellaneous Work in Lower Egypt during the Years 1887–1888* (London, 1890).

[246]Ibid., p. 73

[247]Ibid.

held that the pharaoh had died in the whirlpool, and that a dead pharaoh could indeed transform himself in such a way. For Velikovsky, the above lines represented the after-death apotheosis of the pharaoh, who now takes on the physical characteristics of the gods.

In Velikovsky's opinion, when all elements of the el Arish text are viewed as a whole, it seems highly probable that they are referring to the same events as those recounted in Exodus. "The story of the darkness in Egypt as told in Hebrew and Egyptian sources is very similar. The death of the Pharaoh in the whirling waters is also similar in both Hebrew and Egyptian sources, and the value of this similarity is enhanced by the fact that in both versions the Pharaoh perished in a whirlpool during or after the days of the great darkness and violent hurricane."[248]

But there was one other point of agreement between the el Arish shrine and the Book of Exodus. The march of the pharaoh or god into battle against the whirlpool is connected with a place named Pi-Kharoti. This, Velikovsky noted, was very like Pi-ha-hiroth in Exodus, the spot where pharaoh overtook the Israelites. Pi-ha-hiroth can also be written Pi-ha-Khiroth, or even Pi-Khiroth, since "ha" is merely the Hebrew definite article. In Velikovsky's words, "Pi-Kharoti is Pi-Khiroth of the Hebrew texts. It is the same place. It is the same pursuit."[249]

After the destruction of the god-king in the whirlpool, his son, who is here given the name of Geb, the god of the earth, sets out in search of him. The eyewitnesses from the locality "give him information about all that happened to Ra in Yat Nebes, the combats of the king Thoum [Atum]." The prince, it is said, then flees before the Asiatic invaders before making an unsuccessful attempt to communicate with them.

From the point of view of the historical reconstruction proposed in the present volume, it is apparent that the Egyptians of the Ptolemaic period confused the events of the Exodus with those of the Hyksos Conquest. The confusion of Israelites and Hyksos is amply illustrated in Manetho's work, a confusion which evidently arose from the fact that both peoples were Asiatics who had, at some stage in history, both entered and resided in Egypt. The temple which contained the shrine stood, as we said, at Egypt's eastern border, and was evidently the scene of a special cult designed to protect the country from invasion from that quarter.

Looking at the evidence broadly, it would appear that the el Arish shrine does contain a garbled and confused reference to the events of the Exodus — events which, at the time of the shrine's creation, were part of the hoary

---

[248]Velikovsky, Ages in Chaos, p. 43.
[249]Ibid., p. 44.

past and already heavily mythologized. Knowing as we now do that the Exodus occurred at a remote period in Egypt's history, when the world was still afflicted by great disturbances in the natural order (viewed by the early peoples as the actions of the gods themselves), it is not surprising that the human actors have been confused with the divine. Other traditions, recorded by the Classical authors and deriving from the same epoch as the el Arish inscription, give the king of the time the same name — Typhon — as the comet or cosmic serpent that brought the catastrophe in the first place. The epoch was distant and the events, which involved the direct action of the gods, could not but be encrusted in the glamour of myth.

Thus it would appear that Velikovsky's critics are mistaken and that the Egyptians did indeed recall the drowning of pharaoh during the Exodus. It is incorrect to say that only the Jews knew of it. The Pessimistic Literature, combined with snippets of information contained in classical and Hellenistic sources, as well as the obscure shrine of el Arish, combine to tell us that at a particular point in Egyptian history the land was struck by a terrible calamity of nature. In the midst of this disaster slaves rose in rebellion, and in the ensuing events the pharaoh was killed and royal authority dissolved. Yet in spite of all this, we still do not know the name of the pharaoh involved. Manetho's statement might lead us to believe him to be one of the Akhety kings of the Herakleopolitan Dynasty. However, evidence which I explore in another place[250] makes it very clear that the Akhety monarchs belonged to the Hyksos Age, and the naming of one of them as the pharaoh drowned in the Sea of Passage, which Manetho seems to do, provides yet another example of the confusion which reigned in the minds of later Egyptians with regard to the Exodus and the Hyksos Conquest; two events which, notwithstanding Velikovsky's ingenious arguments, were not contemporary.

The Intermediate Period

The Pessimistic Texts are dated by virtually all scholars to a relatively short period of political and economic instability at the end of the Old Kingdom (after Dynasty 6) known as the First Intermediate Period. This epoch is placed after the reigns of the well-known and powerful pyramid-building kings of Dynasties 4, 5 and 6 for the simple reason that the Pessimistic Texts, as well as other evidence, suggests chaotic conditions in the Nile Valley. The Pessimistic Literature, it is held, must post-date the stable pyramid-building epoch.

---

[250]In my *Pyramid Age* (2nd ed. 2022)

Yet one of the most important of the Pessimistic Texts, the well-known Prophecy of Neferty, is attributed to the time of king Sneferu, the first pharaoh of the Fourth Dynasty, who reigned at the demise of the Third Dynasty. For various reasons, but most especially because Sneferu's time is supposed to have been one of great stability and prosperity, most authorities deny the word of the document and decree that Neferty its author could not possibly have lived when he says he does.

The present writer however holds that not only Neferty, but Ipuwer and perhaps some other Pessimistic authors, lived and wrote during the early reign of Sneferu and they were witnesses to the events which ended the life of Sneferu's immediate predecessor on the Double Throne, Huni.[251] For the Pessimistic Texts record the cataclysmic events that brought to an end the Early Dynastic Age. Thus it was Huni, also known as Ra-nefer-ka, or Ka-nefer-ra (Khenephres), last king of the Third Dynasty, who must be identified with the tyrannical king of the Oppression, the pharaoh who ordered the death of the Hebrew children.

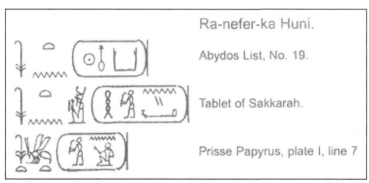

22. Names and titles of Huni (Ra-nefer-ka, or Ka-nefer-ra), last pharaoh of the Third Dynasty, and almost certainly the pharaoh of the Oppression.

This identification is strikingly confirmed by a tradition emanating from Artapanus of Alexandria (third century BC.) and recorded in Eusebius' *Evangelicae Preparationis*. We are told that in an early age a pharaoh named Palmanothes began persecuting the Israelites. His daughter Merris however adopted a Hebrew child who grew up to be Mousos (Moses). Merris herself later became queen when she married pharaoh Khenephres, and Mousos was appointed to administer the land on his behalf. A popular prince, he led a successful military campaign against the invading Ethiopians, a success

---

[251]This is not of course to deny that the texts were not "updated" and added to in later centuries, which they clearly were.

which elicited the jealousy of pharaoh Khenephres. Mousos was therefore forced to flee to Arabia but returned to Egypt to lead the Israelites to freedom when Khenephres died.

It is a strange coincidence, if coincidence is what it is, that the last pharaoh of the Third Dynasty, whom we have, for other reasons entirely, identified as the pharaoh of the Oppression, should bear the same name as the pharaoh identified as the ruler of the Exodus time in an ancient Jewish tradition.

We have already seen how the entire Early Dynastic epoch was punctuated by great upheavals of nature that left their mark both in human tradition and in the record in the ground. Stratigraphic evidence (as for example in Ur in Mesopotamia) shows that the last of these events terminated the Early Dynastic 2 age of that region. Yet the end of the Early Dynastic Age in Mesopotamia is fairly precisely dated to the end of the Third Dynasty in Egypt, and this is demonstrated by very precise cultural parallels. Thus we have the following:

Egypt	Mesopotamia (Ur)
Sixth Dynasty (Pepi I and II)	Akkadian epoch (E. B. 3)
Fifth Dynasty (Sahura)	
Fourth Dynasty (Cheops, Chephren)	Sumerian Early Dynastic 3
	FLOOD EVENT
Second and Third Dynasties	Sumerian Early Dynastic 1 and 2
	FLOOD EVENT
Gerzean (Naqada II) and First Dynasty	Jamdat Nasr
	FLOOD EVENT
Naqada I	Uruk Period
THICK LAYER OF DEBRIS	MAJOR FLOOD, LEAVING DEPOSIT THREE METERS DEEP
Early Badarian (Amratian)	'Ubaid

23. Contemporary cultures and epochs of Egypt and Mesopotamia

Textbook scholarship of course claims to know of no evidence from Egypt or elsewhere suggesting such a dramatic end to the Early Dynastic epoch. The evidence is there in the Pessimistic Literature, but it has been misplaced.

In the chaotic conditions prevailing after the death of pharaoh Huni/ Ka-nefer-ra, local potentates, some related to the royal family, rose to temporary prominence. So, there would indeed have been an "Intermediate" epoch at this time, but it would have been of short duration. After a few months of lawlessness and chaos, order was restored to Egypt by Sneferu. Many of the dignitaries who rose to prominence during the crisis (Neferty's princes who hold sway in the land) held onto their positions under the new regime, and these would later form the basis of the Intermediate Age dynasties, who rose to a really prominent position about 160 years later under the Hyksos. In fact, sometime after the Hyksos Conquest, one of these families, the Inyotefs of Thebes, took on the mantle of freedom fighters. The Akhety princes, however, became clients of the Hyksos, in whose name they waged war against the rulers of Thebes. These events, I suggest, occurred during the time of what is conventionally known as the Sixth Dynasty.

In time, from the ranks of the Theban princes would come the kings who would drive the Hyksos from the land and found the mighty Eighteenth Dynasty.

In another place I have examined the reign of Sneferu in some detail.[252] There it is shown how early in his reign he battled against various desert tribes, as well as Nubians, who sought to exploit Egypt's moment of weakness. One of these tribes was the Amalekites, whom Sneferu repulsed in the Sinai Peninsula. These same Amalekites, an Arabian folk, were the people who had just weeks or perhaps months earlier attacked the Israelites fleeing eastwards out of Egypt. The epic battle at Rephidim, it was said, went in favor of the Israelites so long as Moses could hold his arms aloft. Judging by the complaints of the Pessimistic authors, it would appear fairly certain that the Amalekites (along perhaps with other tribes) actually entered and plundered Lower Egypt. They cannot have found much of value to take from a region so recently dealt such savage blows by nature. In the end, probably no more than a few weeks or months afterwards, Sneferu rallied the Egyptians, expelled the invaders, and restored order.

It seems likely that one of the legends associated with Sneferu, the story of the magician Djadjaemankh, who parted the waters of the royal lake after a servant-girl had lost a hair-pendant in the water, is a vague reflection of the parting of the waters at the Sea of Passage near Pi-Khiroth.

Later generations of Egyptians remembered Sneferu with fondness. He was known as "the Beneficent King" and his epoch viewed as a Golden Age.[253] Indeed, Sneferu himself was recalled in terms not at all dissimilar to those of

---

[252]In *The Pyramid Age* (2006)
[253]See, e.g., M. Rice, op cit., pp. 197-8.

his contemporary Moses. Like Moses, he led his people through an unparalleled crisis to safety and security. But there was one other similarity. Just as Moses gave his people a new religion based on the worship of one invisible god, so the epoch of Sneferu saw in Egypt the abandonment of the old region of planet and star worship, with all its bloody rituals. From the start of the Fourth Dynasty a new type of religion emerged. The Pyramid Texts, which were probably composed in the Fourth Dynasty (though inscribed in the chambers of the Fifth and Sixth Dynasty pyramids), the god Atum is described in terms that verge on monotheism. Furthermore, there is now evidence of a moral development that has astonished scholars. Commoners and kings express an awareness of moral issues hardly less advanced than those of classical Greece or Rome, or Christian Rome, for that matter. "It is," wrote James Henry Breasted, "as it were, an isolated moral vista down which we look, penetrating the early gloom as a shaft of sunshine penetrates the darkness."[254]

The same shaft of sunshine, we might note, penetrated through the Burning Bush at Horeb and enlightened the minds of the Hebrews.

Horeb, the Mountain of God

Both the El Arish shrine and the Book of Exodus identify a place called Pi Khiroth as the site of the dramatic events at the Sea of Passage. Biblical sources also link a place called Baal Zaphon to the same event. Quite possibly Pi Khiroth was on the Egyptian side of the sea, whilst Baal Zaphon, with its Semitic name, was on the opposite shore.

One of the perennial questions of biblical history is the location of this spot, so important to Jewish history. Another, related question, is the location of the Mountain of God, named Horeb or Sinai, on whose summit Moses is said to have received the Ten Commandments shortly after the dramatic escape at the *Yam Suf*. The official site of the latter is what is now called Mount Sinai on the Sinai Peninsula. Yet there is much evidence, both from the Scriptures themselves and from later Jewish tradition (as recorded, for example, in Josephus) which would suggest a location in north-western Arabia — ancient Midian. In fact, the Exodus account itself makes a location in Midian virtually inevitable, as Moses meets his father-in-law, Jethro (of Midian), *before* he ascends the holy mountain (Exodus 18).

The controversy has recently been ignited anew by two American writers/adventurers, Bob Cornuke and Larry Williams, who managed to get

---

[254] J. H. Breasted, *The Development of Religion and Thought in Ancient Egypt* (London, 1912), p. 170.

into Saudi Arabia — where tourism as such is illegal — and investigate the Midian region. What they found there was a strong local tradition about Moses and Jethro and an insistence that the nearby Jebel al-Lawz was Horeb, Moses' Mountain of God.[255] Although the Jebel al-Lawz has long been known to scholars as a possible candidate for Horeb, its claims have never received wide publicity, or been widely supported, owing mainly to the strength of tradition surrounding the so-called Mount Sinai, in the Sinai Peninsula, the location favored by Constantine the Great's mother Helena. After Helena's time, the claims of other sites were pushed into the background and gradually all but forgotten. Nor has the situation improved in recent years, when the attitude of the Saudi authorities has made archeological investigation in the Midian region all but impossible. Indeed, Jebel al-Lawz is now a forbidden region and it is a criminal offence (punishable by a very long jail sentence or perhaps worse) to climb it.

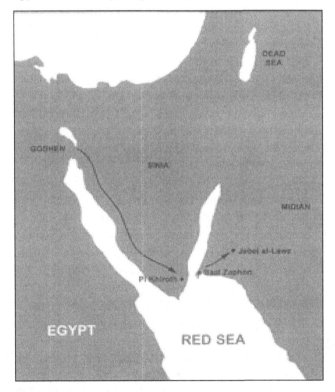

24. Probable route of the Exodus, taking into consideration all available evidence.

[255]Bob Cornuke and Larry Williams, *In Search of the Mountain of God* (Broadman and Holman Books, 2000).

Nevertheless, the mountain and its environs have been investigated by a few daring souls over the past decade and a half. One of these, David Fasold, was apprehended by the authorities and put on trial. Another, Ron Wyatt, did not actually climb the mountain, but he claimed to have found, at the base of the peak, much evidence to corroborate its identification with Horeb/Sinai. The most successful investigation to date, the one that has renewed the debate, was by Cornuke and Williams, whose book, *In Search of the Mountain of God*, has caused something of a sensation. Like Wyatt, Cornuke and Williams appear to have discovered much corroborating evidence in the environs of Jebel al-Lawz, such as for example carved images of an Egyptian-style cow-deity (Hathor), as well as a cyclopean altar upon which sacrifices could have been offered, but it is what they found at the summit that is the most interesting. The peak of the mountain was found to be blackened and scorched, as if by searing heat. The latter fact is actually readily observable from the ground. Now this is most strange, since the mountain is not a volcano. At the summit Williams, a trained geologist, examined some of the rocks, which he deemed to be composed of obsidian (volcanic glass) or a material closely resembling obsidian.[256] But, it is highly significant that, upon splitting the rocks open, the core was found to be unscorched, not obsidian but of the original sandstone-like rock of the mountain.[257]

Cornuke and Williams are both born-again Christians and for them this was nothing less than the physical evidence of one of the Bible's greatest miracles: the actual "Fire of God" which is said to have covered the peak of Horeb during the Israelites' sojourn there.

For the present writer, as a student of catastrophism, the evidence was scarcely less sensational. What force could have melted the rocks at the Jebel's summit, leaving them resembling volcanic glass? The most immediate answer is the immensely powerful thunderbolts which, Velikovsky insisted, were a fundamentally important (and terrifying) part of the phenomena surrounding the Exodus. An elevated spot like a mountain-top would of course be one of the prime targets of such divine bolts. And this is fully confirmed by the Book of Exodus. There we are told:

> Now at daybreak ... there were peals of thunder and flashes of lightning, dense cloud on the mountain and a very loud trumpet blast; and, in the camp, all the people trembled. Then Moses led the people out of the camp to meet God; and they took their stand at the bottom of the mountain. Mount Sinai was entirely wrapped in smoke, because

---

[256]Ibid., pp. 71-78.
[257]Ibid.

Yahweh had descended on it in the form of fire. The smoke rose like smoke from a furnace and the whole mountain shook violently.[258]

So, yet another piece of evidence fits into place. Once again, it is the conventional scholars, and not the catastrophists, who are puzzled. If the Jebel al-Lawz was Horeb, this also means that Pi Khiroth and Baal Zaphon were located on either side of the narrow Strait of Tiran at the southern end of the Gulf of Aqaba. And this brings us onto another important consideration. The Gulf of Aqaba is part of the Great Rift Valley, a tectonic meeting point stretching from the Jordan Valley in the north to central Africa in the south. It is one of the world's most volcanically active regions. Now, it has been suggested by more than one writer that the parting of the waters could have been the result of an immense subterranean telluric force generating a powerful electro-magnetic charge which temporarily separated the shallow sea. And it is here, and here alone, at the Strait of Tiran, the narrow entrance to the Gulf, that the sea is shallow enough to permit such a crossing. As Cornuke and Williams noted, a narrow underwater "causeway", running just a few meters below the sea's surface, connects the southern tip of the Sinai Peninsula with the Arabian coast. On either side of this "causeway", the sea descends sharply into a deep trench. And it is quite possible that this underwater highway had a recent volcanic origin.

But if the Sea of Passage was at the Strait of Tiran, why would Moses (or whoever it was led the fleeing Israelites) have taken the exiles so far south, into what is basically a dead end, at the southern end of the Sinai Peninsula? Could he have intended to ferry his followers across the Strait to his second home, Midian? That is a possibility, though it begs the question: From what materials would the fleeing Israelites have composed their ferries or rafts? The whole area is utterly barren of vegetation, supporting little more than a few acadia bushes in the wadi valleys. It is possible that the Israelites had intended to use inflated buoys made of animal skins. Bearing in mind, however, that in those days the region was not so arid as now, and the Sinai Peninsula, as well as much of North Africa and Arabia, was full of acacia and sycamore forests, it is possible that the intention was to construct wooden rafts or boats with which to effect the evacuation. The arrival of an Egyptian army bent on annihilating the slaves would, of course, have made such an enterprise impossible. It was just at this point, when the terrified fugitives seemed doomed to annihilation, that nature intervened and provided a seemingly miraculous means of escape.

---

[258]Exodus 19: 16-19. It should be noted that the Mount Sinai in the Sinai Peninsula is neither volcanic nor does it display any signs of scorching. On this ground alone it seems a very unlikely candidate for Mount Horeb.

The objection may be raised, as it frequently is, that such an event, happening at just the right time for the Israelites, is just too convenient, and therefore could not have happened. Yet coincidences do happen, and surely it was the extraordinary nature of this coincidence, as well as its timeliness, that convinced future generations of Israelites that they were a "chosen people". If not this, then how to explain such a strange idea?[259]

If the Sea of Passage really was at the entrance to the Gulf of Aqaba, as much evidence seems to indicate, no longer can the Yam Suf be dismissed as a Sea of Reeds. The Israelites, it appears, crossed a real arm of the sea, an event which occurred under catastrophic conditions of some sort.

The End of a World Age

The catastrophic end of the Early Dynastic period, the Age of Sacrifice (as Hindu tradition names it) is very clearly marked in Mesopotamia by a flood layer, a layer which immediately preceded the rise of the Akkadians. No major upheavals of nature, on a similar scale, are reported afterwards. The true nature and extent of his upheaval has already been hinted at. This seems to have been the catastrophe that made a desert of the Sahara and altered the climate and topography of many parts of the world. As we have seen earlier, Velikovsky believed that cosmic upheavals were occurring as recently as the early seventh century BC, and he linked these later events with the god Mars. He argued that Mars had come on a near-collision course with the Great Comet (the Cosmic Serpent), and that a titanic "battle" in the skies, clearly witnessed by the inhabitants of the earth, ensued. As a result of this encounter the serpent lost its tail, or was "decapitated" (hence the world-wide myth of a decapitated dragon), and ceased to be a threat to our planet. However, the encounter between Mars and the comet destabilized the former and led to a further, final series of calamities on the earth.

Whether or not we agree with Velikovsky's analysis, it seems beyond reasonable doubt that some event or rather series of events within the Solar System caused immense disruption on the earth at this time. Events which could dramatically and suddenly change our planet's climate must have been of truly cosmic dimensions. An asteroid or meteorite impact solution will simply not suffice. Furthermore, it has to be stressed that all ancient traditions speak of a time when there was an unstable Solar System, with the members of that system wandering confusedly throughout the firmament.

---

[259]Extra-biblical Jewish tradition, as Velikovsky noted, claimed that many Israelites, as well as their Egyptian enemies, died at the Sea of Passage.

As I have argued in detail elsewhere, Moses is mythologically related to the gods Mars and Mercury and, more specifically, to their alter-egos, Heracles/Perseus.[260] Without going into the details here, it should be noted that, like Heracles, Moses was the enemy of the serpent-god, and his destruction of the two serpents of the pharaoh's magicians recalls Heracles' destruction of the two serpents sent by Hera to kill him in his cradle. Like Heracles, Moses had a mysterious birth, and there is a suggestion of a divine father. Certainly Moses' rescue from the waters of the Nile, to which he had been consigned in a basket, is precisely paralleled by that of Perseus, who was rescued from the sea after being confined, along with his mother, in a sealed chest which his father cast adrift. Heracles' pushing apart of the Pillars at the Straits of Gibraltar, which henceforth bore his name, is rather obviously paralleled by Moses' "pushing apart" of the waters at the Sea of Passage, whilst Moses' end offers a very precise likeness to that of Heracles: Both men did not really die, in the normal sense, but disappeared from the view of men after ascending a mountain: Nebo in the case of Moses and Oeta in the case of Heracles.

In fact, the god/deity Mars or Ares is intimately connected to the whole Exodus drama, as is evinced by the participation in it of Michael, the archetypal dragon slayer. He it was who produced the pillar of fire which blocked the path of the pharaoh's army as it approached the trapped Israelites. Velikovsky admitted the central importance of Michael in the narrative, but curiously failed to identify him as a Mars/Heracles figure. This was no doubt due to the fact that, adhering strictly to the chronology of the Bible, Velikovsky believed the Exodus to have occurred around 1450 BC, at the very time he placed his Ishtar/comet catastrophe. To have placed Moses in what Velikovsky described as the Age of Mars (i.e., the eighth and seventh centuries BC) would have implied a radical questioning of biblical chronology, something he could not countenance.

And this highlights our major point of disagreement with Velikovsky. Whilst Velikovsky more or less accepted the dates provided in the textbooks for the rise of the Near Eastern cultures (i.e., circa 3200 BC) — a date which was, of course, originally founded on biblical time scales — the findings of the present volume suggest that no high civilization existed anywhere before circa 1300 BC. This of course implies a radical reinterpretation of the stratigraphy, as well as a re-examination of the historical events described in Genesis and Exodus, with a view to finding how they relate to stratigraphy. We can agree with Velikovsky that there was an Age of Isthar/Venus in the second millennium BC and an Age of Mars in the tenth to seventh

---

[260]See my *Pyramid Age*

centuries BC, but these World Ages cannot be connected to the biblical events to which they have been linked by Velikovsky. Ishtar/Isis/Venus was the goddess of the Flood, as all ancient mythologies make perfectly clear. Her epoch is rightly placed in the early to mid- second millennium BC but has nothing whatsoever to do with the Exodus, which was clearly linked to Mars/Heracles. This means, in effect, that the last of the catastrophic destructions which left their signature at Ur in Mesopotamia, the disaster which brought to an end the Early Dynastic Age, must be dated around the start of the tenth century BC.

This then marks the last of the great cosmic upheavals. They did not continue into the seventh century BC, as Velikovsky believed, though evidence shows that during the eighth and even seventh centuries our planet continued to be affected by powerful earthquakes and tremors, as the tectonic system gradually stabilized after the last great cosmic quake. Yet these were in the nature of "after-shocks" and cannot be compared with the truly cataclysmic events occurring earlier.

This final cataclysm left its signature throughout the planet. There were immense and sudden changes in climate everywhere. Immense and prolonged earthquake activity accompanied these changes. In some areas land and sea changed places. From this epoch comes the stories, recalled in almost every culture, of sunken or lost kingdoms. These stories are particularly prevalent along the western seaboard of Europe, where for example the Irish told of a sunken land named Hy Brasil or Tir na nOg, the Welsh of the lost regions of Llys Helig and Cantref Gwaelod and the Bretons of the sunken kingdom of Lyonesse. These are well-known, yet every single western European nation, as well as the nations of North Africa, has a similar legend. It might be noted also that the native peoples of the Americas, on the other side of the ocean, have almost identical traditions.

There seems little doubt that these stories are connected with, or perhaps were the source of, the Atlantis myth.

It was not only the Israelites who set out in search of a new home in the midst of these dramatic events. Vast population movements occurred. Traditions in western Europe for example make it abundantly clear that it was these events which spurred the first of the great Celtic migrations. Traditions in both Ireland and Wales insist that the Celtic ancestors of these nations arrived in the British Isles amidst violent upheavals of nature. We are told of great inundations of the sea, of rivers and lakes appearing and disappearing overnight and of frightening portents in the skies.

The same traditions tell us in no uncertain terms that the megalithic structures which still dot the landscape of these regions were raised in the immediate aftermath of these events. It has already been noted of course that the megalith-building epoch is a phenomenon directly related to the final catastrophic episode. These monuments, built securely of enormous polygonal blocks of stone to withstand the seismic disturbances of the period, were intended to be temples cum observatories, where religious rituals were enacted to ensure the continuing stability of the cosmic order.

In this regard it should be noted that in Stonehenge the lintels are secured to the uprights with mortise and tenon joints, a feature completely redundant in the earthquake-free environment of modern Britain but by no means redundant in the environment described in Welsh and Irish literature.

Chapter 6. Moses and His Works

The Authorship of Genesis

According to tradition, the Pentateuch or Torah (i.e., the books of Genesis, Exodus, Leviticus, Deuteronomy and Numbers) was written by Moses. This claim had always been accepted as substantially true until the middle of the nineteenth century, when scholarship turned an increasingly critical eye to the Scriptures. After the Evolution controversy had discredited the first part of Genesis, a whole new genre of biblical exegesis arose. The main proponents of this new thinking were the scholars of the Berlin school, whose work during the last decades of the nineteenth century systematically demolished the credibility of much of the Old Testament. Finally, under the influence of men such as Eduard Meyer, Karl Heinrich Graf and Julius Wellhausen, the very existence of major biblical figures was called into question. It was demonstrated by Graf and Wellhausen that the Torah was the work of more than one author and was a comparatively late composition, probably dating from no earlier than the sixth or seventh century BC. Two main contributors (named the Yahwist and the Elohist authors) were initially identified, though over the years that number has been added to. Modern biblical scholars in fact now talk of at least four contributors or groups of contributors. In addition to the Yahwist and Elohist, two other major traditions are identified: one known as the Deuteronomic, which introduced additions and revisions by Levites after the fall of the Kingdom of Israel; and one the work of editors after the Exile, known as the priestly tradition. One of the latter is named the Redactor and identified (somewhat tentatively) as

Ezra, who is reckoned to have flourished sometime in the fifth century BC or later.

The end result of these discoveries has been a veritable debunking of early Hebrew tradition. We are told that there is no agreement on just how the final Torah was produced. Documentary approaches such as Wellhausen's classic formulation see it as an act of redaction, in which an editor (Ezra) took the four sources — a 9th century Yahwist, 8th century Elohist, and 6th century Priestly source (the Deuteronomist is not present in Exodus) — and combined them with minimal changes. Thus Richard Elliott Friedman's *The Bible with Sources Revealed* (2003) is a modern documentary hypothesis more or less identical with Wellhausen but accepting Yehezkel Kaufmann's dating of the Priestly source to the early 7th century. By contrast, John Van Seters and Rolf Rendtorff see the Torah as a process of progressive supplementation in which generations of authors added to and edited each other, although Van Seters sees the final author as a late, 5th century, Yahwist, whereas Rendtorff views it ultimately as a product of the Priestly school. R. N. Whybray, whose *The Making of the Pentateuch* (1987) was a seminal critique of the methodology and assumptions of the documentary hypothesis, has proposed that the creation of Exodus and the Torah was the action of a single author, working from a host of fragments. The only areas of agreement between these views is that the terms 'Yahwist', 'Priestly' and 'Deuteronomist' do have some meaning in terms of identifiable and differentiable content and style, and that the final Torah emerged in the 5th century BC.[261]

Thus the Torah, it is now accepted, could not possibly be attributed to Moses, even if such a person existed. If however the Exodus occurred early in the tenth century BC, as we claim, the question of the book's authorship takes on an entirely new meaning. If this is correct, it becomes perfectly reasonable to assume that a body of material dating from the time of the Exodus could have formed the foundations of the Torah — even if we accept the later refinements of the various other contributors and editors.

I do not thereby suggest for one minute that these books were written by a man named Moses during years of wandering in the desert. Van Seters for example proved that much of Genesis, including the entire Abraham narrative, can only have received its present form in the seventh century or even later.[262] The whole work is full of anachronisms. One example worthy of mention here is the occurrence of camels in the patriarch stories. Abraham and his contemporaries are said in Genesis to have regularly employed

---

[261]See e.g., John J. Collins, *The Bible after Babel: Historical Criticism in a Postmodern Age* (Eerdmans, 2005)

[262]John Van Seters, *Abraham in History and Tradition* (Yale, 1975).

camels. Yet it is well-known that dromedaries were not domesticated until the seventh century BC.[263] Again, the story of the six days of creation is evidently a late monotheistic attempt to explain why the week has seven days, without recourse to mentioning the celestial gods whom the days were named for (i.e., the five planets visible to the naked eye, plus the sun and moon).

Thus the Book of Genesis almost certainly dates from the period of strictly enforced monotheism — namely the Persian Age or even later; and we can agree with Van Seters that the work we now possess, in the form we have it, dates from that time. The Book of Exodus itself presents similar problems. The story of Moses' birth and infancy, for example, have all the iconographic hallmarks of the mythical divine child, and the story's relationship to other myths of the same type hardly needs to be stressed. Thus Perseus, for example, is also placed in a chest or box and cast into the waters, and this is a fate shared too by the Celtic god Lugh or Lugos. Again, in the present study, we have proposed locating the Exodus narrative in the Early Bronze Age (though we have brought this epoch down into the eleventh and tenth centuries BC), which means that Moses' story too contains many anachronisms. The mention of chariots, for example, both in the Joseph and Moses narratives, can only be anachronistic, since such machines were unknown in Egypt prior to the time of the Hyksos, which we place in the late ninth and eighth centuries BC. And the same may be said of various other details of the two books.

The Berlin scholars were thus correct in saying that the Torah we now possess, in the form that we have it, could not have taken shape before the sixth or even fifth century BC. Nevertheless, it seems reasonable to suppose that the seventh and/or sixth century editors had pre-existing sources upon which to work. If Moses led the Israelites from Egypt at the end of the eleventh century or the beginning of the tenth, it is quite probable that a body of sayings, hymns and poems attributed to the great man were there to be worked upon; and if such a body of material did exist, most or all of it should have entered the Torah in its final form. We would expect to be able to detect such material by its obvious Egyptian influence. Moses, after all, was a prince of Egypt who threw in his lot with the Hebrew slaves, and those slaves themselves had probably, during their long stay in the land of the Nile, absorbed many elements of Egyptian culture.

Does the Torah then display any such influence?

---

[263]The earliest illustration of the domesticated dromedary comes from Neo-Assyrian bas-reliefs believed to date from the seventh century BC. In reality, however, these belong to the fifth century, as the Neo-Assyrian king responsible, Ashurbanipal, is actually an alter-ego of the Persian Darius II. (See my *Egypt's Ramesside Pharaohs and the Persians*, 2021).

Over the past number of years research has demonstrated that the entire Pentateuch is permeated with material of Egyptian origin, a fact that was totally unexpected and which has astonished the critics. The problem is that scholars such as Graf and Wellhausen reached their conclusions before Egyptology had fully matured, and they were unable to identify as Egyptian those elements that are now openly recognized as such. The definitive work on this, A.S. Yahuda's *The Language of the Pentateuch in its Relation to Egyptian*, came out in 1933. As an Egyptologist with intimate knowledge of Hebrew, Yahuda was uniquely qualified to tackle the subject, and what he discovered shattered many of the conclusions of the Berlin exegetes.

Yahuda's great work, which is of such fundamental importance in understanding the Patriarch epoch, has been only grudgingly accepted by the scholarly world. However, a full-blooded reappraisal has now been undertaken by three Australian scholars: Damien Mackey, Frank Calneggia and Paul Money. In an article entitled, "A Critical Reappraisal of the Book of Genesis", Mackey, Calneggia and Money trace the development of Yahuda's thought and add some pertinent observations of their own.[264] Yahuda, they hold, "throws out a challenge" to biblical hypercriticism. His line of argument is that, "if by comparison with Egyptian it could be proved that the Egyptian influence on Hebrew was 'so extensive that the development and perfection of this language can only be accounted for and explained by that influence,' then it would be quite clear that it can only have happened in 'common Hebrew-Egyptian environment!'."[265] The only period in Israelite history "during which there existed the sort of close intimacy necessary for that degree of influence of Egyptian on the Hebrew language ... was the 'Egyptian Epoch'."[266]

Yahuda held that the hundred years or so during which the Israelites were exiled in Egypt must have made a profound impact on the language and culture of the people. The Canaanite dialect which they brought to Egypt could not but have absorbed Egyptian elements, "and in the adaptation to the Egyptian [must] have continued to develop, to extend, and even to modify its original grammatical form and syntactical structure."[267] Yahuda explained that the influence of one language upon another was revealed by three major characteristics:

---

[264]Mackey, Calneggia and Money, "A Critical Reappraisal of the Book of Genesis," Society for Interdisciplinary Studies: Catastrophism and Chronology Workshop No.2 (1987).
[265]Ibid., p. 4
[266]Ibid.
[267] A. S. Yahuda, op cit., p. xxxiii.

1. the adoption of loan-words;
2. the coining of new words and expressions, which could include technical terms, metaphors and turns of speech;
3. the adoption of grammatical elements and some of the syntactical rules of the alien tongue.

Yahuda showed quite clearly that all three conditions were met in early Hebrew, and that this was observable primarily in the language of the Torah, that part of the Bible attributed to Moses.

Egyptian Elements in the Creation and Flood Stories

Contrary to popular belief, the Hebrew account of creation does not owe its origin to the Babylonian. Mesopotamian influences there are, but these are primeval, and do not derive from the period of the Babylonian Exile. Yet, as Mackey, Calneggia and Money demonstrate in some detail, the Hebrew creation story is also heavily permeated with Egyptian elements. As Yahuda himself showed, the only parts of the Bible that actually do show an unmistakable late Babylonian influence are those parts which deal with the Babylonian Exile and events subsequent to it. Mackey, Calneggia and Money remark how, "it is an amazing fact that where there are similar details in the Genesis account of Creation and in the Akkadian myths, almost without exception the Akkadian uses different words and expressions from the Hebrew. Yahuda notes that whilst some Akkadian words and expressions were used in the Hebrew, they do not occur in the Genesis story. But it is quite another matter when we come to consider the dependence of the Genesis narratives on Egyptian. Whilst, perhaps, we may have expected a strong Egyptian influence on that part of the Book of Genesis which deals with Joseph and the 'Egyptian Epoch' of Israel, we find that *the entire book* is saturated with Egyptian elements."[268] The conclusion Yahuda drew from this was that the whole of Genesis was "written from an Egyptian perspective."[269]

The total evidence is substantial, but the following may be regarded as a representative sample.

The Hebrew term *bereshith*, which begins the Creation story, is found on close inspection to be "an exact adaptation of the Egyptian expression *tpy.t*, [which means] ... 'earliest time' or 'primeval time'. Just as *bereshith* is formed from the Hebrew word for 'head', so also is the Egyptian word formed for the word for 'head'."[270]

---

[268] Mackey, Calneggia and Money, loc. cit.
[269] Yahuda, op. cit., p. xxix.
[270] Mackey, Calneggia and Money, loc. cit., p. 5.

Uniquely amongst the Semitic languages, the Hebrew word for "heaven" was supposedly derived from the Akkadian Tiamat, the monster of darkness which Marduk slew and which was reputed to have sent the Flood. However, it is clear that neither Tiamat nor anything resembling such a monster, occurs in the Genesis account. Indeed, since there are virtually no points of similarity between the Hebrew and Babylonian creation stories, "there is [therefore] no intrinsic ground whatever for the identification of tehem with tiamat."[271]

In the Hebrew Garden of Eden there was "every kind of tree that is pleasant to the sight and good for food" (Gen. 2:9). The Egyptians too had their "Garden of God", *ken ntr*, where there grew all kinds of trees with sweet fruits, such as sycamores, figs, dates and vines and other "lovely trees", *ht ndm*.[272] Of even more importance however is the fact that among the trees of the Egyptian Paradise was also the "Tree of Life".[273] Yahuda went into some detail on this and was very explicit that the Egyptian *ht n 'nh*, "Tree of Life", "corresponds literally with the Hebrew phrase in Genesis 2:9."[274]

The term applied to the serpent in Genesis (which is made to crawl on its belly) also has its exact parallel in Egyptian terminology. According to Yahuda, it is the equivalent of the Egyptian *hyr h.t-f*, "that (which goes) on its belly", a term applied to snakes and reptiles generally. Also, the condemnation of the serpent to the eating of dust is paralleled precisely in the Egyptian verse, "Behold their sustenance [food] shall be Geb [earth]".

Yahuda held that the Flood story proved his thesis that the Babylonian legends were later versions of the Hebrew originals, a view which the present author cannot subscribe to. Nevertheless, he does demonstrate fairly convincingly that the Hebrew story is an archaic original, not a late derivation of the Babylonian myth. Crucially, the main feature of the Genesis Flood story, the Ark, is designated neither by an Akkadian word nor a Canaanite one, but an Egyptian one. The Hebrew word used (*tebhah*) has been recognized as deriving from the Egyptian *db.t*, a "box", "coffer", or "chest". In the words of Yahuda, "It is astonishing that a narrative supposedly set in Babylonia, uses for the Ark an Egyptian loan-word!"[275]

---

[271]Ibid., p. 6
[272]Ibid.
[273]Ibid.
[274]Yahuda, op. cit., p. 193.
[275]Ibid., p. 205

25. Sacred Barque of Amon, from the time of Thutmose III. The Ark of the Covenant was almost certainly such a vessel. Note in particular the protective spirits, or angels, whose appearance precisely parallels that of the protective angels of the Ark, as described in Scriptures.

Mackey et al. stress here that the same Hebrew word also occurs in the story of the discovery of the child Moses. We should note too that in Egyptian legend it is in a *db.t* or chest that Osiris is imprisoned before being cast into the Nile by Set, and we have already suggested a close link between some elements in the stories of Moses and Osiris. The very chest of Osiris, we are told by the Egyptians, floated down the Nile and was washed up in Canaan (in Byblos). According to Mackey, Calneggia and Money, the use of the Egyptian term *tebhah* in both the Flood and Moses stories is highly significant and calls for a comparative look at the two accounts. "Such a comparison," they say, "is all the more instructive for our whole thesis as, on the one hand, it clearly reveals the Egyptian character of the Flood narrative and, on a secondary level, shows how much more powerfully Egyptian influences prevailed in the Exodus narrative. Whereas here for the nature of timber and the kind of pitch, the Akkadian words *giparu* and *kupru* are traceable, the Egyptian word *kme*, 'Nile rushes', is used to denominate the material of the ark of Moses."[276]

This of course is just as it should be. Originating in Mesopotamia around 1300 BC, the Hebrews themselves introduced much of the culture of that

---

[276]Mackey, Calneggia and Money, loc. cit., p. 6.

region into Egypt. The Flood was the most important event of early folk-tradition, and we must regard it as highly unlikely that all of the Mesopotamian elements of that story could have been lost, even after a prolonged stay in Egypt. By the time of the Exodus, however, around 1000 BC, the Hebrews had absorbed much of Egyptian culture. The very names of several of the most important Exodus characters, Moses, Aaron, Hur, Assir, Phineas (Phinehas), Hophni, and Miriam, are recognizably Egyptian.[277] Now even events linked to Mesopotamia began to be viewed through the lens of Egyptian culture. Thus the Ark of Noah is called by an Egyptian name; so too, it should be said, is the Ark of the Covenant, wherein the nomadic Israelites house the commandments that Yahweh bequeathed to Moses atop the holy mountain.

The Ark of the Covenant, as a sacred barque, has other links to Egypt. For many ancient peoples the boat had religious connotations. But among the people of the Nile valley the boat was par excellence the vessel in which the gods travelled. Above all, the sun-god was endlessly portrayed in his sacred barque sailing across the skies during the day and in the seas of the Underworld at night. The Ark of the Covenant was almost certainly a vessel of this type.

Thus all of Genesis and Exodus is full of Egyptian phrases, terms, idioms and cultural influence in general. When we look at the Joseph narrative, which takes up almost a quarter of Genesis, we find the same to be true, only more so. Indeed, as we saw in Chapter 3, the Joseph narrative is so thoroughly Egyptian in character that a number of commentators (and not just Yahuda) regard these chapters as based on original Egyptian documentary material.

As we have seen, Joseph's life-story agrees very closely with that of the great Imhotep, who was himself apparently named after the Syrian/Canaanite god Im-Saphon. One important detail of the Joseph narrative not already alluded to is that of Joseph's life span. We are told that he died at the ripe old age of 110. Once again, this reflects Egyptian usage — specifically archaic Egyptian usage. On the famous Papyrus Prisse, for example, which almost certainly dates from the Hyksos period, 110 years is declared to be the ideal lifespan, whilst on the Papyrus Anastasia IV, dating from the same period, we read, "Fulfil 110 years on the earth, whilst thy limbs are vigorous."[278] Also,

---

[277] It is striking that all of these belonged to the Israelite leadership or priestly class, strongly suggesting close connections between the Israelite leadership and the Egyptian priesthood. This is further confirmed by the apparently intimate knowledge of Egyptian religious/magical practice and belief displayed in the account of the confrontation between Aaron and Moses and the Egyptian sorcerers/priests. See e.g., Scott B Noegel "The Egyptian Magicians' Symposium: Envisaging the Exodus Story: Meet the Egyptians, The Torah.com January 2023 www.thetorah.com

[278] Gaston Maspero, *The Dawn of Civilisation* (London, 1884), p. 198.

a granite statue in Vienna is inscribed with a prayer to Isis to grant health and happiness for 110 years.

The fact that the above parallels are with Hyksos-age usage underlines what we have already suggested, namely, that Moses and the Exodus were either contemporary with, or slightly preceded, the Hyksos epoch.

In view of the all-pervading Egyptian influence in Genesis and the rest of the Torah, it must, we conclude, be regarded as perfectly feasible that a figure whom tradition named "Moses" could have composed parts of these texts as a form of epic poem, or rather series of poems, using the traditions of the Hebrews combined with those of the Egyptians. When the Jewish scribes of a later age came to compiling their traditions in an orderly form, they would no doubt then have had at their disposal a large body of "Moses" material, all claiming to date from the time of the great leader but much of which would have been added during the period of Wandering and the Judges. Some of this material they "updated" and "improved", adding, for example, to the Patriarch narratives the mention of camels because at their time all great leaders should have possessed many camels.

Such updating and re-editing no doubt occurred many times before the Torah we now possess took its final shape. But the original ancient core of the literature remained largely untouched and formed the basis of the final version. That ancient core, we suggest, is the work of the "Yahwist" author. Scholarship regards this material as dating from the 9th or 8th century, precisely where we, for other reasons entirely, have placed Moses and the Exodus. Yahweh, as the Torah itself hints on numerous occasions, was peculiarly the God of Moses. It therefore seems perfectly reasonable to suppose that the "Yahwist" work was the body of literature dating from the Exodus or shortly thereafter round which the later Torah was constructed.

Moses the Lawgiver

Moses was the lawgiver *par excellence* of Hebrew history. To him were attributed the voluminous rules, regulations and commandments laid down in the books of Exodus, Leviticus, Numbers and Deuteronomy. The laws and customs governing the lives of pious Jews almost all owe their origin to Moses.

Now the legal and moral code set down in the Torah is by no means unique in the ancient world. Other nations had their legal codes set down in sacred books, and these were also composed by prophets and seers. Thus for example the Persians had their Zend Avesta, written by Zarathustra, founder of Zoroastrianism. In the Greek world, too, there were moral and legal codes set down by prophetic figures. We may mention the laws of Lycurgus of

Sparta, a system that may be regarded as a Greek version of the Mosaic code.[279] Roughly contemporary with Lycurgus was the Athenian lawgiver, Medon. He it was who abolished the monarchy and set up the system of life-archons, as well as establishing many of the customs and institutions by which the Athenians ever-afterwards lived.[280] In Rome, too, we find that Romulus, the semi-legendary founder of the city, was regarded as a great legislator, and many of Rome's most enduring customs and institutions were attributed to him.[281]

The problem with the above figures is that they all date from the eighth or seventh centuries BC. Zarathustra, for example, is said to have been born around 625 BC. The epoch of Lycurgus is less clearly defined, but using the Spartan king-lists of Herodotus we may calculate that he too lived sometime in the seventh century. Romulus is said to have founded Rome in 732 BC.

These facts clearly illustrate something well-known to the Berlin exegetes: namely that the Mosaic Code could not possibly date from earlier than the eighth or seventh century BC. The entire religious, cultural, historical and even linguistic context of the Mosaic Law is clearly that of the eighth/seventh century. It was on precisely these grounds that Wellhausen and the others cast doubt on the historical value of the entire Torah. Since it was obvious that the books of the Mosaic Law belonged to the great epoch of lawmaking and law-giving from the eighth century to the sixth, how could a man named Moses have led the Israelites from Egypt in the fifteenth century, as the Scriptures claimed?

A veritable religious and cultural revolution therefore occurred throughout the ancient world during the eighth and seventh centuries, though why this should be the case has never been adequately explained. Indeed, until Velikovsky, no explanation at all had been forthcoming. However, as we saw in Chapters 1, 2 and 3, Velikovsky's thesis would suggest that catastrophic episodes inspired revolutionary change in all spheres of life. It has been shown, for example, that the cataclysms of the Abraham/Menes epoch (which we date to circa 1300-1200 BC.) helped to inaugurate literate civilization. It was the disasters of that time which initiated the practice of blood sacrifice and prompted the erection of the first temples in which to perform them.

In the same way, then, the great disasters of the eleventh/tenth century inspired another cultural revolution. It can be shown, for example, how the

---

[279]The most extensive description of Lycurgus and his epoch is contained in Plutarch's *Parallel Lives.*

[280]See, e.g., A.R. Burn, *The Lyric Age of Greece* (London, 1967), p. 22.

[281]Livy, *The Early History of Rome* i, 7; "Having performed with proper ceremony his religious duties, he [Romulus] summoned his subjects and gave them laws, without which the creation of a unified body politic would not have been possible."

megalith-building epoch (and I include in this the huge smooth-sided pyramids of Fourth Dynasty Egypt and the tholos tombs of Greece, as well as the megaliths of western Europe) began during the tenth and ninth centuries. These structures were erected of enormous blocks of stone specifically to withstand the continual earth-tremors that were so much a feature of the period. But the reason for building the monuments lay in the skies rather than on the earth. Events in the heavens produced a religious revolution. In his description of Cheops, Herodotus clearly described the builder of the Great Pyramid as a religious reformer. We are told that he closed Egypt's temples and that they remained closed during the reign of his successor Chephren.[282] It was in the temples, of course, that the blood sacrifices which had been the hallmark of the Early Dynastic epoch were performed.[283]

The movement away from blood sacrifice was to become symptomatic of all the religious innovations of the tenth, ninth, and eighth centuries. Thus, in Greece of the Heroic Age (which is properly placed between the ninth and seventh centuries) we find numerous characters involved in abolishing human sacrifice. Theseus, for example, is performing precisely that role when he slays the man-eating Minotaur, housed in the recesses of the Labyrinth at Knossos. The same achievement is repeatedly accredited to the god Hercules (Herakles), a contemporary of Theseus, who is said to have abolished human sacrifice in Egypt, among other places.[284]

The identity of Hercules, and his relationship to the era of Moses, as well as to Samson and the Judges, is a subject I deal with extensively in another place.[285] Here it is sufficient to emphasize that the links between Greece's Heroic Age and the Hebrew Age of the Judges are numerous and compelling and that, furthermore, the various Heroic Age characters of Greece belong after the first Olympiad, an event traditionally placed in the year 776 BC.

Thus the religious innovations of the tenth to eighth centuries BC touched every aspect of human existence, manifesting themselves most visibly in the construction of immense temples and pyramidical structures, as well as in an outpouring of religious, philosophical and legal works. It became an age of sages, seers and prophets, men who had been inspired by the awesome

---

[282]Herodotus, ii, 123

[283]As mentioned earlier, this topic is covered in detail by Gunnar Heinsohn in, "The Rise of Blood Sacrifice and Priest-Kingship in Mesopotamia: A 'Cosmic Decree'?" *Religion* (1992) 22, 109-134.

[284] i.e., when he killed the Egyptian king Busiris, who attempted to offer him as a sacrifice. On Hercules and human sacrifice, see Robert Graves *The Greek Myths* Vol.1 (Pelican Books, 1955), p. 226. Moses, who also abolished human sacrifice ("Thou Shalt not Kill"), shares many features with Hercules. Thus, for example, Hercules strangles two serpents sent to destroy him, whilst Moses' rod devours the two serpents sent against him by the Egyptian priests.

[285]In *The Pyramid Age* (2006)

events of the time. In Egypt, the epoch was marked by the religious reforms of Cheops, as well as by the numerous great sages of the Pyramid Age, whose words continued to inspire men for generations to come.

It was the same story much further afield. In India, this was the age of Krishna, whose timeless wisdom is enshrined in the *Bhagavad Gita*. The latter is a small component of the epic *Mahabharata*, whose images of cosmic battles amongst the celestial gods is rightly celebrated. In China, the same epoch saw the appearance of the Taoist sages, some of whom are also connected to events of cosmic dimensions. Similar stories are told amongst the peoples of western Europe, as well as those of the New World. This epoch of prophecy is a truly universal phenomenon, yet it was not a phenomenon confined to the tenth, ninth and eighth centuries. The forces set in motion at that time continued to throw up great philosophers and thinkers for another two centuries. Thus the Hebrew prophets Elijah and Elisha were prominent in their condemnation of lapses from the Mosaic Law (especially regarding human sacrifice) during the seventh century.[286] By the sixth century the movement away from blood sacrifice reached its apogee, with seers of the time sounding forth in condemnation even of animal sacrifice. In Israel, this movement is represented most clearly by Isaiah, whose attack on blood sacrifice is justly celebrated. Isaiah described these ceremonies as "abominations".[287] In Greece, the movement is represented by Pythagoras, the great seer of the sixth century, who preached vegetarianism.[288] From the same epoch in India we have the Buddha, who of all the seers and prophets of the age was perhaps the most antagonistic towards the religions of cruelty and slaughter that hitherto prevailed.

It is evident then that all the great world religions were formulated between the tenth and sixth centuries BC and that the religion and philosophy attributed to Moses could only, as the Berlin exegetes insisted, have belonged to that epoch.

---

[286]The epoch of the Israelite Kings actually commences around 740 BC., with Solomon for example reigning roughly between 710 and 680 BC. The true position of the Israelite monarchies is subject to a detailed examination in my *Egypt's Ramesside Pharaohs and the Persians* (New York, 2021).

[287]Isaiah 66: 3-4

[288]See, e.g., Ovid, *Metamorphoses* xi,80-470.

EPILOGUE

Our meander through the winding roads of ancient history has led us on a strange path. Our search has brought us face to face with characters and events unknown to conventional history books. We began with the discovery of one cataclysmic upheaval of nature and ended with another. The first of these, we found, preceded, by about a thousand years, the rise of high civilization and the life of Menes, legendary founder of the Egyptian kingdom. And the first pharaoh — whether known as Menes or otherwise — lived shortly after a second great natural catastrophe, one that came to be associated with a celestial Tower or Pillar, a feature which gave rise to the custom of circumcision. It was to this period also that Abraham, father of the Jewish nation, belonged. By synchronizing the stories of these two ancient peoples we were enabled to illuminate the very beginnings of history. Once we accept that world-wide catastrophes actually occurred, it becomes relatively straightforward to synchronize the disparate histories.

Irrespective of whether Abraham was an historical person or a tribal deity, the father of the Jews assumed all the characteristics of the god Thoth/Mercury, who, like Abraham, was accredited with initiating the elements of high civilization. The gods that threatened destruction had to be appeased with sacrifice, and high temples modeled on the Celestial Mountain had to be erected in which to perform these. Also, careful attention had to be paid to the movements of the heavenly bodies in their wanderings through the sky.

Precisely the same forces were operative throughout the globe, and wherever we go in the world we find parallel traditions. Conditions being favorable, settled metal-using cultures sprang up. In this way it is possible to place the beginnings of a Copper Age civilization in Egypt, in Palestine, in

Anatolia, in Mesopotamia, in Europe, in India, in China and in the Americas, around 1300 BC. More work will have to be done on all these areas in order to verify this statement for each culture.

The possibilities thus opened by this "catastrophist chronology" need hardly be stressed. Events from the histories of different nations can be synchronized with an exactness that would otherwise have been impossible. And so we find early biblical history transported from the realms of half-forgotten legend into that of history proper. From the first meeting of Egyptians and Hebrews, recalled in the story of Abraham, the histories of the two peoples now form a perfect match, complementing each other and affording new insights at every turn. Thus Egyptian sources add greatly to our knowledge of Joseph, whose story takes up a quarter of Genesis. In his Egyptian guise of Imhotep we find Joseph being honored not only as a seer and administrator, but also as an architect and physician. In like manner, the Egyptian accounts of the Exodus, preserved in the various "Pessimistic" treatises, fill in various details omitted from the Hebrew Scriptures. We have, for example, been able to identify the pharaoh of the Oppression as Huni, last ruler of the Third Dynasty, the king with whom a World Age came to a close.

We ended our investigation with the Exodus, on the eve of the Israelites' epic journey to their Promised Land, an event we synchronized with the beginnings of Egypt's Pyramid Age, the epoch during which the pharaohs of the Fourth, Fifth and Sixth Dynasties raised the mighty monuments that have become synonymous with the Kingdom of the Nile and its civilization. These monuments were in fact raised specifically to mark the great cosmic events recalled in the Book of Exodus. As the Israelites wandered in the desert and around the fringes of Canaan, the Egyptians were engaged in raising these wonderful structures.

Yet all these events, we found, occurred as recently as the tenth, ninth and eighth centuries BC. Within a hundred and sixty years of the Exodus, Egypt was invaded by the Assyrians, a nation known as Hyksos in the hieroglyphic records. In another place I have demonstrated in some detail how these Hyksos are identical to the dynasty archeologists designate as the Sixth. The Assyrian conquerors adopted Egyptian names and styled themselves as pharaohs. They looked especially to the cosmic dragon Apop as their tutelary deity.

The destruction of Assyrian/Hyksos power in the south saw the rise of Egypt herself, under the mighty Eighteenth Dynasty, as an Imperial Power. It can be shown that these events were contemporary with the establishment of the Hebrew monarchy under Saul and David. Thus the Hebrew United Kingdom, which in conventional history books is placed centuries after the

Egyptian New Kingdom, was in fact contemporary with it. But surely, it might be said, the histories of these two great empires are known in detail. How is it then that they do not refer to each other in their chronicles and inscriptions? Where, for example, do the Egyptians mention Solomon, and where, on the other hand, do the Hebrews mention pharaohs such as Thutmose III?

As a matter of fact, the two rulers mentioned above do figure in the records of both nations. Indeed, the histories of Eighteenth Dynasty Egypt and United Kingdom Israel can be made to agree in a most dramatic way. That agreement was illustrated as early as 1952 in Velikovsky's seminal *Ages in Chaos*. There he demonstrated in great detail how Ahmose, who chased the Hyksos from Egypt, was truly contemporary with Saul and David, who battled against the same nation as well as their allies in Palestine, the Philistines and Amalekites. There also he showed that Queen Hatshepsut, whose greatest feat was to visit the fabulous Divine Land, was actually the Queen of Sheba, who visited Solomon in Jerusalem. There too he illustrated how Thutmose III, who plundered the fabulously opulent temple of Kadesh, was none other than the pharaoh Shishak, who plundered the temple of Jerusalem (Al Kuds) after the death of Solomon.

In *Ages in Chaos*, and in subsequent historical works, Velikovsky adhered to the conventional dating of Hebrew chronology and reduced the antiquity of New Kingdom Egyptian civilization by five centuries in order to correspond with it. In the present study we have found that Hebrew history itself is unnaturally lengthened and that it too needs to be brought forward in the historical time scale. Thus we claim that Saul did not found the Israelite United Kingdom circa 1020 BC, but around 740 BC. The synchronisms identified by Velikovsky in *Ages in Chaos* therefore belong not in the tenth and ninth centuries, as he believed, but in the eighth and seventh.

Velikovsky ended *Ages in Chaos* with the reign of Akhnaton, a pharaoh whom he identified as contemporary with Ahab of Israel and Shalmaneser III of Assyria. Using the measuring-rod of our revised chronology, we are compelled to place these kings near the end of the seventh century. In another volume dedicated to an examination of the Neo-Assyrian kingdom, I have shown how Shalmaneser III was the Assyrian title of a Median king who battled for years against a great king of Lydia, known to contemporary scholarship as Suppiluliumas the Hittite. There it is demonstrated also how Tiglath-Pileser III, who brought a new age of power and prosperity to Assyria, is the Assyrian alter-ego of Cyrus the Persian conqueror of Babylon. In the Hebrew Scriptures, Tiglath-Pileser exacted tribute from Ahaz of Judah, an event normally dated to c. 735 BC. But Cyrus also extended his power towards the borders of Egypt, not in the eighth century, but in the decade 550–540 BC. The king Shalmaneser, who carried the Ten Tribes of Israel into captivity in the cities of the Medes, was actually Cambyses, Persian conqueror of Egypt. Sargon II, who usurped the Assyrian throne, was Darius the Great, who usurped the Achaemenid throne. The last years of the state of Judah correspond to the last years of the Achaemenid state. Thus Nebuchadrezzar, who carried off the people of Jerusalem to Babylon, was the Babylonized Artaxerxes III, who re-established Persian power in the west, whilst the pharaoh Necho, who was defeated by this latter-day Nebuchadrezzar, was actually Nectanebo III, who was defeated by Artaxerxes III.

Thus it was the Persians who destroyed the kingdom of Israel and enslaved the people of Judah, not the Assyrians and Babylonians. Why events of the Persian epoch should have been projected back into the Assyrian epoch of the eighth century is a complex issue, not to be explained in a few sentences.

However, it should be stated here and now that Rabbinical Jewish tradition is in total disagreement with conventional history as regards the antiquity of the Hebrew monarchies. Thus for example the second temple is said to have been erected some time in the fourth century BC, rather than the latter sixth, where it has been placed by orthodox scholarship. The Old Testament is the repository *par excellence* of Jewish tradition, yet it has nothing whatsoever to say about the period between Ezra (mid fifth century) and the Maccabees (early second century). So, in an eventful period from where we should have expected a rich tradition to have survived, the Jews, most assiduous of record-keepers, are supposed to have left not a single sentence.

Nevertheless, the Jewish chroniclers were themselves very much confused by their past. They were not helped by the Achaemenid habit of aping the great kings of yesteryear — particularly those of Assyria and Babylonia. Nor were they assisted by the fact that the Macedonians, in their turn, imitated the Persians.

Thus the monarch who freed the two tribes of Judah from captivity was not Cyrus the Achaemenid by Alexander the Macedonian and his Seleucid successors. Alexander himself was confused with the founder of the Achaemenid Empire in the traditions of many of the Near Eastern peoples, and well before his death his court began to bear striking resemblance to that of the Persian Great Kings. Ultimately, it was this confusion of Macedonians with Achaemenids that added over two and a half centuries to the chronology of the Hebrew kings. The Macedonian Seleucids later became bitter enemies of the Jews, and the Maccabean War of the second century BC was among the most savage conflicts in the entire history of the Jewish people. The fact of the Jews and Seleucids becoming such bitter enemies may have had a bearing on how history was recorded. It is conceivable that the Jewish scribes only with great reluctance may have recalled that it was the ancestors of the Seleucids who had freed their own ancestors. In time, it was completely forgotten.

Thus it was that the monarchs who systematically demolished the states of Israel and Judah came to be viewed as the saviors of the Hebrews, whilst the kings who re-established the Jewish state were cast forever in the roles of villains and tyrants.

Appendix: Compared Stratigraphies And Cultures

Since an important part of the present work has centered round the correction of Egyptian chronology, and since the need for such a correction demonstrated by the inconsistencies in terminologies employed by archeologists with regard to strata and cultures from Egypt and Mesopotamia on the one hand and Syria/Palestine on the other, I regard it as important to include some of this material in the present study. However, as this mainly concerns the somewhat dry topic of pottery styles, etc., whereas the main body of the book forms a historical narrative, I felt it best to include such evidence as an appendix.

As mentioned in Chapter 2, a great natural catastrophe directly preceded the rise of literate civilization throughout the Near East. However, in Mesopotamia and Egypt this disaster is placed immediately before the beginning of the Early Bronze Age, whereas in Syria/Palestine the same disaster is placed near the end of the Early Bronze Age — approximately 1,000 years later. Thus for example the stratigraphy of Ur in southern Mesopotamia is defined thus (after Woolley).

Note that the Late Neolithic culture in Ur, terminated by the "Flood", is named 'Ubaid and is there dated to circa 3300 BC. Compare Ur however with the stratigraphy of Ugarit, as revealed by Claude Schaeffer, where a culture destroyed by a great "Conflagration", supposedly in the second last phase of the Early Bronze Age, is however also designated 'Ubaid; only this 'Ubaid culture is dated to circa 2200 BC — over a thousand years after Mesopotamian 'Ubaid.

The chronology of Egypt, unlike that of Syria/Palestine, is synchronized with that of Mesopotamia; and here too we find a great natural catastrophe immediately preceding the first phase of the Early Bronze Age (Naqada 1).

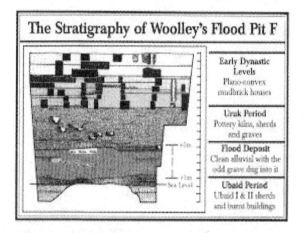

26. The stratigraphy of Ur (after Woolley).

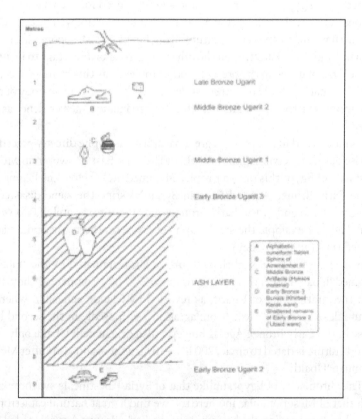

27. The stratigraphy of Ugarit, after Schaeffer.

The same terminological discrepancy, beginning therefore with the earliest phases of high civilization in Egypt and the Fertile Crescent, displays itself again and again in subsequent epochs. In this way, Early Bronze 1 in Mesopotamia, or Jamdat Nasr, shows close parallels with Early Bronze 1 in Egypt, there called Gerzean, or Naqada 1, but with Early Bronze 3/Middle Bronze 1 in Ugarit, there called Khirbet Kerak. The pottery sequences below serve to illustrate the point.

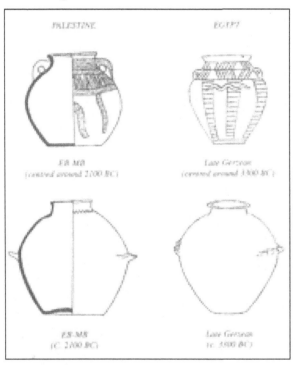

28. Parallel pottery styles from Egypt and Palestine which are however placed over 1000 years apart. (Palestinian pottery from K.M. Kenyon in *The Cambridge Ancient History*, 3rd ed. Vol. 1, part 2, page 573; Egyptian pottery from F. Petrie, *The Making of Egypt* (1939))

The same pattern of misalignment continues right the way through the Bronze Age in the above areas. And so, Middle Bronze 2 in Syria/Palestine, the epoch of the Hyksos, and dated there to circa 1600–1500 BC, is stylistically and stratigraphically equivalent to Early Bronze 3 in Mesopotamia — the epoch of the Akkadians — and there dated to circa 2400–2300 BC. This striking and crucial fact was highlighted as early as 1971 by J. Kaplan, who produced the table below, but has, until now, been virtually ignored by the archeological establishment.

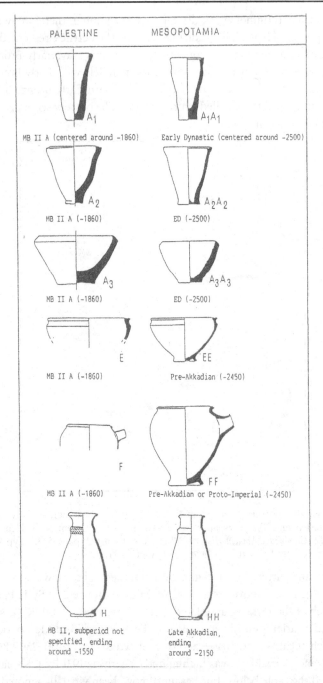

29. Parallel pottery styles from Palestine and Mesopotamia which are however placed 700 years apart. (after Kaplan).

The table below illustrates the point. Epochs in Egypt, Syria/Palestine, and Mesopotamia that can definitely be shown to be contemporary (through identical pottery styles etc.) are shown in linked bubbles).

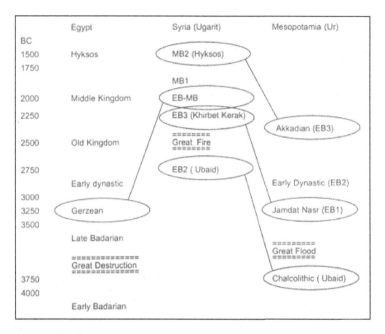

30. Chronological inconsistencies in the archeology of Egypt, Mesopotamia and Syria/Palestine.

Conventional Chronology

BC	EGYPT	ISRAEL
3200	First Dynasty civilization established mainly by immigrants from Mesopotamia. Epoch is associated with phallus-worship and circumcision.	
	Great seer Imhotep, who is High Priest of Heliopolis, solves crisis of seven-year famine by interpreting pharaoh Djoser's dream.	
2500		
	Collapse of Egyptian civilization during a catastrophe which darkens the sun and sees "fire throughout the land".	
2100		Abraham tribe arrives in Egypt and teaches Egyptians rudiments of civilization.
		Great seer Joseph, who is High Priest of Heliopolis, solves crisis of seven-year famine by interpreting pharaoh's dream.
1500		
		Collapse of Egyptian civilization in a catastrophe that darkens the sun and allows the Israelite slaves to escape.

31. Egypt and Israel, Conventional Chronology and Revised Chronology

Revised Chronology

BC	EGYPT	ISRAEL
	Chalcolithic (Naqada 1)	Chalcolithic
1300	NATURAL CATASTROPHE	
	First Dynasty established by immigrants from Mesoptamia. Worship of phallic god Min and custom of circumcision.	"Abraham" tribes from Mesopotamia bring high civilization to Egypt. Phallus-worship and circumcision.
1100	Imhotep solves famine-crisis after interpreting pharaoh Djoser's dream.	Joseph solves famine-crisis after interpreting pharaoh's dream.
1000	NATURAL CATASTROPHE	
	In wake of disaster Sneferu defeats invading desert tribes, founds Fourth Dynasty and launches Pyramid Age	Moses leads Israelites out of Egypt and across the desert of Midian, where they fight migrating desert tribes.
920	Fifth Dynasty, from Elephantine, takes control of Egypt	Nomadic Israelites arrive in Canaan and begin the Conquest of the land under Joshua.
830	Egypt is invaded by the "Old" Assyrians under Sargon I, who establishes Sixth (or Hyksos) Dynasty.	After death of Joshua, Israelites are defeated by Assyrian king Cusham Risathaim (Sargon I).
740	After about 100 years, Sixth or Hyksos Dynasty is defeated and expelled from Egypt by Theban (Eighteenth Dynasty) rulers.	Saul becomes first ruler of Israelite kingdom.

BIBLIOGRAPHY

Books

Albright, William F. *Yahweh and the Gods of Canaan: An Historical Analysis of Two Contrasting Faiths* (New York, 1968).

Allan, D. S. and J. B. Delair. *When the Earth Nearly Died* (London, 1994).

Baikie, James. *A History of Egypt* Vol. 1 (London, 1929)

Breasted, James Henry. *The Development of Religion and Thought in Ancient Egypt* (London, 1912).

Brooks, C. E. P. *Climate through the Ages* (2nd ed, 1940).

Brown, Hugh Auchincloss. *Cataclysms of the Earth* (London, 1967).

Brugsch, Heinrich Karl. *Die biblischen sieben Jahre der Hungersnoth* (Leipzig, 1891).

Brugsch, Heinrich Karl. *Steininschrift und Bibelwort* (Leipzig, 1898)

Burn, A. R. *Minoans, Philistines and Greeks* (London, 1930)

Burn, A. R. *The Lyric Age of Greece* (London, 1967).

Collins, John J. *The Bible after Babel: Historical Criticism in a Postmodern Age* (Eerdmans, 2005)

Cornuke, Bob and Williams, Larry. *In Search of the Mountain of God* (Broadman and Holman Books, 2000).

Cottrell, Leonard. *The Mountains of Pharaoh* (London, 1956)

Courville, Donovan. *The Exodus Problem and its Ramifications: A Critical Examination of the Chronological Relationships between Israel and Egypt* 2 Vols. (Crest Challenge Books, 1987).

Dana, James Dwight. *Manual of Geology* (Philadelphia, 1894).

Dayton, John. *Minerals, Metals, Glazing and Man* (London, 1978).

De Bourbourg, Brasseur. *Histoire des nations civilizes du Mexique* (Paris, 1857-59)

De Cambrey, Leonne. *Lapland Legends* (Yale, 1926).

Fawcett, Percy. *Exploration Fawcett* (London, 1953).

Firestone, R., A. West and S. Warwick-Smith. *The Cycle of Cosmic Catastrophes: How a Stone-Age Comet changed the Course of World Culture* (Bear and Company (2006).

Flint, Richard F. *Glacial Geology and the Pleistocene Epoch* (New York, 1947).

Frazer, Sir James. *Folklore in the Old Testament: Abridged Version* (London, 1918).

Friedman, Richard Elliot. *The Bible with Sources Revealed* (London, 2003)

Garland, H. and Bannister. C. O., *Ancient Egyptian Metallurgy* (London, 1927)

Ginzberg, Louis. *Legends of the Jews* (Philadelphia, 1909).

Graves, Robert. *The Greek Myths* 2 Vols. (Pelican Books, 1955).

Griffith, Francis Llewellyn. *The Antiquities of Tell el Yahudiyeh and Miscellaneous Work in Lower Egypt during the Years 1887-1888* (London, 1890).

Hapgood, Charles. *Earth's Shifting Crust* (London, 1958).

Hapgood, Charles. *Path to the Pole* (London, 1970).

Hancock, Graham and Robert Bauval. *Keeper of Genesis* (London, 1996).

Heinsohn, Gunnar. *Die Sumerer gab es nicht* (Frankfurt, 1988).

Heinsohn, Gunnar. *Wann lebten die Pharaonen?* (Frankfurt, 1990).

Holmes, T. Rice. *Ancient Britain and the Invasions of Julius Caesar* (Clarendon Press, 1907)

Hornung, E. in William Kelly Simpson (ed.). *The Literate of Ancient Egypt* (Yale, 2003)

Hubner, J. *Kurze Fragen aus der politische Historie* (Leipzig, 1729)

Humphreys, A. A. and H. L. Abbot, *Report upon the Physics and Hydraulics of the Mississippi River* (Philadelphia, 1861).

Keller, Werner. *The Bible as History* (London, 1980)

Kovacs, Maureen Gallery. *The Epic of Gilgamesh* (Stanford, 1989)

Kramer, Samuel Noah. *History Begins at Sumer: Thirty-Nine Firsts in Man's Recorded History* (Pennsylvania, 1981).

Lichtheim, Miriam. *Ancient Egyptian Literature: The Late Period* (Berkeley, 2006).

McEnery, J. *Cavern Researches, or discoveries of Organic remains and of British and Roman Relics, in the caves of Kent's Hole, Anstis Cove, Chudleigh and Barry Head* (London, 1859).

Meyer, Eduard and Bernhard Luther. *Die Israeliten und ihre Nachbarstämme* (Halle, 1906)

Montgomery, James A. *Arabia and the Bible* (Philadelphia, 1934).

Morenz, Siegfried. *Egyptian Religion* (Cornell University Press, 1973)

Murray, H. and J. Crawfurd and others. *An Historical and descriptive Account of China* (London, 1836).

Peratt, Anthony L. *Physics of the Plasma Universe* (Springer, 2014).

Petrie, Flinders. *A History of Egypt* Vol. 1 (London, 1894)

Petrie, Flinders. *The Making of Egypt* (London, 1939)

Pritchard, John. (ed.) *Ancient Near Eastern Texts* (Princeton, 1949??).

Powell, J. L. *Deadly Voyager: The Ancient Comet Strike that changed Earth and Human History* (Bowker, 2020).

Reiske, Johann Jacob. *De Arabum Epocha Vetustissima, Sail Ol Arem, id est Ruptura Catarrhactae Marebensis Dicta* (Leipzig, 1748).

Rice, Michael. *Egypt's Making* (London, 1990).

Rohl, David. *Legend: The Origins of Civilisation* (London, 1998).

Rundle Clark, R. T. *Myth and Symbol* (London, 1959)

Schaeffer, Claude. *Stratigraphie comparée et Chronologie de l'Asie Occidentale, 2me et 3me millenaires* (Oxford, 1948).

Shaw, Ian and Paul Nicholson. *British Museum Dictionary of Ancient Egypt* (London, 1995)

Stannard, Brendan. *The Origins of Israel and Mankind* (Lancashire, 1983)

Sweeney, Emmet. *Arthur and Stonehenge: Britain's Lost History* (Domra Publications, 2001).

Sweeney, Emmet. *The Theban Empire: Ages in Chaos Revisited* (Algora, New York, 2020).

Sweeney, Emmet. *The Pyramid Age* (Algora, New York, 2007).

Sweeney, Emmet. *Egypt's Ramesside Pharaohs and the Persians* (Algora, New York, 2021).

Van der Slujis, Rens. *The Mythology of the World Axis* (All-Round Publications, 2007).

Van Seters, John. *Abraham in History and Tradition* (Yale, 1975).

Vandier, Jacques. *La Famine dans l'Égypte ancienne* (Cairo, 1936).

Velikovsky, Immanuel. *Ages in Chaos* (New York and London, 1952).

Velikovsky, Immanuel. *Earth in Upheaval* (New York and London, 1955).

Velikovsky, Immanuel. *Worlds in Collision* (New York and London, 1950).

Vergote, Jozef. *Joseph en Egypte* (1959).

Weigall, Arthur. *A History of the Pharaohs* Vol.1 (London, 1952)

Wellhausen, Julius. *Prolegomena zur Geschichte Israels* (Berlin, 1883).

Wilkinson, J. G. *The Ancient Egyptians* Vol.3 (London, 1878).

Williamson, R. W. *Religious and Cosmic Beliefs of Central Polynesia* Vol. 1 (Cambridge, 1933).

Woolley, Leonard. *Ur of the Chaldees* (Pelican edition, 1950)

Wright, G. F. *The Ice Age in North America and its Bearing upon the Antiquity of Man* (New York, 1891).

Yahuda, Abraham Shalom. *The Language of the Pentateuch in its Relation to Egyptian* (Oxford, 1933).

Zhirov, N. *Atlantis: Atlantology, Basic Problems*, (English ed., London, 1970).

Articles

Arslanov, Kh. A. et al. "Consensus Dating of Remains from Wrangel Island." *Radiocarbon.* **40** (1) (1998).

Barguet, P. *La stèle de la famine à Séhel*, Institut français d'archaéologie orientale - Bibliothéque d'étude Paris, volume 34. Cairo 1953

Bell, Barbara. "The Dark Ages in Ancient History: The First Dark Age in Egypt," *American Journal of Archeology* 75, (1971) 24.

Burkitt, M. C. "Archeological Notes," *Man* Vol. 25 (Jan. 1926).

Butzer, K. W. "Physical Conditions in Eastern Europe, Western Asia and Egypt Before the Period of Agricultural and Urban Settlement," in *The Cambridge Ancient History* Vol. 1 part 1 (3rd ed.).

Chetwynd, Tom. "A Seven Year Famine in the Reign of King Djoser with other Parallels between Imhotep and Joseph," *Catastrophism and Ancient History* IX:1 (January, 1987).

De Alvara, Don Fernando "Ixtlilxochitl." *Obras Historicas* Vol. 1 (Mexico, 1891).

Douglas, Kory C. "Comparing the Genetic Diversity of Late Pleistocene *Bison* with Modern *Bison bison* using Ancient DNA Techniques and the Mitochondrial DNA Control Region," www.baylor-ir.tdl.org

Drower, Margaret S. "Syria Before 2200 BC," in *The Cambridge Ancient History* Vol.1 part 2 (3rd ed.)

Edwards, I. E. S. "The Early Dynastic Period in Egypt," in *The Cambridge Ancient History* Vol.1 part 2 (3rd ed.).

Eissfeldt, O. "Palestine in the Time of the Nineteenth Dynasty: (a) The Exodus and Wanderings," in *The Cambridge Ancient History* Vol. 2 part 2 (3rd ed).

Ewing, Maurice. "New Discoveries on the Mid-Atlantic Ridge," *National Geographic*, Vol. XCVI, No. 5 (November, 1949).

Flesher, John. "Possible mastodon carving found on rock," *Associated Press*, 2007-09-04.

Gardiner, A. H., "New Literary Works from Egypt," *Journal of Egyptian Archeology* 1, (1914) 100-16.

Gardner, E. W. and Caton-Thompson, G. "The Recent Geology and Neolithic Industry of the Northern Fayum Desert," *The Journal of the Royal Anthropological Institute of Great Britain and Ireland*, Vol. 56 (1926).

Gidly, J. W. "Ancient Man in Florida," *Bulletin of the Geological Society of America*, Vol. XL, (1929).

Harvey, G. R. "Abraham and Phallicism," *Society for Interdisciplinary Studies, Chronology and Catastrophism Workshop* (1998) No. 2.

Hayes, W. C. "The Middle Kingdom in Egypt: Internal History from the Rise of the Heracleopolitans to the Death of Ammenemes III," in *The Cambridge Ancient History* Vol.1 part 2 (3rd ed.)

Heinsohn, Gunnar. "The Rise of Blood Sacrifice and Priest-Kingship in Mesopotamia: A 'Cosmic Decree'?" *Religion* (1992) 22.

Hibben, F. C. "Evidence of Early Man in Alaska," *American Antiquity*, VIII (1943), 256.

Hrdlička, Aleš. "Preliminary Report on Finds of Supposedly Ancient Human Remains at Vero, Florida," *Journal of Geology*, XXV (1917).

Jaggard, Victoria. "Yellowstone Supervolcano may rumble to life sooner than thought," *National Geographic*, October, 2017.

Jones, J. Claude. "Geologic History of Lake Lahontan," in *Quaternary Climates*, (Carnegie Institute of Washington, 1925).

Kenyon, K. M. "Syria and Palestine c. 2160-1780 BC: The Archeological Sites," in *The Cambridge Ancient History* Vol. 1 part 2 (3rd ed.).

Lambeck, Kurt. "Late pleistocene, holocene and present sea-levels: constraints on future change," *Palaeogeography, Palaeoclimatology, Palaeoecology*, Vol. 89, Issue 3 (December, 1990)

Lasken, Jesse E. "Towards a New Chronology of Ancient Egypt," *Discussions in Egyptology*, 17 (1990).

Mackey, Damien; Calneggia, Frank, and Money, Paul. "A Critical Reappraisal of the Book of Genesis," *Society for Interdisciplinary Studies: Catastrophism and Chronology Workshop* No. 2 (1987).

Mallowan, Max. "The Early Dynastic Period in Mesopotamia," in *The Cambridge Ancient History* Vol. 1 part 2 (3rd ed.)

Mellaart, James. "Anatolia: c. 4000-2300 BC," in *The Cambridge Ancient History* Vol. 2 part 2 (3rd ed.)

Merriam, J. C. *California University Bulletin*, Department of Geology, VIII (1915), 377-384.

Mewhinney, Sean. "El-Arish Revisited," *Kronos* XI: 2 (Winter, 1986).

Mullen, William. "Myth and the Science of Catastrophism: A Reading of the Pyramid Texts," *Pensée*, Vol. 3, No. 1 (1973).

Ninkovich, Dragoslav. *Earth and Planetary Science Letters*, Vol. 4, No. 2 (1968).

Noegel, Scott B. "The Egyptian "Magicians"' Symposium: Envisaging the Exodus Story: Meet the Egyptians, *The Torah.com* January 2023 www.thetorah.com

Plenck, A. "Das Alter des Menschengeschlechts," *Zeitschrift für Ethnologie*, XL (1908).

Rainey, F. "Archeological Investigation in Central Alaska," *American Antiquity*, V (1940), 305.

Russell, I. "Geologic History of Lake Lahontan," U.S. Geological Survey, Monograph 11.

Salkeld, David. "Old Testament Tale XI: Dysphasia in Genesis?" *Society for Interdisciplinary Studies, Chronology and Catastrophism Workshop*, No. 1 (2007).

Sanderson, Ivan T. "Riddle of the Frozen Giants," *Saturday Evening Post*, No. 39, January, 1960.

Satow, Chris. et al. "Eruptive activity of the Santorini Volcano controlled by sea-level rise and fall," *Nature Geoscience* 14 586-592 (2021)

Schneider, T. "Modern Scholarship versus the Demon of Passover: An Outlook on Exodus Research and Egyptology through the Lens of Exodus 12," in Thomas E. Levy, Thomas Schneider, William H. C. Propp (eds.) *Israel's Exodus in Transdisciplinary Perspective* (Springer, New York, 2015).

Sellards, E. H. "On the Association of Human Remains and Extinct Vertebrates at Vero, Florida," *Journal of Geology*, XXV (1917).

Smith, W. Stevenson. "The Old Kingdom of Egypt and the Beginning of the First Intermediate Period," in *The Cambridge Ancient History* Vol. 1 part 2 (3rd ed.).

Strickling, James E. "The Tower of Babel and the Confusion of Tongues," *Kronos*, Vol. VIII, No. 1 (1982).

Teit, James A. "Kaska Tales," *Journal of American Folklore*, no. 30 (1917).

Van Winkle, Walton. "Quality of the Surface Waters of Oregon," *US Geological Survey, Water Supply* Paper 363 (Washington, 1914).

Vartanyan, S. L. " Radiocarbon Dating Evidence for Mammoths on Wrangel Island, Arctic Ocean, until 2000 BC." *Radiocarbon*. 37 (1) (2000).

Venzke, E (ed.) Global Volcanism Program, 2013. Volcanoes of the World, v. 4.4 10. 4. Smithsonian Institution. Downloaded 16 Dec. 2021. https://doi.org/10.5479/si.GVP.VOTW4-2013

Westgate, John A. *Science*, November, 1982.

White, Mark J. "Things to do in Doggerland when you're dead: Surviving OIS3 at the northwesternmost fringe of Middle Palaeolithic Europe," *World Archaeology*, 38, 4 (2006).

Whitley, D. Garth. "The Ivory Islands of the Arctic Ocean," *Journal of the Philosophical Society of Great Britain*, XII (1910), 35.

Index

Printed in the United States
by Baker & Taylor Publisher Services